D0083898

Teaching with
The Norton Anthology of
Theory and Criticism

A Guide for Instructors

THE EDITORS

Vincent B. Leitch, General Editor
PROFESSOR AND PAUL AND CAROL DAUBE SUTTON CHAIR IN ENGLISH
UNIVERSITY OF OKLAHOMA

William E. Cain
MARY JEWETT GAISER PROFESSOR OF ENGLISH AND AMERICAN STUDIES
WELLESLEY COLLEGE

Laurie Finke
PROFESSOR OF WOMEN'S AND GENDER STUDIES
KENYON COLLEGE

Barbara Johnson
PROFESSOR OF ENGLISH AND COMPARATIVE LITERATURE
FREDRIC WERTHAM PROFESSOR OF LAW AND PSYCHIATRY IN SOCIETY
HARVARD UNIVERSITY

John McGowan
PROFESSOR OF ENGLISH AND COMPARATIVE LITERATURE
UNIVERSITY OF NORTH CAROLINA, CHAPEL HILL

Jeffrey J. Williams
ASSOCIATE PROFESSOR OF ENGLISH
UNIVERSITY OF MISSOURI

Teaching with
The Norton Anthology
of Theory and Criticism

A Guide for Instructors

M. Keith Booker

UNIVERSITY OF ARKANSAS

W. W. NORTON & COMPANY
New York · London

Copyright © 2001 by W. W. Norton & Company, Inc.
All rights reserved.
Printed in the United States of America.
First Edition.

The text of this book is composed in Fairfield Medium LH
with the display set in Bernhard Modern BT.
Composition by PennSet, Inc.
Manufacturing by Victor Graphics

ISBN 0-393-97574-6 (pbk.)

W. W. Norton & Company, Inc., 500 Fifth Avenue, New York, N.Y. 10110
www.wwnorton.com

W. W. Norton & Company Ltd., 10 Coptic Street, London WC1A 1PU

1 2 3 4 5 6 7 8 9 0

Contents

Introduction: Teaching Theory and Criticism with *The Norton Anthology of Theory and Criticism (NATC)*

In his essay "The Archetypes of Literature" (included in *NATC*), Northrop Frye argues that strictly speaking, it is not really possible either to teach or to learn "literature." What teachers teach, and what students learn, in "literature" classes, Frye concludes, is really the criticism of literature, because literature itself cannot be grasped except through some sort of criticism. This insight provides a potentially valuable starting point for any course in literary theory and criticism. It reassures students, who will be mostly literature majors, but who (especially if they are undergraduates) may not have explicitly studied theory and criticism before, that what they are about to study is much the same thing they have been studying all along, but they will be approaching it with a higher degree of self-consciousness.

Put differently, it is quite often useful to start a course on literary theory and criticism by suggesting to students that the choice between reading literature with theory and without theory is a false one. One always reads all texts with some sort of theory; otherwise the words on the page would be no more than a meaningless collection of black marks. Indeed, any student in any college-level course on literary theory and criticism is already certain to have adopted a variety of highly sophisticated (and highly theoretical, if not consciously so) interpretive strategies in decoding the virtually endless barrage of texts and signs with which we are all confronted in the contemporary world. The choice, then, is between being aware of the theoretical approach one is using and not being aware of that approach. The concerted study of literary theory and criticism can help make students more aware of the theoretical choices they are already

1

making. It can also provide them with the information they need to make more informed choices in the future.

Such commonsense arguments can be comforting to students who are just beginning to study theory and criticism. These arguments should not, however, obscure the fact that approaches to literary studies and to the teaching of literature can be controversial and have changed substantially in the past few decades. Moreover, it is important to recognize that those changes are largely associated with a dramatic increase in the self-consciousness with which scholars and teachers of literature have pursued theoretical approaches to their work. Furthermore, attempts to reassure students who initially find theory threatening should not obscure the controversies that have surrounded the word *theory* in North American literary scholarship in the past few decades. In this context, theory has been used to describe a variety of self-conscious approaches to literature that have gained prominence since the late 1960s among scholars seeking an alternative to the enervation of New Critical formalism. This search for alternatives to a method that had, for decades, been virtually equated with criticism itself has led to serious debates about the very nature of literary study. While such a fundamental reexamination of the work of literary scholars and teachers is healthy, it has understandably led to considerable dispute, in part because a well-established system was being powerfully challenged and in part because the challenges to this system were themselves multiple and often at odds with one another.

That very multiplicity is one of the keys to the intellectual excitement that often accompanies the discovery of theory by students; it is also central to the confusion and sense of threat that some students feel on making this discovery. Much recent effort has gone into the search for productive ways to teach theory in the classroom, and a variety of conclusions have been reached.[1] One of the few to have gained fairly widespread acceptance is that the various controversies and debates surrounding various theories can themselves be extremely productive pedagogical resources. The differences and disagreements among different theories should therefore not be ignored or dismissed, but should be used to help bring theories to life for students who might otherwise find them overly abstract or just plain boring.[2] If nothing else, the sometimes passionate disagreements that arise among different theorists can help students un-

---

[1]The collections edited by Sadoff and Cain and by Nelson contain a number of suggestive essays by scholars and teachers who have thought about and been involved in teaching theory. Among other things, the essays in these two volumes contain a great deal of practical advice for instructors who are seeking more productive ways to teach theory in their own classes. The essays in the volume edited by Clifford and Schilb contain interesting explorations of the use of literary theory in teaching composition. See also Scholes for a book-length meditation on the use of literary theory in teaching English. Finally, see Scholes, Comley, and Ulmer for an attempt to develop an introductory textbook on reading literature that draws on and incorporates theory, especially of the poststructuralist variety.

[2]Graff's discussion of "teaching the conflicts" in *Beyond the Culture Wars* is one of the best known and most accessible discussions of this topic.

derstand that theory really matters and that there can be a great deal at stake in choosing among different theoretical approaches to literature and culture.

In addition, an emphasis on disagreements among different theories can help bring the theories into contact with one another. One of the major pitfalls of an anthology as large and diverse as *NATC* arises because in any given course, the material must be organized and grouped in some sort of coherent way. Indeed, this instructor's manual is designed primarily to suggest a number of just such schemes. But this kind of organization, however necessary, can tend to make each subgroup seem an entity unto itself with no relation to the other subgroups. Instructors should therefore work hard to overcome this perception and to help students see that even theoretical approaches that seem vastly different can be related to each other in important ways.

The exploration of such interrelationships can go a long way toward clearing up the confusion that students sometimes feel when confronted with what often seems to them to be a bewildering array of different approaches in the kinds of broad survey courses in which they are typically introduced to theory. As the most comprehensive anthology of theory and criticism yet to be published, *NATC* is obviously meant to accommodate such courses, and *NATC* contains such a large number and wide variety of entries that it offers instructors a great deal of versatility and flexibility in designing the courses in which it is to be the principal text. This instructor's manual is supplied in an effort to provide useful advice to instructors who are planning and teaching such courses.

Of necessity, this manual is oriented primarily toward recommendations of selections to be included in given courses. At the same time, instructors should be aware that especially at the undergraduate level, most of the students in courses that might be taught using *NATC* as a primary text will need to learn some basics about how to read literary theory and criticism before they can begin to appreciate the complexities and implications of the various selections assigned in the course. Instructors might, then, want to start the course with some basic comments on reading theory and criticism, alerting students that they will be confronting a new discourse that operates according to principles with which they might not be fully familiar. It might be helpful, for example, to devote much of the first class period to very brief readings (perhaps even a single paragraph) chosen from the longer selections to be covered later in the course. Students can then be asked to respond to one or more of them in an in-class writing assignment. This assignment need not (and probably should not) be graded, but instructors might want to use the responses as a diagnostic tool. In any case, these assignments can provide the basis for in-class discussions, giving students confidence that they can not only read theory and criticism but also say something useful about it.

In addition to selecting material to cover in courses on theory and criticism, instructors must also choose from among a number of basic strategies for teaching the texts chosen. Some instructors, often in graduate-level courses, choose to concentrate solely on theory and criticism in such courses, assigning no reading of literary works or other supplemental materials. Instructors may assign only primary theoretical and critical texts, such as those included in *NATC*, or may supplement the primary materials with an introductory text (such as those by Booker, Bressler, Selden, or Tyson) that presents cogent overviews of the individual critical schools.

Other instructors may choose to include in their course syllabi one or more literary or cultural texts (not simply books but also film, television, and other sources of cultural material), intending to discuss the application of theory to those texts in class or to structure it into students' outside writing assignments. In examining such supplemental texts, students have an opportunity to exercise the theoretical and critical approaches they have been studying and therefore to develop a more in-depth understanding of those approaches. In addition, students often find their appreciation of the importance and power of theory considerably enhanced when they realize that self-conscious theoretical approaches enable them to discern things in cultural and literary texts that they had not previously seen.

The principal goal of *NATC* is to provide students with convenient access to a wide variety of primary works of literary theory and criticism. However, students should also be urged to make maximum use of the important supplemental material that is included in *NATC*, most notably the extensive headnotes that introduce the individual selections in the anthology. These headnotes offer useful background material concerning the authors' lives and works. In addition, they provide frameworks within which to read the selections, helping in two ways: the expectations they raise provide readers with effective reading strategies and they place the individual selections within larger contexts.

In addition to the headnotes, *NATC* also includes a substantial introduction to Theory and Criticism that helps students understand what literary theory is and why they should be studying it. It underscores that questions such as "what is reading?" and "what is literature?" can, in fact, be complex questions that might be answered in a variety of ways. The introduction also helps students understand that the way one answers such questions depends on the theoretical approach one takes to the reading and study of literature. In addition, introduces students to the notion that there are many such approaches, each involving different assumptions about the nature of literature, culture, history, society, and even reality itself. Finally, the introductory chapter includes what is essentially a brief survey of both the history of theory and the forms of literary theory and criticism that have been prominent, especially in the twentieth century. This survey is too brief, in itself, to convey to students a full understanding of the various theories discussed, especially if they have had no previous experience with these theories, but it does help them see the kinds of questions they will be attempting to answer in the course they are about to take. Ideally, it will help students approach that course with excitement and heightened expectations, and it is probably a good idea, especially with undergraduates, to spend some time discussing this introduction at the beginning of any course on literary theory and criticism.

Furthermore, *NATC* includes a substantial bibliography that provides useful suggestions for students (or, for that matter, instructors) who wish to read further in any of the areas covered by the selections in the anthology. This section of *NATC* includes a useful listing of works in various categories, including bibliographies, anthologies, histories, handbooks/encyclopedias, and introductions/guides. It includes as well bibliographic essays on a variety of contemporary schools and movements. These essays can be particularly valuable for students who are pursuing research projects; they also help students appreciate the variety and scope of work that has been done in those areas.

The following four chapters in this instructor's manual contain descriptions of four different types of courses that might be taught with *NATC*. The final chapter presents less-detailed outlines of several additional courses in which *NATC* might be effectively used. Individual instructors will, of course, wish to consider their own experience and interests, as well as the experiences and interests of their students, in designing specific courses. The courses described in this instructor's manual should provide useful starting points for a variety of courses.

In all cases, the course designs are provided in a modular format. Each module includes a list of selected readings, with individual entries prioritized according to the amount of time devoted to that particular module in teaching the course. For example, a typical module might be designed to take anywhere from one to three weeks of class time.[3] The entries will then be grouped according to priority, with the highest priority texts included in all versions of the module, the lowest priority only in the fullest. The listings of suggested readings are arranged to show not only the priority groupings but also the order in which the texts in any given group should be taught. While usually that order is chronological, it sometimes reflects the delayed influence in the West of an author (e.g., Bakhtin) or the logic of the ideas presented (especially in chapter 3).

The times suggested for the various versions of each module are intentionally ambitious in their brevity especially for undergraduate courses. They assume that the selections from *NATC* will constitute most if not all of the assigned reading for the course. Instructors who wish to employ a substantial amount of additional material (whether supplemental readings in theory and criticism or readings in literary and other cultural texts) should adjust their syllabi accordingly. In addition, instructors who wish

---

[3]A "week" in this scheme is a typical week for a three-credit-hour course: three 50-minute classes or two 75- to 80-minute classes. For courses worth more than three hours of credit or deviating from the norm in some other way (e.g., compressed summer sessions), instructors should adjust the recommended assignments accordingly.

to devote significant class time to reviews of material previously covered, in-class examinations, or other activities will probably need to adjust their syllabi.

This modular format has a number of advantages. It adjusts easily to courses of varying length, such as ten-week quarter courses or fifteen-week semester courses. Thus, an instructor teaching in the quarter system might teach the two-week versions of five different modules, an instructor teaching in a semester system might teach the three-week versions of the same five modules, and so on. Each chapter includes charts that suggest various standard modular combinations, but the format allows instructors to combine the different modules in an almost unlimited number of ways.

Together with the lists of suggested readings, the chapters in this manual include a number of specific teaching tips and other suggestions that are designed to help instructors in teaching individual selections and in placing different selections in dialogue with one another. Because chapters 2 and 3 include almost all the selections in *NATC*, discussion questions are not generally included in chapters 4 and 5; instructors relying on them are referred back earlier to chapters to find questions for particular selections.

These questions, which are broad and basic, are designed to serve a number of purposes. Students who have read and understood the selection and its accompanying headnote should be able to answer them adequately; conversely, students who can answer these questions adequately have probably read and understood the selection and its headnotes. The discussion questions might help instructors prepare their own teaching materials by conveniently suggesting the main ideas covered in each selection. Some instructors might, in fact, wish to distribute these questions (or similar questions that they have developed) to their students before the relevant selections are read. In that case, the questions will help students structure their reading, and could also help structure class discussions of the selections. Some instructors might also wish to assign students to prepare written answers to some of these discussion questions (or similar questions of their own). Finally, such questions might also be used to help construct take-home or in-class written examinations.

Chapters 2–5 also include lists of key terms and additional essay topics for each module. The essay topics generally involve more than one selection and are thus not encompassed by the discussion questions that accompany the individual selections. The topics are intended to be used in the same ways as the discussion questions: for classroom discussion, as exam questions, or as out-of-class writing assignments. Finally, each module in chapters 2 and 3 includes a list of advanced research topics that might be pursued as major out-of-class assignments for graduate or advanced undergraduate students. These suggested projects generally require a significant amount of additional research beyond the assigned selections from *NATC*.

CHAPTER 2

Sample Course: Historical Survey of Theory and Criticism

Broad historical surveys of major works are among the most commonly taught courses in literary theory and criticism in universities. Such courses have the advantage of introducing students to a wide variety of important ideas about theory and criticism, while at the same time providing a sense of the historical evolution of these ideas. Indeed, establishing coherent narratives of development is one of the best ways for instructors to overcome the major disadvantage of such courses—the possibility that students might be overwhelmed by the sheer amount of material that needs to be covered. Instructors should consider the following course modules as suggestions to help them construct coherent syllabi according to their own strategies for organizing such courses. Note that the introduction to Theory and Criticism provides a useful historical survey of theory that can be used to accompany such a course. See also the recent survey by Harland.

Course Modules

   I.   Classical Theory and Criticism (1–3 weeks)
  II.   Medieval Theory and Criticism (1–3 weeks)
 III.   Renaissance Theory and Criticism (1–3 weeks)
 IV.   Enlightenment Theory and Criticism (1–4 weeks)
  V.   Nineteenth-Century Theory and Criticism (1–4 weeks)
 VI.   Modern Theory and Criticism (1–4 weeks)
VII.   Contemporary Theory and Criticism (1–4 weeks)

Course Modules

I. Classical Theory and Criticism (1–3 weeks)

While numerous works of classical commentary on literature and literary criticism are now lost, many of those that have survived have exercised a powerful influence on subsequent critics and theorists. It is thus often useful to begin the historical survey of literary theory and criticism by considering some of the major works from the classical period, both because those works are of interest in themselves and because they provide an important background for later works.

TEACHING TIP: In addition to the selections listed below, some instructors might wish to emphasize the role of classical theory and criticism in the work of later critics and theorists. Selections in the *NATC* that reflect this engagement (such as Corneille's "Of the Three Unities" or the excerpt from Nietzsche's *Birth of Tragedy*) might productively be taught in conjunction with the module on classical theory and criticism. A variation on this approach would be to pair classical and contemporary texts, such as Derrida's *Dissemination* and Plato's *Phaedrus*, Baudrillard's *Precession of Simulacra* and Plato's *Republic*, or Todorov's "Structural Analysis of Narrative" and Aristotle's *Poetics*.

Suggested Readings		
1-week module	2-week module	3-week module
Plato	Gorgias	Gorgias
Republic VII & X	Plato	Plato
Aristotle	*Republic* VII & X	*Ion*
Poetics	*Phaedrus*	*Republic* II & III
Horace	Aristotle	*Republic* VII & X
	Poetics	*Phaedrus*
	Horace	Aristotle
	Longinus	*Poetics*
		Rhetoric
		Horace
		Longinus
		Quintilian
		Plotinus

SUGGESTED READINGS AND DISCUSSION QUESTIONS

■ Gorgias, from *Encomium of Helen*
   1. In what ways does the selection from Gorgias reinforce its argument about the power of speech through its own use of a flamboyant rhetorical style?

2. Summarize and comment on Gorgias's argument concerning the power of speech.

■ Plato, *Ion*
1. What are some of the implications of Socrates' argument that poetry is a form of divinely inspired madness?
2. Summarize and comment on Socrates' extension of this argument to include criticism as well as poetry.
3. In what ways do Plato's warnings about the power of speech complement or contradict Gorgias's earlier argument about the same power?

■ Plato, from *Republic*, Books II and III
1. Who are the "Guardians" and what role do they play in Plato's ideal republic?
2. Summarize and comment on the program outlined by Plato for the education of the Guardians.
3. What fundamental attitude toward literature is suggested by this educational program?

■ Plato, from *Republic*, Books VII and X
1. Briefly summarize and interpret the allegory of the cave in Book VII.
2. In what ways does this allegory constitute a warning about the dangers of literature?
3. Summarize and comment on Plato's warnings concerning imitation in Book X.

TEACHING TIP: Plato's suspicion of poetry (really, any literature) is one of the seminal statements on the subject in the Western tradition. Any number of later thinkers have felt the need to respond to Plato's criticisms and to defend poetry against his charges. It might be useful when teaching Plato to indicate the existence of these replies, many of which may be taught in this course. For example, the selections from Gorgias, Aristotle, Piotinus, Macrobius, Boccaccio, Sidney, Mazzoni, Vico, Arnold, and Pater all contain suggestions of the positive value of art that can be productively read in dialogue with Plato. See also Derrida's famous critique of Plato in *Dissemination*.

■ Plato, from *Phaedrus*
1. Summarize the contrast between writing and speaking that is suggested in this dialogue.
2. In what ways does the suspicion toward writing in this dialogue resemble the suspicion toward poetry shown in *Republic*?

TEACHING TIP: The suspicion displayed in this dialogue toward writing as less authentic than speaking has been adduced by Jacques Derrida as a crucial example of "logocentric thought" and of the "metaphysics of pres-

ence" that, according to Derrida, pervades the Western philosophical tradition. Instructors might want to bring up this issue, especially if they will
be teaching Derrida in their course. (The selection from *Dissemination* in
NATC contains much of Derrida's commentary on Plato.) For a good discussion of Derrida's treatment of Plato, see chapter 3 in Norris.

■ Aristotle, *Poetics*
   1. Summarize and comment on Aristotle's discussion of the three uni-
      ties.
   2. Discuss the role of catharsis in Aristotle's discussion of tragedy.
   3. What are the elements of plot in Aristotle's theory? Do you think
      these elements adequately encompass the various aspects of plot?

TEACHING TIP: Aristotle's work has been immensely influential on virtually all subsequent Western theories of literature. This influence should
be stressed in presenting his work. It might be a good idea to place special
emphasis on Aristotle's status as an authority in the Middle Ages and Renaissance, which provides an excellent link between the classical and the
medieval and Renaissance modules in this course. It is also a good idea to
point out the central role played by Aristotle's treatment of the unities of
time, place, and action in subsequent discussions. See, for example, the
selections in *NATC* by Corneille and by Samuel Johnson (on Shakespeare).

■ Aristotle, from *Rhetoric*
   1. Explain what Aristotle means by *rhetoric*.
   2. What, according to Aristotle, are the three elements of persuasion
      (or *pisteis*) in public speech?
   3. Summarize and comment on Aristotle's discussion of the three
      species of rhetoric or kinds of public speeches.
   4. In what ways does Aristotle's commentary in *Rhetoric* anticipate the
      later development of reader-response theory?

■ Horace, *Ars Poetica*
   1. Explain Horace's concept of decorum and the role it plays in poetry.
   2. Summarize and comment on Horace's comparison between poetry
      and painting.
   3. Summarize and comment on Horace's discussion of the relative im-
      portance of genius and craft in producing good poetry.

■ Longinus, from *On Sublimity*
   1. Explain the concept of sublimity, especially as it is used by Longi-
      nus.
   2. What, according to Longinus, are the five sources of sublimity in lit-
      erature?
   3. Summarize and comment on Longinus's discussion of the distinc-
      tion between genius and mediocrity.

■ Quintilian, from *Institutio Oratoria*
  1. What, according to Quintilian, is the role of tropes in oratory?
  2. Summarize and comment on Quintilian's emphasis on the importance of virtue for the orator.
  3. What, according to Quintilian, is the relationship between oratory and philosophy?

■ Plotinus, from *Enneads*
  1. What, according to Plotinus, is the distinction between the intelligible world and the sensible world?
  2. Summarize Plotinus's description of the three *archai*, or causes, of the intelligible world.
  3. Compare and contrast Plotinus's Neoplatonic view of the relationship between art and truth with Plato's view.

Key Terms and Concepts

catharsis	rhetoric
decorum	the sublime
idealism	the three unities
mimesis	tragedy
plot	trope
poetics	

Essay Topics

1. Compare and contrast the attitudes toward poetry expressed by Plato and Aristotle.
2. Comment on the role played by the poetry of Homer in the selections from classical criticism you have read.
3. Summarize and comment on the role of rhetoric in the various selections from classical criticism you have read.
4. Compare and contrast the attitudes shown by the Greek thinkers included in *NATC* with the Roman thinkers included in the anthology.
5. Discuss the social justifications for literature developed by classical theorists.

Research Projects

1. Plato's *Republic* has long functioned as one of the founding texts of the tradition of utopian literature. Do some research on this topic and write an essay that describes the role of Plato's text as background for later utopian writers, such as Sir Thomas More, Francis Bacon, Edward Bellamy, Tomaso Campanella, and H. G. Wells. *Suggestion*: See Mumford and Walsh for beginning information regarding this topic. For brief descriptions of many of the major utopian works, see Booker's *Dystopian Literature*. *Hint*: It might be a good idea to focus on views of the arts in these utopian texts.

2. Historians of language have argued that the classical emphasis on rhetoric implies a fundamentally different understanding of language than the modern view of language as representation. Do some research on this topic and write an essay summarizing your findings. *Suggestion*: Lanham provides a good starting point for this project.

3. Look at a major work of classical Greek literature, such as Sophocles' *Oedipus the King*. Which selections from Greek theory and criticism in *NATC* seem best to illuminate this work, and why?

4. Plato's discussion, in *Ion*, of poetic creativity as divinely inspired madness seems to contradict the traditional view of the classical Greeks as rational thinkers. Do some research on this topic and write an essay summarizing your conclusions. *Suggestion*: See Dodds.

5. Read Derrida's critique of *Phaedrus* in Dissemination and write an essay that summarizes your own view of the validity of Derrida's critique. *Suggestion*: Because Derrida's work is difficult, it might be useful to consult a secondary work on Derrida's critique of Plato, such as chapter 3 in Norris.

II. Medieval Theory and Criticism (1–3 weeks)

The Middle Ages have come to be known for a worldview—and views of art, literature, and language—strikingly different from that of the modern era. For this reason, students may find medieval texts both confusing and illuminating, and instructors should take advantage of the different perspectives of the medieval period to raise questions about literature and language whose answers might otherwise have seemed obvious to some students. At the same time, the medieval period has often been misrepresented as more foreign (and especially as more rigid and intellectually impoverished) than it was. Instructors might, for example, note the way in which sophisticated medieval meditations on sign theory anticipated developments in structuralist and poststructuralist criticism and theory in the twentieth century.

TEACHING TIP: Instructors who have done little work in the medieval period might find it helpful to consult a general survey of medieval aesthetics, such as Eco. A general survey of the period, such as that by Bishop, might also be helpful. Probably the best-known study of late medieval society is Huizinga's *Autumn of the Middle Ages* (long known in an abridged translation as *The Waning of the Middle Ages.*)

SUGGESTED READINGS AND DISCUSSION QUESTIONS

■ Augustine, from *On Christian Doctrine* and *The Trinity*
  1. Summarize and comment on Augustine's distinction between signs and things; between natural and conventional signs; between literal and figurative conventional signs.

Suggested Readings		
1-week module	2-week module	3-week module
Augustine	Augustine	Augustine
Moses Maimonides	Macrobius	Macrobius
Dante	Moses Maimonides	Hugh of St. Victor
	Aquinas	Moses Maimonides
	Dante	Geoffrey of Vinsauf
		Aquinas
		Dante

2. In what ways does Augustine's theory of the sign show the medieval Christian orientation of his thought? In what ways does it anticipate modern semiotics?
3. In what ways does Augustine seek to guarantee the stability of reference of figurative signs?
4. Describe the role of sound in Augustine's discussion of signs in *The Trinity*.

TEACHING TIP: Augustine's work can be seen either as the culmination of the classical period or the start of the medieval one. It thus provides a convenient transition, helping students to understand the continuities and discontinuities between the two periods.

■ Macrobius, from *Commentary on the Dream of Scipio*
  1. In what ways does Macrobius's discussion of the interpretation of dreams suggest that fictional texts may yield a special access to truth?
  2. Summarize Macrobius's catalog of the five kinds of dreams.
  3. In what ways does Macrobius's discussion suggest that his technique of reading dreams might also be applied to literary texts?

■ Hugh of St. Victor, from *The Didascalicon*
  1. In what ways does Hugh's discussion suggest the special importance of figurative language?
  2. Explain Hugh's notion that textual exposition includes three different steps: the letter, the sense, and the inner meaning. Explain Hugh's related notion of the special three-level mode of signification at work in biblical texts.
  3. In what ways does Hugh's discussion factor in the value of broad education and knowledge for the interpretation of texts?

■ Moses Maimonides, from *The Guide of the Perplexed*
  1. Explain Maimonides' argument that the meanings of biblical texts are complicated by such texts' being "equivocal," "derivative," and "amphibolus."

2. Summarize and comment on Maimonides' argument that some parables must be interpreted through close reading word by word, while others must be grasped as a whole.

3. In what ways does Maimonides' emphasis on the indeterminacy of the meaning of biblical texts anticipate modern theories of interpretation?

4. In what ways does Maimonides' work, rooted in the tradition of Jewish hermeneutics, differ from that of medieval thinkers whose work is rooted in the Catholic tradition?

■ Geoffrey of Vinsauf, from *Poetria Nova*

1. Summarize and comment on Geoffrey's suggestions concerning the proper ordering of narrative material.

2. What, according to Geoffrey, is the role of ornamentation in poetry?

3. In what ways does Geoffrey's discussion suggest a view of poetry as a craft to be learned by careful training? In what ways does this view suggest an important role for literary criticism?

4. Compare and contrast the view of poetics expressed by Geoffrey with that expressed by Horace in *Ars Poetica*.

■ Thomas Aquinas, from *Summa Theologica*

1. Summarize the system of fourfold exegesis of biblical texts propounded by Aquinas.

2. Discuss the significance of Aquinas's emphasis on the literal level of interpretation in relation to the other three levels.

3. Summarize and comment on Aquinas's discussion of the difference between the use of figurative language in poetry and in the Bible.

■ Dante Alighieri, from *II Convivio* and the Letter to Can Grande

1. Summarize the system of fourfold exegesis that Dante propounds in these selections.

2. Discuss the significance of Dante's extension of this mode of biblical exegesis to the interpretation of secular texts.

3. In what ways does Dante's discussion suggest an acceptance of multiple meanings of a kind that has served him or other exemplary writers well as a literary resource?

KEY TERMS AND CONCEPTS

allegory	literacy
commentary	literal language
figurative language	Neoplatonism
fourfold exegesis	philology
gloss	sign
grammar	trivium
hermeneutics	vernacular

ESSAY TOPICS

1. In what ways do these selections challenge the conventional notion that the medieval period consisted of "Dark Ages" dominated by ignorance and superstition?
2. In what ways does the preoccupation with fundamental issues concerning language and signification in these medieval selections anticipate developments in contemporary literary theory?
3. Write a brief description of the basic characteristics of Neoplatonism, based on the selections you have read.
4. Summarize and comment on medieval notions about the fourfold exegesis of sacred texts.

RESEARCH PROJECTS

1. Much medieval literary criticism is deeply concerned with the implications of reading and writing. Do some research on the topic of literacy and write an essay that summarizes your findings. *Suggestions*: Stock would be a good starting point for this project.
2. Write an essay about your overall perception of medieval sign theory. *Suggestion*: See Vance.
3. Write an essay discussing the ways in which medieval attitudes toward language differ fundamentally from modern and/or contemporary attitudes. *Suggestion*: Colish provides a good starting point for this project.
4. Read Dante's *Inferno*. Then write a detailed exegesis of one of the books, noting the way in which the poem invites reading via the medieval theory of fourfold exegesis. *Suggestion*: See Hollander, *Allegory* and "Babytalk."
5. The line between poetry and criticism appears less clear in the medieval period than it has generally seemed in modern times. Research this topic and write an essay that summarizes your findings. *Suggestion*: See Spearing. On the literary criticism embedded in the poetry of Dante, see Barolini. On the literary criticism embedded in the poetry of Chaucer, see Wetherbee.

III. Renaissance Theory and Criticism (1–3 weeks)

In Western culture, the Renaissance enjoys the reputation of being marked by a particular flowering of intellectual and artistic endeavor. Specifically, it marks the emergence of many attitudes (humanism, individualism, etc.) that remain distinctively modern, even centuries later. Instructors should note this special position of the Renaissance in Western intellectual history. At the same time, they should note that this vision of the Renaissance was created largely by eighteenth- and nineteenth-century historians, who were seeking to justify the new prominence of the ascendant middle classes in Western society, a justification that was furthered by a depiction of the Renaissance as a time of reborn enlightenment. In particular, the Renaissance was painted by these historians in stark contrast with the medieval period, seen as a dark time of ignorance and superstition (and as a time dominated by the Catholic Church and European aristocracy). For a classic nineteenth-century historical account of the Italian Renaissance, see Burckhardt. For a representative account that focuses on art and culture, see Pater.

TEACHING TIP: The transition between the medieval and Renaissance periods was not a sudden event but a gradual change that occurred at different times and at different rates in different parts of Europe. Instructors should encourage students to look for continuities between the two eras, rather than simply thinking of them as radically different. Some authors (such as Boccaccio, Christine de Pizan, and Dante) can be seen as transitional figures that might be included in either period.

Suggested Readings		
1-week module	2-week module	3-week module
Boccaccio	Boccaccio	Boccaccio
du Bellay	Giambattista Giraldi	Christine de Pizan
Sidney	du Bellay	Giambattista Giraldi
	Mazzoni	du Bellay
	Sidney	Ronsard
		Mazzoni
		Sidney

Suggested Readings and Discussion Questions

■ Giovanni Boccaccio, from *Genealogy of the Gentile Gods*
  1. Summarize and comment on Boccaccio's reversal of the common medieval privileging of philosophy over poetry as a discourse of authority.
  2. What, for Boccaccio, is the distinction between poetry and rhetoric?
  3. How does Boccaccio defend poetry against charges of obscurity?

■ Christine de Pizan, from *The Book of the City of Ladies*
  1. In what ways is Christine's attitude typically medieval? In what ways does it anticipate more modern feminist concerns?
  2. Summarize and comment on Christine's elaboration of the obstales that had, to that time, limited women's ability to become writers.
  3. Summarize and comment on Christine's defense of women against the various charges that were widely leveled against them in medieval writing.

■ Giambattista Giraldi, from *Discourse on the Composition of Romances*
  1. Summarize and comment on Giraldi's argument that romances possess an organic unity despite their multiple plot lines.
  2. Summarize and comment on Giraldi's argument in favor of pursuing new forms of artistic expression appropriate to the present historical moment rather than merely imitating classical artistic forms.
  3. Summarize and comment on the social and political vision embodied in Giraldi's commentary.

■ Joachim du Bellay, from *The Defence and Illustration of the French Language*
  1. In what ways can du Bellay's defense of the French language be taken as a defense of vernacular languages in general?
  2. According to du Bellay, what changes must take place before poetry written in French can take its place beside the classics of Greek and Latin poetry?
  3. Summarize and comment on du Bellay's discussion of imitation in poetry.

■ Pierre de Ronsard, from "A Brief on the Art of French Poetry"
  1. What advice does Ronsard give young poets on how to live their lives in order to become the type of person worthy of being a poet?
  2. Summarize and comment on Ronsard's emphasis on the imitation of classical forms as the proper mode for poetry.
  3. What does Ronsard mean by *invention* and what role does it play in his vision of poetry?

■ Giacopo Mazzoni, from *On the Defense of the "Comedy" of Dante*
  1. Summarize and comment on Mazzoni's discussion of the "idol." What does this discussion tell us about his view of literary and artistic representation?
  2. What, according to Mazzoni, are the three different "modes" in which poetry functions?
  3. Summarize and comment on Mazzoni's discussion of the instructional value of poetry.

■ Sir Philip Sidney, *An Apology for Poetry*
  1. What is Sidney's argument for the superiority of poetry to history and philosophy?
  2. How does Sidney defend against the charge that poets are liars who mislead their audience?
  3. Summarize and comment on Sidney's discussion of the current state of English poetry in his day.

KEY TERMS AND CONCEPTS

ancients vs. moderns   rhetoric
humanism   romance
imitation   style
Renaissance   vernacular language

ESSAY TOPICS

1. Describe and comment on the role assigned to rhetoric in the selections you have read from Renaissance criticism.
2. Compare and contrast the treatment of rhetoric in Renaissance criticism with that in classical criticism.
3. Renaissance thinkers often envisioned their innovative work as a return to the Greek and Roman classics. Based on the selections you have read, discuss the impact of classical theory on Renaissance criticism and theory.
4. In what ways do the selections you have read from Renaissance theory and criticism resemble those you have read from the medieval period? In what ways are they different?
5. Compare and contrast the fundamental concerns and attitudes expressed in the selections from French writers with those from English writers during this period.

RESEARCH PROJECTS

1. Christine de Pizan, as a fourteenth-century woman writer, is often regarded as an anomaly. Do some additional research on this topic and write an essay that describes the extent to which women wrote in the Middle Ages and early Renaissance. *Suggestion*: Finke might be a good place to begin research on this topic.
2. Choose a work of Renaissance literature and write an essay describing the ways in which it exemplifies Renaissance notions about literature and rhetoric. *Suggestion*: Sidney's *Astrophil and Stella* (1591) might be a good choice for this project because it provides an opportunity for comparison with Sidney's *Apology*. For excellent beginning observations on this project, see William J. Kennedy.
3. The plays of Shakespeare are generally considered the peak literary achievement of the Renaissance in England. In what ways do these plays indicate typical Renaissance attitudes reflected in Renaissance criticism and theory?
4. Much of the most influential criticism of Renaissance culture in recent years has taken an approach known as New Historicism. Do some research on this contemporary critical movement and comment on some of its findings with regard to our understanding of Renaissance society and culture. *Suggestion*: Stephen Greenblatt, a selection from whom is included in *NATC*, is probably the most in-

fluential figure in this movement. For a good survey of the movement, see Montrose. See also the book-length study by Brannigan
and the essays collected in Veeser and in Cox and Reynolds.

5. A great deal of recent criticism on the Renaissance has involved re-
examining the role of gender in that period. Do some research on
this topic and write an essay that summarizes your findings. How
might these findings cause you to reevaluate some of your ideas
concerning Renaissance theory and criticism? *Suggestion*: The essays in the volume edited by Goldberg provide a good starting point
for this project.

IV. Enlightenment Theory and Criticism (1–4 weeks)

The term *Enlightenment* is sometimes used as a rough designation for the
historical period between the Renaissance and the nineteenth century.
But the Enlightenment was also a more specific historical phenomenon
that had to do with the rise of science and reason as the dominant modes
for solving intellectual and material problems in the West. Students
should be made aware of both uses of the term. In the second sense, the
Enlightenment is conventionally seen as the beginning of a genuinely
modern sensibility. As such, the Enlightenment involves a number of in-
terrelated phenomena, including not only the rise of science as a discourse of authority but the rise to dominance of market-based economics,
middle-class ideology, and individualist notions of the self. These phenomena are all still powerful, and the influence of many of the major
ideas of Enlightenment thinkers can easily be detected in the work of today's critics and theorists. At the same time, students should be asked to
explore connections between the selections from the Enlightenment and
those from earlier periods. For example, the emergence of neoclassicism
(called classicism in France) indicates a link to ideas from the classical
period, while the roots of the growing Enlightenment emphasis on individualism can easily be seen in the Renaissance.

TEACHING TIP: The Enlightenment, as a formal philosophical and social movement, tends to be characterized by certain fairly consistent
philosophical ideas, such as a reliance on reason and rationality and the
use of a scientific epistemology to seek the truth about the world. It is
probably a good idea to introduce this module with a lecture describing
some of the central characteristics of Enlightenment thought in order to
provide students with the context needed to better understand the individual selections. A good, accessible introduction to the Enlightenment is
Outram.

Suggested Readings

1-week module	2-week module	3-week module	4-week module
Corneille	Corneille	Corneille	Corneille
Vico	Vico	Dryden	Dryden
Pope	Pope	Vico	Behn
Kant	Samuel Johnson	Addison	Vico
	Shakespeare	Pope	Addison
	Hume	Samuel Johnson	Young
	Kant	*Shakespeare*	Pope
	Edmund Burke	Hume	Samuel Johnson
		Kant	*Shakespeare*
		Edmund Burke	misc. selections
		Lessing	Hume
			Kant
			Edmund Burke
			Lessing

SUGGESTED READINGS AND DISCUSSION QUESTIONS

■ Pierre Corneille, "Of the Three Unities of Action, Time, and Place"
1. In what ways does Corneille's argument in this piece suggest modifications to Aristotle's strict emphasis on the unity of time, place, and action in drama?
2. How does Corneille use the three unities as a tool for criticizing the excesses of the baroque theater?
3. Summarize and comment on Corneille's emphasis on verisimilitude in this piece.

TEACHING TIP: Corneille should be introduced within the context of French classicism (see Greenberg). In addition, a discussion of this movement naturally leads to a consideration of the parallel movement of English neoclassicism, in relation to selections by such thinkers as Pope. For a good introduction to neoclassicism in the arts, see Irwin. Both of these movements can also be used effectively to introduce the historical transition from the Renaissance to the Enlightenment.

■ John Dryden, various selections
1. Summarize and comment on Dryden's discussion of Shakespeare and Jonson.
2. Why does Dryden feel that poetry functions as an especially effective form of instruction?
3. Summarize and comment on Dryden's discussion of translation.

■ Aphra Behn, "Epistle to the Reader" from *The Dutch Lover* and Preface
to *The Lucky Chance*
   1. What, according to Behn's "Epistle to the Reader," is the function
      and purpose of drama? How does this view challenge the elitism of
      the literary establishment of her day?
   2. Summarize and comment on the role of gender in Behn's argument
      in the Preface to *The Lucky Chance*.
   3. Compare and contrast the arguments and tones of the two selec-
      tions from Behn.

TEACHING TIP: Behn is a contradictory figure. While her own career as
a professional woman writer certainly points toward modernity, it is a
good idea to make clear to students that Behn's political ideas remain
rooted in aristocratic privilege and rule. She can therefore be seen as a
kind of transitional figure between early periods and the Enlightenment.

■ Giambattista Vico, from *The New Science*
   1. Briefly summarize the basic elements of Vico's universal model of
      the history of human societies.
   2. Summarize and comment on Vico's discussion of the first men in
      the age of the gods. What implications does this discussion have for
      our understanding of art and literature?
   3. In what ways does Vico's discussion suggest the special importance
      of poetry in human history and society?

■ Joseph Addison, from *The Spectator*
   1. What, exactly, does Addison mean by *wit*?
   2. Explain and comment on Addison's distinction between true and
      false wit.
   3. Summarize and comment on Addison's discussion of the sublime.
   4. Compare and contrast Addison on the sublime with other theorists,
      including Longinus, Kant, and Burke.

TEACHING TIP: Addison is representative of his time in a number of
ways, not least that his prominence as an intellectual figure owed a great
deal to the rise of print culture, which facilitated the distribution of his
ideas through such venues as *The Spectator*. His work might then provide
instructors with an opportunity to discuss the crucial role of print culture
in the historical evolution of the Enlightenment. A good source on this
phenomenon is McLuhan. See Goldgar for an excellent discussion of the
role of print culture in promoting the free exchange of ideas during the
Enlightenment. See also the brief selections from Habermas in *NATC*
concerning the role of print culture in the development of the public
sphere.

■ Edward Young, from "Conjectures on Original Composition"
   1. Summarize and comment on Young's discussion of the "ancients vs. moderns" debate. *Suggestion*: This debate was one of the central cultural issues in the first half of the eighteenth century, especially in a rapidly modernizing England. Major figures such as Swift and Pope took the side of the ancients, thus opposing the position represented by Young. For an interesting discussion of this debate within the context of the rise of science, see Jones.
   2. In what ways does Young's discussion mark him as a predecessor of the Romantics?

■ Alexander Pope, *An Essay on Criticism*
   1. Summarize and comment on Pope's assessment of the bad criticism he sees as rampant in his age.
   2. Explain and comment on the role of nature in Pope's vision of poetry and criticism.
   3. Summarize and comment on the role of the classics in Pope's "essay."
   4. In what ways is the impact of this piece different because it is written in verse, rather than prose? (Recall that earlier major critical works from Horace and Geoffrey of Vinsauf were also composed in verse.)

TEACHING TIP: Pope offers instructors a good opportunity to introduce the Augustan movement to their students. For Pope's leading role in that movement, see Mack's biography. Note, however, that Pope and the Augustans were largely conservative figures who opposed most of the historical currents associated with the Enlightenment. Pope, Swift, and others were, for example, highly suspicious of print culture, feeling that it led to the production and distribution of debased and spiritually impoverished works. For an influential take on the evolution of print culture that includes discussions of the opposition of Swift and Pope, see McLuhan.

■ Samuel Johnson, from *Shakespeare*
   1. What, according to Johnson, are the special virtues of Shakespeare's plays?
   2. Summarize and comment on Johnson's defense of Shakespeare against the charge that his plays are flawed because they mix comic and tragic modes.
   3. How does Johnson defend Shakespeare against the charge that his plays are flawed because they violate the classical unities of action, time, and place?
   4. In what ways might Johnson's discussion of Shakespeare, however laudatory, be seen as condescending, as a sign that Johnson regards himself as living in a more advanced and enlightened era than Shakespeare's?

■ Samuel Johnson, from *The Rambler, Rasselas,* and *Lives of the English Poets*
 1. How does Johnson react to the emerging genre of the novel in the selection from *The Rambler?*
 2. In what ways does the selection from *Rasselas* suggest that the author of this novel might have also been a literary critic?
 3. Summarize and comment on Johnson's discussion of metaphysical poetry in the selection from *Lives of the English Poets.*

■ David Hume, "Of the Standard of Taste"
 1. Briefly describe the major premises of Hume's empiricist philosophy.
 2. Summarize and comment on the argument by which Hume concludes that there may, in fact, be absolute and universal measures of aesthetic beauty.
 3. How does Hume account for variations in taste, given that there are universal standards of beauty?

■ Immanuel Kant, from *Critique of Judgment*
 1. Describe Kant's vision of the autonomy of the work of art and of art's "purposiveness without purpose."
 2. Explain Kant's notions of the beautiful and the sublime and discuss the ways in which they contribute to the overall impact of the work of art. *Suggestion:* For an interesting discussion of the significance of this aspect of Kant's aesthetics from a Marxist perspective, see the chapter on Kant in Eagleton's *Ideology of the Aesthetic.* Eagleton's analysis offers instructors, among other things, the chance to introduce the role played by the spread of capitalism in the culture of Enlightenment.
 3. Discuss the notion of the wholeness of the work of art and the role that this notion plays in Kant's philosophy of aesthetics.

TEACHING TIP: While Kant's work can be seen as one of the pinnacles of Enlightenment thought, his work also provides the background for many later critics and theorists. For example, Kant's aesthetic philosophy provides an important background to formalist criticism, though students typically find his work difficult. Instructors who do not choose to assign the selection from Kant directly should consider at least giving students an introduction to his ideas via a lecture, emphasizing the three points covered by the above discussion questions. The headnote to the Kant selection provides useful information for the preparation of such a lecture. Instructors who wish to read further to prepare to teach Kant might also consult some of the essays in the volumes edited by Guyer and by Ted Cohen and Guyer. The best brief single-volume introduction to Kant is probably Kemp. Kant's immensely influential work can be taught in dialogue with a number of later theoretical positions on aesthetics, almost all of which have felt the need to engage Kant in some way. For example, while formalist approaches all draw on Kant in some way, the selections in *NATC* from Bourdieu and Barbara Herrnstein Smith engage Kant's work from perspectives that challenge his basic premises of the autonomy of art and the universality of aesthetic judgments. Derrida's *Truth in Painting* engages Kant from a poststructuralist perspective, though for nonspecialists this dialogue is perhaps better approached via secondary criticism, such as Carroll (135–44).

■ Edmund Burke, from *A Philosophical Enquiry into the Origin of Our Ideas of the Sublime and Beautiful*
1. In what ways does Burke seem to regard taste as a universal category? In what ways does he account for variations in individual taste?
2. What, according to Burke, is the key to developing good taste? *Suggestion*: One can detect, in Burke's discussion of this topic, the conservatism that made him something of an anti-Enlightenment figure. Indeed, Burke's notorious opposition to the French Revolution is part of a larger opposition to many of the central ideas of the Enlightenment.
3. Summarize and comment on Burke's discussion of the sublime and its sources.

TEACHING TIP: Burke's discussion of the sublime can be placed in useful dialogue with Kant's. Note also the treatment of this topic in selections by Longinus and Addison. The sublime is also a key category for Romanticism and thus provides a crucial link between Enlightenment theory and nineteenth-century theory. For an overview of various eighteenth-century theories of the sublime, see the volume edited by Ashfield and De Bolla.

■ Gotthold Ephraim Lessing, from *Laocoön*
1. How does Lessing distinguish between "bodies" and "actions" as the objects of artistic representation?
2. Summarize and comment on Lessing's discussion of the relationship between poetry and painting.
3. In what ways does Lessing's discussion of poetic language anticipate modern sign theory?

KEY TERMS AND CONCEPTS

aesthetics	modernity
ancients vs. moderns	neoclassicism
the beautiful	philology
capitalism	print culture
classicism	rationality
didactic theory	the sublime
the Enlightenment	the three unities
individualism	universalism

ESSAY TOPICS

1. Summarize your understanding of the basic characteristics of neo-classicism, as gleaned from your readings in Enlightenment theory and criticism.
2. In what ways does English neoclassicism resemble French classicism? In what ways do the two movements differ? *Suggestion*: The selections from Pope and Corneille in *NATC* can be taken as respectively representing these two movements.
3. In what ways do the Enlightenment selections you have read reflect the increasing authority of scientific and rational thinking during this period? *Suggestion*: One might approach this topic by discussing the attempt to explain aesthetic response within the framework of a larger philosophical system, as in Kant or Hume. One might also look at such topics as the tendency toward categorization in thinkers such as Lessing.
4. Based on your readings from *NATC*, how do you see criticism and theory in the Enlightenment differing from those in earlier periods?
5. Compare and contrast the discussions of the sublime in the selections by Addison, Kant, and Burke.

RESEARCH PROJECTS

1. Do some research on the eighteenth-century "ancients vs. moderns" debate and write an essay that summarizes your findings on the topic. *Suggestion*: This debate was one of the central cultural issues in England at the end of the seventeenth century and beginning of the eighteenth century. Major figures such as Swift and Pope took the side of the ancients, thus opposing the position represented by Young. On Swift's role in this debate, see Pinkus. For an interesting discussion of this debate within the context of the rise of science, see Jones. On the same debate within the context of French culture at the end of the seventeenth century, see DeJean.
2. Several observers in recent decades have debated fundamental questions about the Enlightenment, such as whether it is over or still under way and whether it was a success or a failure. Do some research on this topic and write an essay that summarizes your findings. *Suggestion*: Gray provides a provocative starting point for this project.
3. The eighteenth century, generally seen as the height of the Enlightenment, is also conventionally seen by literary historians as the century of the emergence of the novel to prominence as a genre in Western literature. What aspects of the Enlightenment might have contributed to the rise of the novel in this era? *Suggestion*: See Watt.
4. Read a work of literature from the Enlightenment that seems to embody the ideas of that period. Then write an essay describing the ways in which it does so or does not do so. *Suggestion*: Diderot's *Jacques the Fatalist* (1796) should be an excellent choice for this project.

5. Max Horkheimer and Theodor Adorno wrote a famous essay titled "The Concept of Enlightenment" that strongly challenges conventional ideas about the Enlightenment, arguing that Enlightenment science and reason functioned more as techniques of domination than as methods of rational inquiry into truth. Read this essay (included in *Dialectic of Enlightenment*) and write an essay summarizing your response to it. *Suggestion*: This essay is challenging, and it will probably be useful to consult some secondary material, including Habermas's response to Horkheimer and Adorno.

V. Nineteenth-Century Theory and Criticism (1–4 weeks)

The nineteenth century was particularly rich not only in technological developments but also in the development of ideas that have remained central to Western thought into the twenty-first century. Instructors who have not done extensive work in the nineteenth century might want to consult some basic histories in order to further their appreciation of its importance. For this purpose, the best history of the nineteenth century is arguably Eric Hobsbawm's three-volume sequence, *The Age of Revolution, The Age of Capital,* and *The Age of Empire.*

Suggested Readings

1-week module	2-week module	3-week module	4-week module
Coleridge	Schiller	Schiller	Schiller
Gautier	Schleiermacher	Wollstonecraft	Wollstonecraft
Marx & Engels	Coleridge	Schleiermacher	de Staël
Communist	Shelley	Hegel	Schleiermacher
Manifesto	Poe	Wordsworth	Hegel
Arnold	Gautier	Coleridge	Wordsworth
Nietzsche	Marx & Engels	Shelley	Coleridge
Birth of Tragedy	*Communist*	Emerson	Peacock
	Manifesto	Poe	Shelley
	Arnold	Gautier	Emerson
	Pater	Marx & Engels	Poe
	Nietzsche	*Communist*	Gautier
	Birth of Tragedy	*Manifesto*	Marx & Engels
		Baudelaire	*Communist*
		Arnold	*Manifesto*
		Pater	Baudelaire
		James	Arnold
		Nietzsche	Pater
		Birth of Tragedy	James
			Nietzsche
			Birth of Tragedy
			Wilde

SUGGESTED READINGS AND DISCUSSION QUESTIONS

■ Friedrich von Schiller, from *On the Aesthetic Education of Man*
  1. In what ways do Schiller's comments suggest a sense of social and cultural crisis?
  2. Summarize and comment on Schiller's notion of the proper role of the artist in society.
  3. What is Schiller's advice to artists concerning the kind of art they should seek to produce?
  4. What aspects of Schiller's comments identify him as a Romantic thinker?

TEACHING TIP: Schiller can be effectively taught in dialogue with English Romantics, such as Wordsworth, Coleridge, and Shelley, to help students think about the nature and implications of Romanticism. On the character of Romantic thought, see Abrams, *The Mirror and the Lamp*.

■ Mary Wollstonecraft, from *A Vindication of the Rights of Woman*
  1. Discuss the ways in which *A Vindication of the Rights of Woman*, written in the midst of the French Revolution, might have been influenced by that historic event.
  2. Wollstonecraft consistently uses slavery as a metaphor for the condition of white, middle-class women. Discuss the implications of this usage.
  3. Discuss the ways in which, according to Wollstonecraft, women are complicit in their own domination by men. In what ways is this complicity influenced by the social conditioning of women from early childhood on?

■ Germaine Necker de Staël, from "Essay on Fictions" and from *On Literature Considered in Its Relationship to Social Institutions*
  1. In what ways is de Staël's attitude in both of these essays influenced by Romanticism? In what ways does it differ from typical Romantic attitudes?
  2. Summarize and comment on de Staël's recommendations regarding the novel as a genre in the first selection.
  3. Summarize and comment on de Staël's discussion of the plight of the woman intellectual in the second selection.

■ Friedrich Schleiermacher, from "Outline of the 1819 Lectures"
  1. What, according to Schleiermacher, constitutes "good" interpretation?
  2. Summarize and comment on Schleiermacher's categorization of various types of interpretation.
  3. Summarize and comment on Schleiermacher's discussion of "misunderstanding" in interpretation.

▪ Georg Wilhelm Friedrich Hegel, from *The Phenomenology of Spirit and Lectures on Fine Art*
1. Explain the concept of the dialectic as it functions in Hegel's philosophy.
2. Summarize and comment on Hegel's discussion of the Master-Slave (lord/bondsman) dialectic in relation to the achievement of self-consciousness in individuals.
3. What, according to Hegel, is the epistemological function of art?
4. In what ways does Hegel's discussion of art defend art from charges that it is relatively frivolous and inferior to philosophy as an intellectual pursuit? In what ways does Hegel's discussion nevertheless maintain the primacy of philosophy?

TEACHING TIP: As with the work of Kant, many students, unaccustomed to the technical language of philosophy, will find the crucial work of Hegel challenging to follow. Instructors might want to introduce the selections from Hegel with a brief overview of his work. Indeed a useful way to structure this lecture might be to set Hegel against Kant. The headnote to Hegel can help in preparing this lecture. Instructors who feel they need a better general understanding of Hegel might also want to consult Houlgate or *The Cambridge Companion to Hegel,* edited by Beiser. Kaminsky provide a useful introduction to Hegel's aesthetics, while the chapter on Fichte, Schelling, and Hegel in Eagleton's *Ideology of the Aesthetic* provides a useful Marxist approach to Hegel's aesthetics.

▪ William Wordsworth, Preface to the Second Edition of *Lyrical Ballads*
1. Summarize and comment on Wordsworth's specific recommendations for the writing of poetry.
2. In what ways can this Preface be taken as a manifesto of Romanticism? *Suggestion*: Note the very self-conscious way in which Wordsworth and Coleridge, in *Lyrical Ballads,* see themselves as creating a new and revolutionary type of poetry.
3. In what ways can this Preface be taken as an explanation and defense of Wordsworth's own poetic practice?
4. In what ways does this preface show the clear influence of the historical context in which it was written? *Suggestion*: Wordsworth clearly sees both the Enlightenment rise of science as a discourse of authority and the aftermath of the French Revolution as crucial to his project.

▪ Samuel Taylor Coleridge, from *Biographia Literaria* and *The Statesman's Manual*
1. How does Coleridge distinguish between imagination and fancy in *Biographia Literaria?*
2. Summarize and comment on Coleridge's discussion of the notion of organic form in *Biographia Literaria.*
3. What, according to Coleridge, are the distinctive features of a poem that set it apart from, say, a work of science?

4. Summarize and comment on Coleridge's discussion of the distinction between symbol and allegory in *The Stateman's Manual*.

TEACHING TIP: As the most important founding figures of English Romanticism, Wordsworth and Coleridge can be effectively taught together. In addition, either functions well as an introduction to English Romanticism. Some instructors may want to choose a representative poem or two by either author to discuss in class in relation to their selections in *NATC*. Wordsworth's "Tintern Abbey" (1798) and "Ode: Intimations of Immortality" (1807) and Coleridge's "The Rime of the Ancient Mariner" (1798) and "Kubla Khan" (1816) should work well for this purpose. On the basic characteristics of Romantic thought, see Abrams's *The Mirror and the Lamp*.

■ Thomas Love Peacock, "The Four Ages of Poetry"
   1. Briefly describe the four ages of poetry as set forth by Peacock.
   2. How does the progression of these four ages challenge the heroic models of the history of poetry often put forth by poets themselves?
   3. Summarize and comment on Peacock's description of the contemporary role of the poet in his society.
   4. Summarize and comment on Peacock's description and assessment of Romantic poetry.

■ Percy Bysshe Shelley, from *A Defence of Poetry*
   1. What is Shelley's vision of the role of the poet in society?
   2. Summarize and comment on Shelley's description of the history of poetry.
   3. In what ways can Shelley's essay be taken as a manifesto of Romanticism? *Suggestion*: On the character of Romantic thought, see Abrams's *The Mirror and the Lamp*.

TEACHING TIP: Shelley's "defence" was written largely as a response to Peacock's "Four Ages of Poetry," so these two selections can be taught very effectively in dialogue with one another.

■ Ralph Waldo Emerson, from "The American Scholar" and "The Poet"
   1. Summarize the basic characteristics of Transcendentalism as represented in Emerson's essays.
   2. Summarize and comment on Emerson's description of the reading process in "The American Scholar."
   3. Summarize and comment on Emerson's description of the process of poetic creation in "The Poet."

TEACHING TIP: Emerson is perhaps the leading exemplar of American Transcendentalism and can be usefully understood in that context. However, it is also a good idea to make clear the many links and parallels between American Transcendentalism and European Romanticism. On the

Romantic aspects of Emerson's thought, see Ellison. For a useful discussion of Emerson's Transcendentalist thought in its historical context, see Howe.

■ Edgar Allan Poe, "The Philosophy of Composition"
   1. Summarize and comment on Poe's recommendations for constructing a plot.
   2. Summarize and comment on Poe's recommendations concerning the ideal length of a work of literary art.
   3. In what ways does Poe's attitude show the influence of Romanticism?
   4. What aspects of Poe's account of poetic craft might be identified as formalist in nature?

■ Théophile Gautier, from Preface to *Mademoiselle de Maupin*
   1. In your opinion, does the "art for art's sake" attitude taken by Gautier elevate art by lifting it above reality, or does it diminish art by making it seem pointless or irrelevant?
   2. Gautier claims that "nothing is really beautiful unless it is useless" and that "the most becoming activity for a civilized man seems to me to be inactivity." How do these claims suggest Gautier's privileged economic status and how might they be criticized from the view point of less privileged individuals?

■ Karl Marx and Friedrich Engels, from *The Communist Manifesto*
   1. Explain the historical background of *The Communist Manifesto*. *Suggestion:* Instructors who feel that they need more background on the revolutions of 1848 might want to consult Postgate or Robertson.
   2. Summarize and comment on the description in this selection of the role of the bourgeoisie in history.
   3. How does this discussion of the bourgeoisie, together with the vision of all history as the history of class conflict, demonstrate the Marxist dialectic?
   4. In what ways are the accounts of capitalism's global destiny and its desacralizing forces relevant to conditions in our time?

TEACHING TIP: It is clearly impossible, within a single brief selection, to represent effectively the breadth, scope, and historical importance of the work of Marx and Engels. Instructors should probably spend some time emphasizing this topic, perhaps calling attention not only to the tradition of Marxist criticism that Marx and Engels founded but also to the impact of Marxist thought on other modern critical approaches, including cultural studies and postcolonial studies. The book by Demetz contains helpful information on the work of Marx and Engels as the founding texts of Marxist criticism. Useful dialogues can also be established by considering the influence of Hegel's dialectical method on Marx.

Instructors who feel that they need a firmer grounding in Marxist theory before teaching this module might start by reading the chapter on Marxism in Booker (*Practical Introduction*). Eagleton's *Marxism and Literary Criticism* also provides a succinct basic introduction to the application of Marxist theory to literature. The anthology edited by Tucker is probably the best collection of writings by Marx and Engels themselves. McLellan provides a good biographical introduction to Marx and his world in *Karl Marx*, and an overview of Marx's most important ideas in *The Thought of Karl Marx*. For a particularly good recent biography, see Wheen. For other useful suggestions, see the essay on Marxism included in the bibliography section of *NATC*.

■ Charles Baudelaire, from "The Painter of Modern Life"
  1. How does Baudelaire define beauty in this essay?
  2. Summarize and comment on Baudelaire's discussion of Constantin Guys (Monsieur G.).
  3. How does Baudelaire's describe modernity in this essay?
  4. Summarize and comment on Baudelaire's discussion of women.

■ Matthew Arnold, "The Function of Criticism at the Present Time" and from "Sweetness and Light" (*Culture and Anarchy*)
  1. In what ways does Arnold's discussion of the function of criticism suggest that critics bear a special moral responsibility in modern society?
  2. Summarize and comment on Arnold's view of the special importance of criticism in the context of late-nineteenth-century England.
  3. Explain the source and implication of the title of the essay "Sweetness and Light."
  4. In what ways does Arnold appear to see culture as a substitute for religion amid the increasingly materialistic context of Victorian England?

■ Walter Pater, from *Studies in the History of the Renaissance*
  1. Summarize and comment on Pater's arguments for the importance of art in human society.
  2. Compare and contrast Pater's aesthetic vision with that of Arnold.
  3. In what ways does the tendency toward relativism in *The Renaissance* suggest tensions typical of the Victorian age? *Suggestion*: See the discussion in the *NATC* headnote of the controversy over Pater's original conclusion to the book.

■ Henry James, "The Art of Fiction"
  1. Comment on James's notion that the "quality of the mind of the producer" is the most important and "deepest quality of the work of art."
  2. Summarize and comment on the aspects of James's argument that suggest that the novel should be viewed as genuine art and not merely popular entertainment.

3. In what ways does James's essay suggest that literary criticism can
    play a positive role in the development of the art of fiction?

■ Friedrich Nietzsche, from *The Birth of Tragedy*
   1. In what ways does Nietzsche's attitude in this essay point back to
       predecessors such as the Romantics? In what ways does it mark a
       change that points forward toward the twentieth century?
   2. In what ways does Nietzsche return to early Greek models in his
       thought? In what ways does he challenge certain Greek models, es-
       pecially the work of Plato?
   3. How does the aestheticism of this essay resemble that of other
       nineteenth-century thinkers in *NATC*, such as Gautier and Pater?
       How does Nietzsche's approach to the aesthetic differ from that of
       most of his contemporaries?

KEY TERMS AND CONCEPTS

aestheticism	ideology
aesthetics	imperialism
art for art's sake	industrial revolution
commodification	Marxism
commodity fetish	realism
dialectical materialism	Romanticism
dialectics	Victorian era

ESSAY TOPICS

1. Write a brief discussion of your understanding of the basic charac-
    teristics of Romanticism.
2. Based on your readings in *NATC*, how does German Romanticism
    differ from English Romanticism?
3. Compare and contrast the major ideas of English Romanticism with
    those of American Transcendentalism. *Suggestion*: On the Romantic
    aspects of Emerson's thought, see Ellison. For a useful discussion of
    Emerson's Transcendentalist thought in its historical context, see
    Howe. For additional interesting information on cultural links be-
    tween Britain and America during this period, see Weisbuch.
4. In what ways do the ideas of Victorian thinkers, such as Arnold and
    Pater, differ from those of Romantic thinkers, such as Wordsworth
    and Coleridge?
5. In what ways do the nineteenth-century selections you have read
    suggest the impact of the Industrial Revolution and of the accompa-
    nying transformation of European society on the culture of that
    century?
6. Discuss the contributions of women critics during the nineteenth
    century, based on your readings in *NATC*.

RESEARCH PROJECTS

1. Read one of the volumes of Hobsbawm's history of the nineteenth century and write an essay that comments on the volume, keeping in mind the selections you have read from nineteenth-century criticism and theory. In what ways does Hobsbawm's history illuminate those selections?

2. Read several poems by an important Romantic poet who also wrote criticism, then write an essay discussing the ways in which that poet's poetry embodies (or not) the ideas expressed in his poetry. *Suggestion*: Schiller, Wordsworth, Coleridge, Shelley, Poe, Baudelaire, Arnold, and Mallarmé might be good choices for this project.

3. Do some research on the role of women writers in nineteenth-century European culture and then write an essay that summarizes and comments on your findings. *Suggestion*: Books by Gilbert and Gubar (*The Madwoman in the Attic*) and by Showalter provide suggestive beginning points for this project.

4. Do some research on the impact of the French Revolution and its aftermath on nineteenth-century European culture and then write an essay that summarizes and comments on your findings. *Suggestion*: Lukács's *Historical Novel,* which emphasizes the impact of the French Revolution on the evolution of nineteenth-century realism, is an excellent place to begin this project. Hobsbawm's *Age of Revolution* provides good historical background. In addition to powerfully influencing nineteenth-century French history and being treated at length by major nineteenth-century French historians such as Michelet and de Tocqueville, the Revolution was also a major concern of English thinkers of the period. Among the early English studies of the French Revolution, several are regarded as masterpieces of polemical history; indeed, they are often read as literature. See, for example, Edmund Burke's *Reflections on the Revolution in France* (1790), which provided an immediate (and horrified) conservative reaction. (Thomas Paine's *Rights of Man* [1792] was a response to Burke.) Thomas Carlyle's *History of the French Revolution* (1837) is especially literary and is often compared with the novels of Sir Walter Scott; it is also late enough to treat the Revolution in a fairly positive way. Carlyle is strongly influenced by Romanticism while conducting a spirited polemic against conventional histories. For a good, brief recent history of the French Revolution, see Rudé.

5. Imperialism was a central defining characteristic of nineteenth-century European life, especially in major imperial powers such as England and France. Comment on the ways in which imperialism might have influenced the development of criticism and theory during this century. *Suggestion*: Said's *Orientalism* is the seminal study of the impact of colonialism on nineteenth-century discourses of various kinds. See Viswanathan for a discussion of the ways in

which the growth of English studies was spurred by a desire to promote English colonial power in India.

VI. Modern Theory and Criticism (1–4 weeks)

While observers conventionally think of the period from the 1960s forward as informed by an explosion in discourse concerning literary theory, the groundwork for this explosion was being laid throughout the earlier decades of the century. The selections from 1900 to 1960 included in *NATC* should strike most students as distinctively modern, far less foreign to their own sensibilities than even the nineteenth-century selections. Yet it is still important to place these modern selections in historical context and not to assume that students, especially undergraduate students, are familiar with the conditions underpinning these texts.

TEACHING TIP: Rather than being arranged chronologically, the selections below have been grouped together roughly according to the schools of criticism and theory represented by the various selections. Instructors will probably find it convenient to use these groupings to help students organize the large amount of material covered in this module. The selections for contemporary theory and criticism (the following module) have been organized similarly. Some instructors might wish to combine these two modules, teaching all selections from a single school (formalism, Marxism, feminism, etc.) together as a unit. Instructors should consult chapter 3 of this guide for a more thorough grouping of the twentieth-century selections in *NATC* according to critical school. Surveys of modern literary theory (such as those by Booke [*Practical Introduction*], Bressler, Selden, or Tyson) generally contain individual chapters that provide introductions to the different schools.

TEACHING TIP: The synthesizing essay by Kenneth Burke, "Kinds of Criticism," succinctly maps many of the main contending critical approaches of the modern period. It can, incidentally, be contrasted effectively with Cleanth Brooks's "Formalist Critics" and Georges Poulet's "Phenomenology of Reading," as well as Boris Eichenbaum's "Theory of the 'Formal Method'" and Edmund Wilson's "Marxism and Literature." All of these selections provide introductory surveys of various modern critical approaches.

SUGGESTED READINGS AND DISCUSSION QUESTIONS
Psychoanalytic Theory and Criticism

- Sigmund Freud, "The 'Uncanny'"
    1. Briefly describe the experience Freud refers to as "uncanny."
    2. Summarize and comment of Freud's conclusions concerning the source of uncanny feelings.

	Suggested Readings		
1-week module	2-week module	3-week module	4-week module
Freud "The 'Uncanny' "	Freud "The 'Uncanny' "	Freud "The 'Uncanny' "	Freud "The 'Uncanny' "
Bakhtin	Eichenbaum	Saussure	Jung
Gramsci	Eliot	Eichenbaum	Frye
Du Bois	Bakhtin	Eliot	Saussure
Woolf	Gramsci	Ransom	Jakobson
	Benjamin	Bakhtin	Eichenbaum
	Poulet	Lukács	Eliot
	Du Bois	Gramsci	Ransom
	Woolf	Benjamin	Brooks
		Horkheimer & Adorno	Bakhtin
		Poulet	Lukács
		Du Bois	Gramsci
		Woolf	Wilson
		Beauvoir	Benjamin
			Horkheimer & Adorno
			Poulet
			Hirsch
			Fish
			Du Bois
			Hughes
			Woolf
			Beauvoir

3. In this essay, Freud concludes that writers can produce uncanny feelings because they are able to control the return of the repressed in literature. What might this conclusion imply about Freud's general notion of the source of artistic creativity?

4. In what ways does Freud's focus on literature in this essay suggest the applicability of psychoanalysis to the interpretation of literature in general?

TEACHING TIP: Freud is easily the most important founding figure of psychoanalysis, and most students will be at least vaguely familiar with his work. However, instructors should not assume too much familiarity, especially by undergraduate students, for whom a good basic introduction to Freud's work should be very useful. Wright provides helpful introductory information, especially on the application of Freud's work by literary theorists and critics.

■ Carl Gustav Jung, "On the Relation of Analytical Psychology to Poetry"
1. Explain Jung's notions of the collective unconscious and archetypes. What roles, according to Jung, do these notions play in artistic creativity?
2. Explain and comment on Jung's distinction between "introverted" and "extraverted" forms of artistic creation.
3. In what does Jung's essay challenge and criticize potentially impoverishing forms of psychoanalytic interpretation of literary texts?

■ Northrop Frye, "The Archetypes of Literature"
1. Describe the ways in which Frye's notion of archetypes draws on concepts from Jungian psychoanalysis.
2. What, exactly, does Frye mean by a *literary archetype*? What might be some of the objections to Frye's hypothesis that all literary genres are derived from the quest-myth?
3. In what ways is Frye's attitude, as expressed in this essay, reminiscent of American New Criticism? In what ways does Frye suggest important limitations in formalist approaches such as New Criticism?

TEACHING TIP: Frye's work, with its use of the notion of archetypes, draws on the work of Jung in obvious ways. In addition, Frye's penchant for categorization has much in common with the impulses behind structuralism and thus provides a good transition to a discussion of that movement.

Structuralist Theory and Criticism

■ Ferdinand de Saussure, from *Course in General Linguistics*
1. Explain Saussure's concepts of *langue* and *parole*.
2. Explain Saussure's notions of synchronic and diachronic analysis.

TEACHING TIP: Saussure's work on linguistics is widely regarded as the most important theoretical inspiration behind the development of structuralism. Note that Saussure's emphasis on language itself provides a good opportunity for instructors to call attention to the linguistic focus of structuralism and to note, among other things, the extensive points of connection between structuralism and formalism.

■ Roman Jakobson, from "Linguistics and Poetics"
1. Summarize and comment on Jacobson's discussion of the "poetic function" in language.
2. Summarize and comment on the communication model used by Jacobson to describe the workings of language.
3. Explain Jacobson's concept of metalanguage and summarize the role it plays in his discussion.

TEACHING TIP: Instructors who wish to spend more time on structuralism might also consider including in their syllabi selections in *NATC* from such thinkers as White, Althusser, Lacan, and Todorov, who employed structuralist approaches in history, Marxism, psychoanalysis, and analysis of narrative, respectively. In any case, it is a good idea to emphasize the historical importance of structuralism, especially in Europe. Culler's *Structuralist Poetics* is probably the best introduction to the use of structuralism in analyzing literature. Hawkes is also an excellent introduction. See the two volumes by Dosse for a history of structuralism; Kurzweil might be helpful in this regard as well.

Formalism

■ Boris Eichenbaum, "The Theory of the 'Formal Method' "
1. Discuss the Russian formalist notion of literariness and of the ways in which literary objects and literary language are distinct from the nonliterary. What role does the phenomenon of "defamiliarization" play in this notion of the literary?
2. Discuss the distinction between "story" (*fabula*) and "plot" (*syuzhet*) in Russian formalist aesthetics.
3. Discuss the notion of the dominant and its role in the Russian formalist model of literary history.

■ T. S. Eliot, "Tradition and the Individual Talent" and "The Metaphysical Poets"
1. What is Eliot's vision of poetic tradition? Does Eliot's particular notion of tradition tend to connect poetry to larger historical processes, or does it isolate the world of poetry from the world of social reality?
2. Describe Eliot's notion of the artist as catalyst within the context of his vision of the impersonality of great art and literature.
3. How does Eliot's notion of the dissociation of sensibility, combined with his notion of tradition, inform his vision of literary history and of history as a whole?
4. In what ways might the attitudes expressed in Eliot's essays identify him as a predecessor of the formalism of the New Critics?

TEACHING TIP: Eliot's essays might provide a useful focal point for considering the modernist movement and its close relationship with the rise of formalist criticism, especially American New Criticism, then leading into a discussion of the work of Ransom and Brooks. There is a vast (and sometimes contradictory) literature on modernism. For a variety of perspectives on the movement, see the volumes edited by Brooker, by Bradbury and McFarlane, and by Chefdor, Quinones, and Wachtel. For an introduction to modernism from an essentially New Critical perspective, see Spears. For a broad general discussion of modernism in the arts, see Nicholls. For a discussion of modernism within the context of other modern artistic movements, such as postmodernism and the avant-garde, see Calinescu. For further discussions of modernism in relation to post-modernism, see Fokkema and Huyssen.

■ John Crowe Ransom, "Criticism, Inc."
1. Explain Ransom's distinction between scholars and critics. What reasons does he give for preferring the work of critics to that of scholars?
2. Ransom argues that criticism must become "more scientific, or precise and systematic." What do you think he means by this statement, in light of the consistently antagonistic attitude toward science shown by most of the major New Critics?
3. Describe Ransom's vision of the role of universities, and especially English departments, in modern culture.

TEACHING TIP: The Ransom selection, with its focus on the professionalization of literary studies, provides a good introduction to this aspect of New Criticism, as well as to debates about professionalization that are still raging today. Instructors might want to consult Robbins's *Secular Vocations* for a cogent overview of this subject.

■ Cleanth Brooks, "The Heresy of Paraphrase" (*The Well Wrought Urn*)
1. Why, for Brooks, is it "heretical" to believe that one can capture the essence of a work of literature by paraphrasing it? What does this attitude say about Brook's vision of the nature of literary art?
2. What does Brook's attitude in these essay suggest about the nature of literary canonicity?
3. Describe and comment on Brook's emphasis on the notion of unity in the literary work.
4. Describe and comment on the role of irony in Brook's view of literature and literary criticism.

■ Mikhail M. Bakhtin, from "Discourse in the Novel"
1. What does Bakhtin mean by *heteroglossia*?
2. Summarize and comment on Bakhtin's distinction between the dialogic nature of the novel and the monologic nature of poetry.
3. Summarize and comment on Bakhtin's notion that the true object of representation in the novel is language itself. Why, for Bakhtin, is the novel nevertheless intensely engaged with social and historical reality?
4. In what ways does Bakhtin's discussion of the novel resemble structuralist approaches?
5. What, according to Bakhtin, is wrong with "stylistics" as it is usually practiced?

TEACHING TIP: Bakhtin is among the most important literary theorists of the twentieth century, but his work, which has points of contact with Russian formalism, structuralism, Marxism, and cultural studies, is difficult to categorize and does not fit well in any given school. Teaching Bakhtin in conjunction with formalism enables the instructor to pay attention to the ways in which his work both grows out of that movement and deviates from it. A good source of information on this topic is Bennett, which sees Bakhtin as a bridge between Russian formalism and Marxism. The best general introduction to Bakhtin's work is by Morson and Emerson. The critical biography by Clark and Holquist is useful as well.

Marxist Theory and Criticism

TEACHING TIP: It is useful, especially in a brief introduction to such a broad phenomenon as Marxism, to help students place various Marxist ideas and approaches into categories. For example, see the chapter on Marxism in Booker's *Practical Introduction* for a suggestion that modern Marxist theorists and critics, at least in the West, can be broadly grouped into two categories: Lukácsian Marxists, who maintain a focus on the economic base and on alienation, commodification, and other classic Marxist "mediatory codes," and Gramscian Marxists, who focus their inquiries more on the superstructure (i.e., on the realm of culture and ideology).

■ György Lukács, "Realism in the Balance"
   1. Explain and comment on Lukács's emphasis on the notion of totality in this essay.
   2. What, according to Lukács, are the principal shortcomings of expressionism and other forms of modernist art?
   3. What, according to Lukács, are the principal advantages of realism in art?
   4. Explain and comment on the Popular Front as a historical phenomenon and as the background for this essay.

TEACHING TIP: Though this essay engages in a specific debate with Ernst Bloch over the merits of literary expressionism, it also participates in a general defense of realism and critique of modernism that represented Lukács's contribution to what is often called the "Brecht-Lukács debate," Brecht being a leading defender of modernism on the Left. For more on this important argument, see Lunn and the essays collected in the volume edited by Taylor.

Instructors who feel they need a better understanding of expressionism might consult Sheppard's essay or Nicholls's chapter on expressionism.

■ Antonio Gramsci, from the *Prison Notebooks*
   1. Explain Gramsci's distinction between "civil society" and "the State," and relate this distinction to the two different levels at which official power works to help the dominant bourgeois class maintain its control over capitalist society.
   2. Explain Gramsci's notions of the intellectual and the organic intellectual.

3. Explain Gramsci's notion of hegemony and identify ways in which it suggests a particularly important role for intellectuals in society.

TEACHING TIP: Gramsci's work has been particularly influential in recent decades, especially in the development of cultural studies. See, for example, the selection by Hall in *NATC*, which discusses the importance of Gramsci to the British cultural studies movement.

■ Edmund Wilson, "Marxism and Literature"
  1. Summarize and comment on Wilson's review of the role played by literature in the works of major Marxist thinkers from Marx to Trotsky.
  2. Summarize and comment on Wilson's arguments for the value of Marxism as a framework within which to interpret literature.
  3. Summarize and comment on Wilson's discussion of proletarian literature and of the view of literature as a weapon in the class struggle. *Suggestion*: Note that Wilson's position on this issue is essentially that of a group of thinkers who were aligned with the journal *Partisan Review*; this position was diametrically opposed to that held by Michael Gold, Granville Hicks, and other American Marxists associated with the journal *New Masses*. On this debate, see Murphy.

TEACHING TIP: For American instructors, Wilson's essay provides a convenient starting point for a discussion of the history of Marxism in the United States, and in particular of the prominence of Marxist thought in American culture in the 1930s. Instructors who wish to pursue this topic might want to read some of the excellent recent scholarship on the American cultural Left in the 1930s. The studies by Foley and Denning are particularly useful starting points.

■ Walter Benjamin, "The Work of Art in the Age of Mechanical Reproduction"
  1. Explain Benjamin's notion of the aura of the work of art and describe his understanding of the implications of the "decay" of the aura in modern culture.
  2. Explain the role of film in Benjamin's discussion of the antiauthoritarian potential of modern art.
  3. In what ways does the phenomenon of fascism affect and motivate Benjamin's essay?

■ Max Horkheimer and Theodor W. Adorno, from "The Culture Industry: Enlightenment as Mass Deception" (*Dialectic of Enlightenment*)
  1. This essay was written before television had become the dominant force in mass culture. In what ways does this essay anticipate the later rise of television?
  2. In what ways, according to Horkheimer and Adorno, does the cul-

ture industry make true individualism impossible while at the same time reinforcing the illusory claims of bourgeois society to respect the individual?

3. In what ways is this essay influenced by the historical phenomenon of German Nazism? What relationships do Horkheimer and Adorno see between German Nazism and American popular culture?

TEACHING TIP: Because there will probably be relatively little time to discuss the phenomenon of cultural studies in a course of this type, instructors might want to take advantage of "The Culture Industry" to introduce cultural studies to their students, especially if the course contains little in the way of more contemporary cultural studies. See the module on cultural studies in chapter 3 of this manual for more information and suggestions.

Phenomenology, Hermeneutics, and Reader-Response Theory

■ Georges Poulet, "Phenomenology of Reading"
1. Summarize and comment on Poulet's argument that books represent a unique category of objects.
2. Explain Poulet's vision of the reading process as a mingling of the minds of the reader and the author.
3. In what ways does Poulet's vision of the reading process conflict with structuralist and poststructuralist reading practices?

■ E. D. Hirsch Jr., "Objective Interpretation"
1. Summarize and comment on Hirsch's insistence that the meaning of a text must coincide with the intention of the author. Contrast Hirsch's conclusion with the rejection of authorial intention by the New Critics.
2. Explain and comment on Hirsch's distinction between meaning and significance in a literary text.
3. Summarize Hirsch's engagement with such European philosophers of phenomenology as Husserl and Heidegger.
4. Explain and comment on Hirsch's concept of historical "horizon."

■ Stanley Fish, "Interpreting the *Variorum*"
1. Summarize and comment on Fish's critique of formalist criticism.
2. Fish's approach depends on descriptions of the activities of "the reader." Who, exactly, is this "reader" and how does Fish know what he or she will do when encountering a specific text?
3. Explain Fish's notion of interpretive communities. How are these communities, for Fish, constitutive of meaning in the literary text?

TEACHING TIP: For an accessible introduction to reader-response theory as a whole, see Freund. See also the essays in the volume edited by Tompkins.

Race and Ethnicity Studies

■ W. E. B. Du Bois, "Criteria of Negro Art"
   1. Summarize Du Bois's description of the white "culture industry" and of the ways in which that industry contributes to the stereotyping of African Americans, denying them equal access to venues of self-expression and self-representation.
   2. Summarize Du Bois's vision of the role of the artist in the African American struggle for emancipation.
   3. Discuss Du Bois's conclusion that "all art is propaganda." How does this notion differ from conventional white American visions of art, especially as promulgated in formalist criticism and theory?

■ Langston Hughes, "The Negro Artist and the Racial Mountain"
   1. Discuss Hughes's emphasis on the importance of the production of "racial art" by African American artists.
   2. Discuss some of the ways in which Hughes's argument suggests an interrelationship between race and class in American society.
   3. In what ways does Hughes suggest that African American art might provide a powerful weapon in the struggle against white ideological domination?

TEACHING TIP: Hughes's essay can serve, among other things, as an opportunity to introduce the phenomenon of the Harlem Renaissance. On the intersection of the Harlem Renaissance and modernism, see Hutchinson. On the Marxist inclinations of the members of the Harlem Renaissance, see Maxwell.

Feminist Theory and Criticism

■ Virginia Woolf, from *A Room of One's Own*
   1. In what ways does Woolf's fable of Judith Shakespeare suggest broader historical phenomena regarding the obstacles encountered by women who would seek to gain recognition as writers or artists?
   2. Discuss the ways in which Woolf's treatment of gender in the fable of Shakespeare's sister also involves class and addresses the difficulties faced by working-class individuals who would seek to become writers or artists, regardless of their sex.

TEACHING TIP: Instructors might want to emphasize the importance of Woolf's work (both her novels and her nonfiction writings) to later feminist critics. It is also helpful to note that Woolf's discussion of language and style (the "woman's sentence") in *A Room of One's Own* makes her a precursor of French feminism. On the other hand, her discussion of the social and economic restrictions that have limited the production of women writers makes her a precursor of Anglo-American feminism.

■ Simone de Beauvoir, from *The Second Sex*

   1. Discuss Beauvoir's argument that Western tradition tends to depict the woman as a locus of mystery and otherness. In what way, according to Beauvoir, is this depiction useful to men?
   2. What implications might Beauvoir's discussion have for our understanding of Western dualistic thinking in general?

Key Terms and Concepts

alienation	*langue*
ambiguity	linguistics
archetype	modernism
aura	modernity
commodification	monologic
culture industry	New Criticism
dialogic	*parole*
dream-work	phenomenology
ego	psychoanalysis
extrinsic/intrinsic criticism	Russian formalism
fetishism	semiotics
the Harlem Renaissance	signified
the heresy of paraphrase	signifier
heteroglossia	structuralism
id	stylistics
irony	superego

Essay Topics

1. Summarize the fundamental differences between Marxist criticism and formalist approaches to criticism.
2. What aspects of the selections from modern theory and criticism clearly set them apart from the selections from the nineteenth century?
3. Compare and contrast the basic premises of Russian formalism and New Criticism.
4. Choose one of the basic critical approaches (psychoanalytic, structuralist, Marxist, formalist, or feminist) from modern theory and criticism. Write an essay that comments on what you see as the major strengths and weaknesses of this approach.
5. Choose any one of the selections from modern theory and criticism and write an essay that explains why that particular selection could not have been written at any time before the twentieth century.

Research Projects

1. As the essay by Habermas demonstrates, twentieth-century cultural critics have been particularly concerned with critical analyses of the phenomenon of modernity. Do some additional research into analy-

ses of modernity and present a survey of some of the major findings of the critics and theorists. If you choose, you might bring discussions of postmodernism into your essay as well. *Research hint*: See the issue of *New German Critique* (no. 26, 1982) devoted to the Frankfurt School's engagement with the phenomenon of modernity. Other useful works to consult include Therborn and Marshall Berman.

2. The canon of Western literature from the Renaissance onward has been dominated by works that Marxist critics would describe as bourgeois in their orientation. Yet many works of Western literature, especially those published during the 1930s, have been written from specifically antibourgeois and anticapitalist stances. Read a novel or other major literary work written from a perspective opposed to bourgeois ideology and comment, using the insights of Marxist theory, on the ways in which this work differs from typical Western canonical literature. *Suggestion*: Some important literary works with a Marxist or socialist orientation include Robert Tressell, *The Ragged Trousered Philanthropists* (1955); Lewis Jones, *Cwmardy* (1937) and *We Live* (1939); Michael Gold, *Jews without Money,* (1930); Jack Conroy, *The Disinherited* (1933); John Steinbeck, *The Grapes of Wrath* (1939); Richard Wright, *Native Son* (1940); and Meridel Le Sueur, *The Girl* (1978). Numerous British and American leftist novels are described in Booker, *The Modern British Novel of the Left* and *The Modern American Novel of the Left*. For an excellent critical study of American leftist literature that offers insights on leftist aesthetics, see Foley.

3. Do some research on modernism and write an essay that summarizes what you find to be the basic characteristics of modernist literature. *Suggestion*: There is a vast (and sometimes contradictory) literature on modernism. For discussions of the movement from a variety of perspectives, see the volumes edited by Brooker, by Bradbury and McFarlane, and by Chefdor, Quinones, and Wachtel. For an introduction to modernism from an essentially New Critical perspective, see Spears. For a broad general discussion of modernism in the arts, see Nicholls. For a discussion of modernism within the context of other modern artistic movements, such as postmodernism and the avant-garde, see Calinescu. For further discussions of modernism in relation to postmodernism, see Fokkema and Huyssen.

4. Do some additional research and write an essay tracing the historical impact of structuralism on Western thought in a variety of disciplines. *Suggestion*: Culler's *Structuralist Poetics* is probably the best introduction to the use of structuralism in analyzing literature. Hawkes is also an excellent introduction. See the two volumes by Dosse for a history of structuralism; Kurzweil might be helpful in this regard as well.

VII. Contemporary Theory and Criticism (1–4 weeks)

The 1960s and subsequent decades marked a genuine explosion in the discourses of literary theory and criticism, even though all these theoretical developments had roots in earlier decades, if not centuries. Nevertheless, the amount and variety of published criticism and theory began expanding at an unprecedented rate. As a result, students are faced with a potentially bewildering barrage of material when they first attempt to study contemporary theory and criticism. Instructors should seek to make this material as accessible as possible, without minimizing the genuine difficulty and complexity of much contemporary theory. One very useful way of doing so in a historical survey course is to emphasize the continuities between these texts and the earlier works that students will have already studied in the course.

TEACHING TIP: The selections below have been arranged roughly according to leading contemporary schools of criticism and theory represented by the various selections. Instructors will probably find it convenient to use these groupings to help students organize the large amount of material covered in this module. The selections in this module are, of necessity, extremely selective. Instructors should consult chapter 3 of this guide for a more thorough grouping of the twentieth-century selections in *NATC* by critical school. Individual instructors may, of course, want to vary the order in which the selections are taught in order to serve their own pedagogical goals.

SUGGESTED READINGS AND DISCUSSION QUESTIONS

Structuralist and Poststructuralist Theory and Criticism

■ Jacques Lacan, from "The Agency of the Letter in the Unconscious"
   1. Summarize and comment on Lacan's suggestion that language and its structures are prior to and constitutive of the individual subject.
   2. Explain and comment on Lacan's notion of the "signifying chain."
   3. What distinction does Lacan make between metaphor and metonymy?

TEACHING TIP: Lacan's work, though extremely difficult, is indispensable to fully understand contemporary psychoanalytic theory or the impact of structuralism on literary theory and criticism. It is useful, however, to introduce Lacan's major ideas (the Symbolic, Imaginary, and Real orders; the mirror stage of subject formation) in a form more accessible than his own writing. In addition to the headnote in *NATC*, instructors preparing such a lecture might want to consult a brief summary of Lacan's ideas, such as that contained in Booker (*Practical Introduction*, 35–37) or Wright (107–22). Perhaps the most accessible book-length introduction to Lacan's work is Benvenuto and Kennedy. Ragland-Sullivan is also useful. Instructors should note not only Lacan's distinctive appl-

Suggested Readings

1-week module	2-week module	3-week module	4-week module
Barthes "Death of the Author"; "From Work to Text"	Lacan "Agency of the Letter"	Lacan "Agency of the Letter"	Lacan "Agency of the Letter"
Foucault *Discipline and Punish*	Barthes "Death of the Author" "From Work to Text"	Barthes "Death of the Author" "From Work to Text"	Barthes "Death of the Author" "From Work to Text"
Jameson "Postmodernism"	Derrida *Of Grammatology*	Derrida *Of Grammatology*	Derrida *Of Grammatology*
Fanon "Pitfalls"	Foucault *Discipline and Punish*	Lyotard	de Man "Semiology and Rhetoric"
Butler	Althusser "Ideology"	Foucault *Discipline and Punish*	Lyotard
	Jameson "Postmodernism"	Althusser "Ideology"	Foucault *Discipline and Punish*
	Greenblatt	Habermas "Modernity"	Althusser "Ideology"
	Fanon "Pitfalls"	Jameson "Postmodernism"	Williams
	Said	Greenblatt	Habermas "Modernity"
	Sedgwick	Fanon	Jameson "Postmodernism"
	Butler	Said	Hebdige
		Bhabha	Iser
		Cixous	Fish
		Sedgwick	Greenblatt
		Butler	Fanon
			Said
			Bhabha
			Cixous
			Foucault *History of Sexuality*
			Sedwick
			Barbara Smith
			Butler

ication of structuralist methods to psychoanalysis but also his important
influence on movements such as French feminism.

TEACHING TIP: Instructors who want to emphasize the interdisciplinary
nature of structuralism might want to look at other selections in *NATC* by
such thinkers as White, Althusser, and Todorov who employed structuralist approaches in history, Marxism, and analysis of narrative respectively.

■ Roland Barthes, "The Death of the Author" and "From Work to Text"
   1. Explain what Barthes means by the *author*. Within this context,
      what is Barthes's concept of the *scriptor*?
   2. Describe Barthes's poststructuralist notion of intertextuality.
   3. What, for Barthes, distinguishes a "text" from the more traditional
      notion of the "work"?
   4. What are the implications of Barthes's notion of the text for the
      reading of literature?

■ Jacques Derrida, from *Of Grammatology*
   1. Explain Derrida's conceptualization of the "science" of grammatol-
      ogy.
   2. What does Derrida mean by *logocentrism*?
   3. Summarize and comment on Derrida's discussion of the "supple-
      ment" in this selection.
   4. What does Derrida mean when he writes that "there is nothing out-
      side the text"?

TEACHING TIP: Derrida was the single most important philosophical influence on Anglo-American deconstructive criticism, which was particularly prominent in the 1970s. (Paul de Man was the leading theoretical
force behind the specific development of U.S. deconstruction.) Instructors who teach Derrida's work will want to be sure that they understand
that phenomenon; they may find introductory discussions such as Culler's
On Deconstruction and (especially) Leitch's *Deconstructive Criticism* particularly valuable reading. A study of poststructuralism offers students an
opportunity to begin to understand these widespread influences. Norris
offers a good introduction that focuses specifically on Derrida's work.

■ Paul de Man, "Semiology and Rhetoric"
   1. What are the implications of de Man's presentation of the instability
      of rhetoric for the interpretation of literary texts?
   2. In what ways does de Man's reading of Yeats's "Among School Chil-
      dren" suggest a challenge to the Aristotelian tradition of "either/or"
      logic?
   3. In what ways does de Man's essay suggest that literary texts are al-
      ways already engaged in their own deconstruction?

■ Jean-François Lyotard, "Defining the Postmodern"
  1. Summarize and comment on Lyotard's distinction between modernist and postmodernist architecture.
  2. Summarize and comment on Lyotard's discussion of the status of the idea of progress in the postmodern era.
  3. Summarize and comment on Lyotard's notion that the postmodern era is a time for analyzing and reflecting on the past. In what ways is his vision here a poststructuralist one?

TEACHING TIP: Lyotard is one of the leading theorists of postmodernism. The brief selection in *NATC* does not make entirely clear that Lyotard is best known for his idea, expressed in *The Postmodern Condition*, that postmodernism is marked by "incredulity toward metanarratives," where *metanarratives* are totalizing theories of the workings of history, society, and epistemological inquiry. Instructors might want to familiarize themselves with Lyotard's argument in that book before teaching his work. Lyotard's work also has much in common with that of such poststructuralist thinkers as Derrida and Foucault. See, for example, Carroll.

■ Michel Foucault, from *Discipline and Punish*
  1. Describe Foucault's vision of the way in which the modern prison has come to function as a representative manifestation of "normative" power in modern society as a whole.
  2. Explain Foucault's notion that the "productive" techniques of power employed within modern carceral society actually exercise more effective and thoroughgoing control of individual behavior than did the "repressive" techniques of earlier eras.
  3. In what ways does Foucault's notion of the carceral resemble Althusser's notion of ideology? In what ways is Foucault's notion different?

TEACHING TIP: Foucault joins Derrida as one of the most important thinkers of poststructuralism. Therefore, instructors should make sure that students gain some appreciation for the scope and importance of Foucault's work. The chapter on Foucault in Booker's *Practical Introduction* provides a good overview of his career for instructors (or students) who feel that they need a better understanding of his work. In addition, there is a vast secondary literature on Foucault. *The Cambridge Companion to Foucault*, edited by Gutting, contains essays that are particularly helpful as an introduction to various aspects of Foucault's work.

Marxist Theory and Criticism and Cultural Studies

■ Louis Althusser, from "Ideology and Ideological State Apparatuses"
  1. Describe Althusser's concept of the Ideological State Apparatus (ISA).
  2. Discuss Althusser's notion of interpellation. What does it suggest about the difficulty of resistance to official ideology in a modern bureaucratic society?

3. In what ways is Althusser's understanding of the concept of ideology and the construction of the subject structuralist in nature?

TEACHING TIP: Though Althusser's work is Marxist in its orientation, his methodology is structuralist. Instructors might want to emphasize this fact to help students understand the broad influence of structuralism, as well as the frequency with which specific critics and theorists use hybrid approaches. In addition, Althusser's structuralism (an approach typically seen as synchronic) potentially conflicts with his Marxism (with its diachronic emphasis on history). Indeed, Althusser's work triggered an extensive debate on the role of historicism in Marxist thought. See, for example, Thompson's *Poverty of Theory* for a critique of Althusser. Jameson's *Political Unconscious* is, among other things, an attempt to mediate between Althusser's structuralism and the more traditional historicism of dialectical Marxists such as Lukács.

■ Raymond Williams, from *Marxism and Literature*
  1. Discuss Williams's vision of "dominant, residual, and emergent" elements in society. How does this vision clarify and enhance the traditional Marxist notion of history as a sequence of periods, each dominated by a given mode of production?
  2. Discuss Williams's notion of structures of feeling. Compare this notion to more traditional Marxist concepts, such as ideology.
  3. What is the principal goal, according to Williams, of a Marxist "sociology of culture"?

■ Jürgen Habermas, "Modernity—An Incomplete Project"
  1. What does Habermas mean by *modernity*? In what sense, according to Habermas, is the project of modernity incomplete?
  2. Discuss Habermas's notion of the fragmentation of modern bourgeois society into separate, seemingly autonomous spheres of activity. What are the implications of this fragmentation?
  3. In what sense does Habermas believe supposedly radical thinkers such as Foucault and Derrida to be "neoconservatives"?

■ Fredric Jameson, "Postmodernism and Consumer Society"
  1. Summarize some of the key characteristics of postmodernist culture as described by Jameson in this essay.
  2. Discuss Jameson's use of Lacan's figuration of schizophrenia as a metaphor for postmodern textuality and postmodern experience as a whole.
  3. Summarize and comment on Jameson's key conclusion that postmodernism replicates the logic of consumer capitalism.

TEACHING TIP: Jameson is probably the most important theorist of postmodernism in the United States, and his contributions in that area should not be ignored; he presents these ideas more fully in his book *Postmodernism*. Jameson was also a central figure in the turn toward more detailed consideration of social, political, and historical issues in U.S. criticism of the 1980s and 1990s. For a discussion of Jameson's importance as the thinker who "made Marxism stick in the United States," see Walter Cohen. Instructors might also consider constructing a unit on modernity and postmodernity, employing selections from such theorists as Foucault, Lyotard, Habermas, Jameson, Baudrillard, and hooks.

■ Dick Hebdige, from *Subculture*
  1. Summarize Hebdige's discussion of the term *culture*.
  2. Discuss the ways in which, according to Hebdige's Marxist analysis, the dominant culture in any society at any given time reflects the ideology of the ruling class of that society.
  3. Hebdige argues that "there is an ideological dimension to every signification." How might this notion affect our methods of reading and interpreting literary texts?

TEACHING TIP: Hebdige was an important figure in the evolution of the British cultural studies movement, as were Raymond Williams, Stuart Hall, and Laura Mulvey, all of whom are represented in *NATC*. For more on this movement, see Dworkin.

Reader-Response Theory and Criticism

■ Wolfgang Iser, "Interaction between Text and Reader"
  1. Summarize and comment on the role played by textual "gaps" or "blanks" in Iser's description of the reading process.
  2. Explain and comment on Iser's notion of the repertoire of a literary text.
  3. Contrast Iser's reader-response approach to that put forth by Fish via the notion of interpretive communities.

■ Stanley Fish, "Interpreting the *Variorum*"
  1. Summarize and comment on Fish's critique of formalist criticism.
  2. Fish's approach depends on descriptions of the activities of "the reader." Who, exactly, is this "reader" and how does Fish know what he or she will do when encountering a specific text?
  3. Explain Fish's notion of interpretive communities. How are these communities, for Fish, constitutive of meaning in the literary text?

TEACHING TIP: For an accessible introduction to reader-response theory as a whole, see Freund. See also the essays collected in the volume edited by Tompkins.

New Historicist Theory and Criticism

■ Stephen Greenblatt, Introduction to *The Power of Forms in the English Renaissance*
  1. In what ways does Greenblatt's description of New Historicism set it apart from the "old" historicism, as embodied in the work of such critics as J. Dover Wilson?

2. In what ways does Greenblatt's description of New Historicism set it apart from New Criticism and other forms of formalist criticism?
3. What aspects of New Historicism can be identified as postmodern?

TEACHING TIP: Greenblatt is the leading practitioner of New Historicism, a critical movement that reached great prominence in the 1980s and 1990s. It is a good idea to introduce and discuss that movement when teaching Greenblatt's work. Instructors might want to consult his books *Renaissance Self-Fashioning* and *Shakespearean Negotiations* to get a better feel for his work. For an introduction to New Historicism, see the chapter on it in Booker (*Practical Introduction*). See also Montrose, Brannigan, and the volumes of essays edited by Veeser and by Cox and Reynolds.

TEACHING TIP: Michel Foucault is probably the most important theoretical influence on Greenblatt and on New Historicism as a whole. Instructors might therefore wish to introduce some of Foucault's work in conjunction with a discussion of the movement.

Postcolonial Theory and Criticism

TEACHING TIP: Recent work on postcolonial theory and criticism is closely related to work in race and ethnicity studies. Instructors might wish to emphasize this link when presenting postcolonial studies.

■ Frantz Fanon, from "The Pitfalls of National Consciousness" (*The Wretched of the Earth*)
1. In what ways, for Fanon, is national consciousness a useful tool in the anticolonial struggle?
2. What are the "pitfalls" of this consciousness, especially in the postcolonial era?
3. Describe Fanon's characterization of the colonial and postcolonial bourgeoisie.

■ Frantz Fanon, from "On National Culture" (*The Wretched of the Earth*)
1. How does Fanon define *national culture*?
2. What, according to Fanon, is the role of nationalism and national culture in the fight against colonial domination?
3. What, according to Fanon, are the principal pitfalls of a focus on nationalism as a mode of anticolonial resistance?
4. Summarize and comment on Fanon's discussion of the "native intellectual."

TEACHING TIP: Instructors might want to emphasize to their students that Fanon is probably the most important third world anticolonial thinker of the twentieth century. His work has been immensely influential not only for other critics and theorists but also for numerous postcolonial novelists, especially in Africa.

■ Edward W. Said, from *Orientalism*
1. Discuss Said's use of the Foucauldian notion of discourse to describe the legacy of colonialist tendencies in Western thought and
   to define Orientalism as an institution.
2. Describe the motivations behind and basic characteristics of the discourse of Orientalism.
3. Though Said's analysis focuses primarily on nineteenth-century
   texts, his conclusions have far-reaching implications that remain
   relevant at the beginning of the twenty-first century. Describe the
   contemporary relevance of Said's ideas for ethnic studies, as well as
   for postcolonial studies and for scholarly work more generally.

TEACHING TIP: As what many regard as the founding text in the field of
colonial discourse analysis, *Orientalism* is one of the most influential
works of criticism and theory to be published in the last quarter of the
twentieth century. Instructors with relatively little background in postcolonial studies might want to study *Orientalism* in more detail before teaching
Said's work as an example of the analysis of colonialist discourses. They
might also want to underscore the influence of Foucault on this work.

■ Homi K. Bhabha, "The Commitment to Theory"
1. Bhabha espouses a belief that "theory" can be valuable tool for postcolonial critics. On the evidence of this essay, what kinds of theory
   does he himself seem to draw on?
2. Bhabha seeks, in this essay, to refute the charge that the application
   of Western theory to postcolonial culture is a potential form of cultural imperialism that runs counter to the economic and political interests of the formerly colonized world. Is he successful in this
   argument? In what ways might Bhabha's argument be criticized?
3. Explain and comment on the crucial notion of hybridity that informs Bhabha's argument in this essay (and in his work elsewhere).

Gender Studies and Feminist Theory and Criticism

■ Hélène Cixous, "The Laugh of the Medusa"
1. Describe the characteristics that for Cixous set *écriture féminine*
   (women's writing) apart from more conventional, masculine modes
   of discourse.
2. Summarize the ways in which Cixous sees writing as central to the
   emancipation of women.
3. In what ways is Cixous's thought clearly poststructuralist? How does
   her work differ from that of important poststructuralist predecessors
   such as Jacques Derrida?

■ Michel Foucault, from *The History of Sexuality*
1. What is the "repressive hypothesis"? How does Foucault's critique
   of this hypothesis reflect his fundamental theory of the productive
   nature of power in modern bourgeois society?

2. On what basis does Foucault believe the repressive hypothesis to be an inaccurate description of the role played by sexuality in Victorian society?

3. Explain Foucault's notion that the functioning of sexuality in Victorian society produced not only discourse on sexuality but also a variety of forms of "perversion."

■ Eve Kosofsky Sedgwick, from *Between Men* and from *Epistemology of the Closet*

1. Summarize Sedgwick's attempt to differentiate among the terms *sex, gender,* and *sexuality.* How might the distinctions made in queer theory and in feminist theory be different?

2. How, according to Sedgwick, might the very concept of gender be biased toward heterosexual assumptions?

3. Explain the distinction made by Sedgwick between homosexual and homosocial behavior. How and why does this distinction function differently for men than for women?

■ Barbara Smith, "Toward a Black Feminist Criticism"

1. Summarize and comment on Smith's critique of the approaches taken by previous critics to literature by black women, and particularly by black lesbians.

2. What are the basic principles that Smith suggests might be used by black feminist critics?

3. Smith suggests that literary critics can play important social and political roles and that in fact they have a responsibility to do so. Summarize her discussion of the social and political importance of literary critics. Do you agree with her argument?

■ Judith Butler, from *Gender Trouble*

1. In what ways does Butler's vision of the social construction of individual identities challenge the identity politics common to Anglo-American feminist thought in the past few decades?

2. How does Butler's discussion challenge the very notion of "woman" as it has conventionally been used in feminist theory and criticism?

3. Summarize and comment on Butler's discussion of the ways in which socially constructed identities might be challenged by "subversive bodily acts."

TEACHING TIP: Butler's work has been particularly influential in the emerging gender studies and queer theory movements of recent years. Her work thus provides an excellent point of departure for discussing the transformation of feminist criticism and theory into gender studies in the 1990s.

KEY TERMS AND CONCEPTS

cultural studies   New Criticism
écriture féminine   New Historicism
gender studies   postcolonial
essentialism   postmodernism
formalism   postmodernity
hegemony   poststructuralism
Ideological State Apparatus (ISA)   queer theory
intertextuality   reader-response theory
modernism   structuralism
modernity   subjectivity

ESSAY TOPICS

1. Briefly describe your understanding of the basic characteristics and assumptions of New Criticism.
2. Briefly describe your understanding of the basic characteristics and assumptions of structuralism.
3. Briefly describe your understanding of the basic characteristics and assumptions of poststructuralism.
4. Briefly describe your understanding of the basic characteristics and assumptions of feminist criticism.
5. Briefly describe your understanding of the basic characteristics and assumptions of gender studies.
6. Briefly describe your understanding of the basic characteristics and assumptions of cultural studies.
7. Briefly describe your understanding of the basic characteristics and assumptions of Marxist literary theory and criticism.
8. Briefly describe your understanding of the basic characteristics and assumptions of race and ethnicity studies.
9. Briefly describe your understanding of the basic characteristics and assumptions of postcolonial studies.
10. Briefly describe your understanding of the basic characteristics and assumptions of reader-response theory.
11. Briefly describe your understanding of the basic characteristics and assumptions of New Historicism.
12. Briefly describe your understanding of the basic characteristics and assumptions of queer theory.
13. What, according to such theorists as Foucault and Said, are the appropriate roles that should be played by intellectuals in modern society?

RESEARCH PROJECTS

1. The canon of Western literature has been dominated by works by male writers. And, as numerous feminist critics have pointed out, these works often represent women in negative and biased ways.

Read a novel or other major literary work written from an explicitly feminist perspective and comment, using the insights of feminist theory, on the ways in which this work differs from Typical Western canonical literature. *Suggestion*: The novels of Virginia Woolf, especially *Orlando* (1928) should serve well for this project.

2. The canon of Western literature has been dominated by works by white, European writers. And, as numerous race and ethnicity critics have pointed out, these works often represent nonwhite people in negative and biased ways. Read a novel or other major literary work by an African American or other self-consciously ethnic American author and comment, using the insights of race and ethnicity theory, on the ways in which this work differs from typical Western canonical literature. *Suggestion*: The novels of Richard Wright and Toni Morrison should serve well for this project. Gates's *The Signifying Monkey* might be a good place to look for ideas concerning the intersection between literary theory and African American literature.

3. The canon of Western literature has been dominated by works by white, European writers. And, as numerous postcolonial critics have pointed out, these works often represent non-European people (especially those in the colonies formerly ruled by European imperial powers) in negative and biased ways. Read a novel or other major literary work written by a colonial or postcolonial writer and comment, using the insights of postcolonial theory, on the ways in which this work differs from typical Western canonical literature.

4. Much commentary surrounding postmodernism has involved attempts to differentiate that movement from modernism. Research the debate on this issue and write an essay that summarizes some of the most important points that have been made. *Suggestion*: The appendix to Booker's *Vargas Llosa* summarizes much of this debate. The essays contained in the collection edited by Brooker, as well as the volumes by Fokkema and Huyssen, might also provide useful starting points for this project. Hassan is an especially valuable starting point.

5. Marxist theorists and critics have been particularly concerned with the phenomenon of postmodernism and its relationship to capitalism. Research Marxist commentaries and write an essay that summarizes your findings. *Suggestion*: Jameson is probably the most important of the many Marxist thinkers and critics who have addressed postmodernism, generally from a critical perspective that sees it as the cultural equivalent of capitalism in its global, consumerist phase. Instructors might want to consult Jameson's book on the subject, *Postmodernism*, before teaching a module on this topic. Jameson draws on a characterization of global capitalism that can be found in Ernest Mandel's *Late Capitalism*. For other Marxist commentaries on postmodernism, see Harvey and Callinicos.

6. The cultural studies movement has been at the heart of the recent "culture wars" that have sparked sometimes heated debates over the nature and purpose of literary scholarship and teaching. Research these culture wars and write an essay describing your conclusions concerning them. *Research hints*: Useful volumes in this debate include Allan Bloom; Levine; Gates, *Loose Canons*; and Graff, *Beyond the Culture Wars*.

7. The emerging field of body studies takes its inspiration from the work of Foucault and Butler, among others. Examine the recent work of Susan Bordo and Lennard Davis in *NATC* and elsewhere to sample this new area of inquiry. Write an essay that summarizes and comments on the strengths and weaknesses of current body theory.

CHAPTER 3

Sample Course: Major Schools of Modern and Contemporary Theory and Criticism

The following course outline presents suggestions for teaching a course in major schools of modern and contemporary criticism and theory, using *NATC* as the primary text. This course might be enhanced through the use of a supplemental introductory text (such as those by Booker [*Practical Introduction*], Bressler, Selden, or Tyson) that presents cogent overviews of the individual critical schools. Some instructors might also wish to use the introduction to *NATC* as the introductory text. Such a text might be taught in parallel with the related selections. Alternatively, some instructors might prefer to spend the first part of this course surveying various schools with the help of an introductory text, then follow with specific readings, perhaps in areas selected by the students themselves based on their experience with the initial overview of different schools.

The suggested primary modules below can be used to construct a full semester course of fifteen weeks or a full quarter course of ten weeks. Some instructors, however, may spend less than the full three weeks on the primary course modules so that some of the alternative modules can be used. Others may substitute one or more of the alternative modules for some of the suggested primary modules. For example, as formalist criticism is now somewhat passé, some instructors may wish to spend their time on a more currently vital approach (such as psychoanalytic criticism) instead of formalism.

Primary Course Modules

 I. Formalism (including New Criticism) (1–3 weeks)
 II. Marxist Criticism and Theory (1–3 weeks)
 III. Feminist Criticism and Theory (1–3 week)
 IV. Poststructuralist Criticism and Theory (1–3 weeks)
 V. Ethnicity and Race Studies (1–3 weeks)

Additional or Alternative Modules

 I. Psychoanalytic Criticism and Theory (1–3 weeks)
 II. Structuralist Criticism and Theory (1–2 weeks)
 III. Cultural Studies (1–3 weeks)
 IV. Phenomenological, Hermeneutic, and Reader-Response Criticism and Theory (1–2 weeks)
 V. Postmodern Criticism and Theory (1–2 weeks)
 VI. Postcolonial Criticism and Theory (1–2 weeks)
 VII. Gender Studies and Queer Theory (1– 2 weeks)

Primary Course Modules

I. Formalism (including New Criticism) (1–3 weeks)

Formalist approaches provide an excellent beginning point for any survey of modern critical schools. For one thing, New Criticism was dominant in U.S. literary studies for such a long time that many of its premises will still seem almost like common sense to many American students. For another, most of the other schools that came to prominence in North American literary studies from the 1960s to the 1990s were populated by critics who saw them largely in opposition to New Criticism and as responses to perceived inadequacies in the New Critical formalist approach. Outside the United States, formalist approaches were also influential

Suggested Readings

1-week module	2-week module	3-week module
Eichenbaum	Eichenbaum	Kant
Ransom	Bakhtin	Eichenbaum
Brooks	Eliot	Bakhtin
Eagleton	Ransom	Eliot
	Wimsatt & Beardsley	Ransom
	Brooks	Wimsatt & Beardsley
	Kenneth Burke	Brooks
	Eagleton	Kenneth Burke
		Trotsky
		Eagleton

through much of the period following World War II, but were subsequently challenged. Thus, a similar dynamic applies.

SUGGESTED READINGS AND DISCUSSION QUESTIONS

■ Immanuel Kant, from *Critique of Judgment*
  1. Describe Kant's vision of the autonomy of the work of art and of art's "purposiveness without purpose."
  2. Discuss the notion of the organic wholeness of the work of art and the role that this notion plays in Kant's philosophy of aesthetics.

TEACHING TIP: Kant's work provides an important background to formalist criticism, though students typically find it difficult. Instructors who do not choose to assign the selection from Kant directly should consider at least giving students an introduction to his ideas via a lecture, emphasizing the points covered by the above discussion questions. The headnote to the Kant selection provides information useful in preparing such a lecture. Instructors who wish to read further might also consult some of the essays in the volumes edited by Guyer and by Ted Cohen and Guyer. The best brief single-volume introduction to Kant is probably Kemp. Kant's immensely influential work can be taught in dialogue with that of a number of later theorists on aesthetics, almost all of whom have felt the need to engage Kant in some way. For example, while formalist approaches all draw on Kant in some way, the selections in *NATC* from Bourdieu and Barbara Herrnstein Smith engage Kant's work from perspectives that challenge his basic premises of the autonomy of art and the universality of aesthetic judgments. For an interesting discussion of Kant's aesthetics from a Marxist perspective, see the chapter on Kant in Eagleton's *Ideology of the Aesthetic*. Derrida's *Truth in Painting* engages Kant from a poststructuralist perspective, though for nonspecialists this dialogue is perhaps better approached via secondary criticism, such as Carroll (135–44).

■ Boris Eichenbaum, "The Theory of the 'Formal Method' "
  1. Discuss the Russian formalist notion of literariness and of the ways in which literary objects and literary language are distinct from the nonliterary. What role does the phenomenon of "defamiliarization" play in this notion of the literary?
  2. Discuss the distinction between "story" (*fabula*) and "plot" (*syuzhet*) in Russian formalist aesthetics.
  3. Discuss the notion of the dominant and its role in the Russian formalist model of literary history.

■ Mikhail M. Bakhtin, from "Discourse in the Novel"
  1. Explain Bakhtin's key concepts of 'dialogism' and heteroglossia. How are these two concepts different? How are they similar?
  2. Summarize and comment on Bakhtin's distinction between the dialogic nature of the novel and the monologic nature of poetry.

3. Summarize and comment on Bakhtin's notion that the true object of representation in the novel is language itself. Why, for Bakhtin, is the novel nonetheless intensely engaged with social and historical reality?
4. In what ways can one detect, in Bakhtin's discussion of the novel, the influence of Russian formalism? In what ways does Bakhtin's approach challenge the basic premises of formalism?

TEACHING TIP: Bakhtin is among the most important literary theorists of the twentieth century, but his work, which has points of contact with Russian formalism, structuralism, Marxism, and cultural studies, is difficult to categorize and does not fit well in any given school. Teaching Bakhtin in conjunction with Russian formalism allows the instructor to pay attention to the ways in which his work both grows out of that movement and deviates from it. A good source of information on this topic is Bennett, which sees Bakhtin as a bridge between Russian formalism and Marxism. The best general introduction to Bakhtin's work is by Morson and Emerson. The critical biography by Clark and Holquist is useful as well.

■ T. S. Eliot, "Tradition and the Individual Talent" and "The Metaphysical Poets"
1. Describe Eliot's vision of poetic tradition. Does Eliot's particular notion of tradition tend to connect poetry to larger historical processes, or does it isolate the world of poetry from the world of social reality?
2. Describe Eliot's notion of the artist as catalyst within the context of his vision of the impersonality of great art and literature.
3. Describe Eliot's notion of the dissociation of sensibility. How does this notion, combined with his notion of tradition, inform his vision of literary history and of history as a whole?
4. In what ways might the attitudes expressed in Eliot's essays identify him as a precursor of the New Critics?

■ John Crowe Ransom, "Criticism, Inc."
1. Explain Ransom's distinction between "scholars" and "critics." What reasons does he give for preferring the work of critics to that of scholars?
2. Ransom argues that criticism must become "more scientific, or precise and systematic." What do you think he means by this statement, in light of the consistently antagonistic attitude toward science shown by most of the major New Critics?
3. Describe Ransom's vision of the role of universities, and especially English departments, in modern culture.

TEACHING TIP: Because of the importance of New Criticism in the institutionalization of literary studies in the United States, instructors should consider devoting a certain amount of class time to a discussion of this phenomenon, paying attention to New Criticism's cultural politics in addition to its features as a method for reading literature. The Ransom selection, with its focus on the professionalization of literary studies, provides a good introduction to this aspect of New Criticism, as well as to debates about professionalization that are still raging today. Instructors might want to consult Robbins for a cogent overview of this subject. The Eagleton selection in *NATC* contains useful comments on the cultural politics of New Criticism, from a strongly opposed ideological perspective. Instructors who want to read further before teaching this aspect of New Criticism should consult the chapter on New Criticism in Booker (*Practical Introduction*) or Leitch (*American Literary Criticism*). See also Jancovich.

■ William K. Wimsatt Jr. and Monroe C. Beardsley, "The Intentional Fallacy" and "The Affective Fallacy"
   1. Define the *intentional fallacy*. How does this notion relate to Eliot's insistence on the impersonality of poetry?
   2. Define the *affective fallacy*. How does this notion relate to Ransom's notion of the professionalization of literary studies?
   3. Wimsatt and Beardsley use the term *fallacy* to describe certain techniques of interpretation, thereby implying that those techniques are incorrect. Are they suggesting that the New Critical approach is, by contrast, "correct"? What does this suggestion say about the nature of the New Critical project?

■ Cleanth Brooks, "The Heresy of Paraphrase" (*The Well Wrought Urn*) and "The Formalist Critics"
   1. Why, for Brooks, is it "heretical" to believe that one can capture the essence of a work of literature by paraphrasing it? What does this attitude say about Brooks's vision of the nature of literary art?
   2. What does Brooks's attitude in these essay suggest about the nature of literary canonicity?
   3. Describe and comment on Brook's emphasis on the notion of unity in the literary work.
   4. Describe and comment on the role of irony in Brooks's view of literature and literary criticism.

■ Kenneth Burke, "Kinds of Criticism"
   1. Burke is sometimes loosely grouped with the New Critics, though the relationship between his work and theirs is tenuous at best. Discuss the ways in which this essay engages with New Criticism and challenges its premises.
   2. Describe and comment on Burke's notion of the "Criticism of Criticism."
   3. Discuss Burke's distinction between "genetic" and "implicational" types of extrinsic criticism. What critical schools might be included in these two categories, respectively?

■ Leon Trotsky, from *Literature and Revolution*
   1. Summarize Trotsky's critique of formalism, by which he primarily
      means Russian formalism. How might this critique also apply to
      American New Criticism?
   2. What is Trotsky's attitude toward the idea of proletarian art and the
      role of art in the life of the proletariat?
   3. Summarize Trotsky's vision of the relationship between art and pol-
      itics. How might this vision have been influenced by Trotsky's own
      context, as he and the other leaders of the new Soviet Union sought
      to transform the backward and oppressive society of czarist Russia
      into a modern workers' state?

■ Terry Eagleton, from *Literary Theory*
   1. Describe Eagleton's view of the nationalistic motivations behind the
      rise of "English" studies in the early decades of the twentieth cen-
      tury.
   2. Describe the relationship between British formalist criticism and
      American New Criticism, as suggested by Eagleton's discussion.
   3. Explain why Eagleton is skeptic of the New Critical project. Why
      might Eagleton, a Marxist, feel this way?

KEY TERMS AND CONCEPTS

the affective fallacy	heteroglossia
Agrarians	the intentional fallacy
ambiguity	intrinsic and extrinsic criticism
canon	irony
close reading	literariness
defamiliarization	metaphor
dialogism	*fabula*
dominant	poetics
fabula	*syuzhet*
figurative language	tradition
the heresy of paraphrase	

ESSAY TOPICS

1. Compare and contrast the basic premises of Russian formalism and
   New Criticism.
2. Discuss some of the possible limitations of the New Critical emphasis on the "words on the page" as the source of meaning in the literary text.
3. Summarize formalist notions that literary language functions differently than language in nonliterary texts. What criticisms might be
   leveled against such ideas?
4. What, in your view, are the principal strengths and weaknesses of
   New Criticism or of formalism in general?

RESEARCH PROJECTS

1. In what ways is Kant a forerunner of modern formalism?
2. Consult the selections in *NATC* from Trotsky, Burke, Bakhtin, and Eagleton. What, according to these selections, are the limitations of formalism? Do you agree with them?
3. Read T. S. Eliot's poem *The Waste Land* (1922). Discuss the ways in which this poem relates to Eliot's theoretical and critical comments on literature. You might make reference to published criticism on this poem, especially as it relates to Eliot's work as a critic.
4. Read the entire text of at least one book-length work of New Criticism. (Brooks's *Well Wrought Urn* might be a good choice.) Discuss this book, focusing on its goals and the ways in which it achieves them, while at the same time it seeks to promote the New Criticism as a method.
5. Research the cultural history of New Criticism, referring to works such as Graff, *Professing Literature*; Jancovich, Leitch, *American Literary Criticism*; and Lentricchia. Write a brief history of New Criticism, describing the impact of that movement on American literary criticism, and especially its institutionalization in English departments.

II. Marxist Criticism and Theory (1–3 weeks)

Beginning with the work of Marx himself, the tradition of Marxist analysis now stretches more than 150 years. As a result, it is in many ways the most venerable of the schools still prominent in contemporary literary studies. The Marxist tradition is rich and diverse, but decades of cold war propaganda have given it a lingering reputation for dogmatism and narrow-mindedness. Discussions of Marxist theory and criticism can thus be particularly valuable in a survey of critical schools, not just because of its intrinsic importance but also because its reception raises crucial issues about cultural politics and the conditioning of cultural judgments by factors outside the realm of culture proper. Marxist theory also intersects other critical schools in key ways. It has been especially important in the evolution of cultural studies, for which the work of Marxist critics such as Benjamin, Gramsci, and Horkheimer and Adorno provides a crucial background. Similarly, Marxist feminists such as Beauvoir and Spivak have been central to the evolution of gender studies, while third world Marxist thinkers such as Fanon and Ngugi have been central to the development of postcolonial studies. All of these intersections need to be taken into account when planning and designing a course.

TEACHING TIP: Marxist criticism and theory can be taught very effectively in conjunction with formalist criticism and theory, creating a dialogue between the formalist focus on the autonomous text and the Marxist focus on understanding literature in social and historical contexts. This opposition can also effectively introduce the important notion that Marxist theory concerns not merely the reading of literature but the workings of history and human societies. Because Marxism is broader in scope than most of the other approaches covered in this course, it is especially valuable to begin this module with a general overview of Marxist theory. Note that in addition to the readings suggested below, many other selections in *NATC* are by thinkers who have been strongly engaged with the Marxist tradition, including Du Bois, Hughes, Bakhtin, Howe, Ohmann, Hall, Spivak, and Davis.

Instructors who feel that they need a firmer grounding in Marxist theory before teaching this module might start by reading the chapter on Marxism in Booker (*Practical Introduction*). Eagleton's *Marxism and Literary Criticism* also provides a succinct basic introduction to the application of Marxist theory to literature. The anthology edited by Tucker is probably the best collection of writings by Marx and Engels themselves. McLellan provides a good biographical introduction to Marx and his work in *Karl Marx,* and an overview of Marx's most important ideas in *The Thought of Karl Marx.* For a particularly good recent biography, see

Suggested Readings

1-week module	2-week module	3-week module
Marx & Engels	Marx & Engels	Marx
German Ideology	*German Ideology*	Preface to *Critique*
Communist Manifesto	*Communist Manifesto*	*Manuscript of 1844*
Gramsci	Marx	Marx & Engels
Benjamin	*Capital* ("Fetishism")	*German Ideology*
Althusser	Lukács	*Communist Manifesto*
"Ideology"	Gramsci	Marx
Jameson	Benjamin	*Grundrisse*
Political Unconscious	Horkheimer & Adorno	*Capital* ("Fetishism")
	Althusser	*Capital* ("Struggle")
	"Ideology"	Engels
	Williams	Lukács
	Habermas	Wilson
	"Modernity"	Gramsci
	Jameson	Benjamin
	Political Unconscious	Horkheimer & Adorno
		Althusser
		"Ideology"
		"Letter on Art"
		Williams
		Habermas
		"Modernity"
		Jameson
		Political Unconscious

Wheen. For other useful suggestions, see the essay on Marxism included in the bibliography section of *NATC*.

Suggested Readings and Discussion Questions

■ Karl Marx, from Preface to *A Contribution to the Critique of Political Economy and from Economic and Philosophic Manuscripts of 1844.*
   1. In what ways does the first of these two selections reflect a materialist conception of history?
   2. Explain the Marxist concept of alienation, as discussed in the second of these selections.
   3. What, according to the second selection, are the sources of alienation in a capitalist economy?
   4. Summarize and comment on Marx's critique, in the second selection, of the discipline of political economy in his day.

■ Karl Marx and Friedrich Engels, from *The German Ideology*
   1. In what ways does this selection imply that people make their own history rather than being merely the passive objects of larger historical forces?
   2. In what ways does this selection demonstrate the Marxist emphasis on materialism and opposition to idealism?
   3. What do Marx and Engels mean when they say ideology has no history? *Suggestion*: For a succinct introduction to the Marxist critique of ideology, see McLellan's *Ideology*.

■ Karl Marx and Friedrich Engels, from *The Communist Manifesto*
   1. Explain the historical background of *The Communist Manifesto*. *Suggestion*: Instructors who feel that they need more background on the revolutions of 1848 might want to consult Postgate or Robertson.
   2. Summarize and comment on the description in this selection of the role of the bourgeoisie in history.
   3. How does this discussion of the bourgeoisie, together with the vision of all history as the history of class conflict, demonstrate the Marxist dialectic?

■ Karl Marx, from *The Grundrisse*
   1. What, according to Marx, is the source of mythology?
   2. Why, according to Marx, is the modern world antithetical to myth?
   3. Summarize and comment on Marx's discussion of the reasons why many people in the modern world still enjoy classical Greek art, even though it is rooted in a very different world.

■ Karl Marx, from *Capital* ("The Fetishism of Commodities")
   1. Briefly explain the phenomenon of commodification as conceptualized by Marx.

2. Summarize and comment on Marx's explanation of the source of the "mystical character" of commodities, and thus of commodity fetishism.
3. Summarize and comment on Marx's treatment of religion in this selection.
4. Summarize and comment on Marx's use of *Robinson Crusoe* as an example in this selection.

■ Karl Marx, from *Capital* ("The Struggle for a Normal Working-Day")
1. Explain Marx's concept of "labour-power."
2. Discuss Marx's conclusions concerning the implications of the reduction of workers to the abstract notion of labor power.
3. In what ways is Marx's description of the "struggle" for a shorter working day representative of his dialectical vision of history as a whole?

■ Friedrich Engels, from his Letter to Joseph Bloch
1. Summarize and comment on Engel's defense in this letter against the charge that Marxism is based on a simplistic notion of economic determinism.
2. Summarize and comment on Engel's discussion of the role of the state in society.
3. In what ways does Engel's attitude in this letter indicate the scientific and rationalist orientation of Marxism?

■ György Lukács, "Realism in the Balance"
1. Explain and comment on Lukács's emphasis on the notion of totality in this essay.
2. What, according to Lukács, are the principal shortcomings of expressionism and other forms of modernist art?
3. What, according to Lukács, are the principal advantages of realism in art?
4. Explain and comment on the Popular Front as a historical phenomenon and as the background for this essay.

TEACHING TIP: Though this essay engages in a specific debate with Ernst Bloch over the merits of literary expressionism, it also participates in a general defense of realism and critique of modernism that represented Lukács contribution to what is often called the "Brecht-Lukács debate," Brecht being a leading defender of modernism on the Left. For more on this argument, see Lunn and the essays collected in the volume edited by Taylor. Their exchanges were part of an extended and lively discussion that took place in the 1920s and 1930s among leftists concerned with finding the form of art that could best contribute to the growth of socialism and, especially in the latter years of the 1930s, to the Popular Front's battle against fascism. For more on these debates, see Murphy.

For a discussion of the impact of the Popular Front on American culture, see Denning. See the selection from Wilson in *NATC* for an example of American Popular Front literary commentary.

Instructors who feel they need a better understanding of expressionism might consult Sheppard's essay or Nicholls's chapter on expressionism.

The crucial importance of Lukács as one of the founding figures of Western Marxism can perhaps best be appreciated by calling attention to the influence of his work on other figures included in *NATC*, ranging from Benjamin and Horkheimer and Adorno to Jameson. In any case, Western Marxism might best be introduced via Lukács. On this phenomenon, see the volume by Anderson. For a good anthology of writings by its major figures, see the volume edited by Gottlieb.

■ Edmund Wilson, "Marxism and Literature"
   1. Summarize and comment on Wilson's review of the role played by literature in the works of major Marxist thinkers from Marx to Trotsky.
   2. Summarize and comment on Wilson's arguments for the value of Marxism as a framework within which to interpret literature.
   3. Summarize and comment on Wilson's discussion of proletarian literature and of the view of literature as a weapon in the class struggle. *Suggestion*: Note that Wilson's position on this issue is essentially that of a group of thinkers who were aligned with the journal *Partisan Review*; this position was diametrically opposed to that held by Michael Gold, Granville Hicks, and other American Marxists associated with the journal *New Masses*. On this debate, see Murphy.

TEACHING TIP: For American instructors, Wilson's essay provides a convenient starting point for a discussion of the history of Marxism in the United States, and in particular of the prominence of Marxist thought in American culture in the 1930s. Instructors who wish to pursue this topic might want to read some of the excellent recent scholarship on the American cultural Left in the 1930s. The studies by Foley and Denning are particularly useful starting points.

■ Antonio Gramsci, from *The Prison Notebooks*
   1. Explain Gramsci's distinction between "civil society" and "the State" and relate this distinction to the two different levels at which official power works to help the dominant bourgeois class maintain its control over capitalist society.
   2. Explain Gramsci's notions of the intellectual and the organic intellectual.
   3. Explain Gramsci's notion of hegemony and identify ways in which this notion suggests a particularly important role for intellectuals in society.

TEACHING TIP: It might be useful to call attention to the important influence of Gramsci on later Marxist thinkers, such as Althusser and Raymond Williams. For example, the selection in *NATC* by Hall emphasizes the importance of Gramsci for the British cultural studies movement. In addition, Gramsci has been influential for postcolonial scholars such as the Indian Subaltern Studies group and for "post-Marxism," epitomized by the work of Laclau and Mouffe. For more theoretical discussions of the role of intellectuals, see the essays in the volume edited by Robbins, many of which directly engage Gramsci's important formulation of this topic.

■ Walter Benjamin, "The Work of Art in the Age of Mechanical Reproduction"
   1. Explain Benjamin's notion of the "aura" of the work of art and describe his understanding of the implications of the "decay" of the aura in modern culture.
   2. Explain the role of film in Benjamin's discussion of the antiauthoritarian potential of modern art.
   3. In what ways does the phenomenon of fascism affect and motivate Benjamin's essay?

■ Max Horkheimer and Theodor Adorno, from "The Culture Industry: Enlightenment as Mass Deception" (*Dialectic of Enlightenment*)
   1. In what ways, according to Horkheimer and Adorno, does the "culture industry" make true individualism impossible while at the same time reinforcing the illusory claims of bourgeois society to respect the individual?
   2. In what ways is this essay influenced by the historical phenomenon of German Nazism? What relationships do Horkheimer and Adorno see between German Nazism and American popular culture?
   3. This essay was written before television had become the dominant force in mass culture. In what ways does this essay anticipate the later rise of television?

TEACHING TIP: The work of Horkheimer and Adorno needs to be presented within the context of their participation in the Frankfurt School. See Jay for a history of the early decades of the Frankfurt School, when Horkheimer and Adorno were its leading figures. See also the studies by Russell Berman, Kellner, and Held.

■ Louis Althusser, from "Ideology and Ideological State Apparatuses"
   1. Explain Althusser's concept of the Ideological State Apparatus (ISA).
   2. Discuss Althusser's notion of interpellation. What does it suggest about the difficulty of resistance to official ideology in a capitalist society?
   3. Discuss Althusser's understanding of the concept of ideology.

■ Louis Althusser, "A Letter on Art in Reply to André Daspre"
  1. Summarize and comment on Althusser's distinction between ideology and science.
  2. What distinction does Althusser make between art and science?
  3. Explain Althusser's argument that art is particularly effective at revealing the workings of ideology.

■ Raymond Williams, from *Marxism and Literature*
  1. Summarize and comment on Williams's overview of the historical development of the notion of literature.
  2. In what ways, according to Williams, are the concepts of literature and literary tradition ideological ones?
  3. What, according to Williams, is the proper role of Marxist literary criticism?

TEACHING TIP: Williams's extremely influential work is difficult to appreciate from any single selection. It can best be understood within the context of the central role played by Williams in the postwar British New Left and of the rise of the British cultural studies movement after the war. For more background on Williams's work, see the collection edited by Eagleton. For more on Williams's cultural and intellectual context in postwar Britain, see Dworkin.

■ Jürgen Habermas, "Modernity—An Incomplete Project"
  1. What does Habermas mean by *modernity*? In what sense, according to Habermas, is the project of modernity incomplete?
  2. Discuss Habermas's notion of the fragmentation of modern bourgeois society into separate, seemingly autonomous spheres of activity. What are the implications of this fragmentation?
  3. In what sense does Habermas believe supposedly radical thinkers such as Foucault and Derrida to be "neoconservatives"?

TEACHING TIP: Habermas is the leading contemporary figure in the Frankfurt School. It is a good idea to contextualize his work by referring to Frankfurt School predecessors, such as Horkheimer and Adorno. See Jay for a history of the early decades of the Frankfurt School; see Held for a discussion of the Frankfurt School that extends to the work of Habermas. For studies of the Frankfurt School in relation to the question of modernity, see Russell Berman and Kellner.

■ Fredric Jameson, from *The Political Unconscious*
  1. What does Jameson mean when he calls for critics and theorists to "always historicize"?
  2. Describe and comment on Jameson's argument for the "priority" of political (i.e., Marxist) approaches to the interpretation of literary texts.
  3. Summarize and comment on Jameson's conclusions concerning the

ideological nature of literature, particularly the ideological nature of the process of canonization.

4. Summarize and comment on Jameson's use of non-Marxist theoretical positions to supplement his fundamentally Marxist argument.

TEACHING TIP: Jameson was probably America's most important Marxist theorist and critic of the late twentieth century. As such, he was also a central figure in the turn toward more detailed consideration of social, political, and historical issues in American criticism of the 1980s and 1990s, and there is a substantial secondary literature on Jameson's work. For a brief discussion of Jameson's importance as the thinker who "made Marxism stick in the United States," see Walter Cohen.

KEY TERMS AND CONCEPTS

alienation	Frankfurt School
aura	hegemony
base and superstructure	Ideological State Apparatus
bourgeoisie	ideology
class consciousness	interpellation
commodification	mode of production
cultural materialism	organic intellectual
culture industry	proletariat
dialectical materialism	reification
division of labor	totality

ESSAY TOPICS

1. Summarize the fundamental differences between Marxist criticism and formalist approaches to criticism.
2. Relate Althusser's concept of the ISA to Gramsci's notion of hegemony.
3. Summarize the base and superstructure model of society. In what ways does this model influence Marxist theory and criticism of literature? In what ways do Marxist theory and criticism suggest complications in this model?
4. In what ways does Marxist criticism challenge the Arnoldian notion that canonical cultural works tend to pass on the "best" thoughts of a society, expressed in the "best" ways?

RESEARCH PROJECTS

1. Marxism is a theory of history and of the workings of human society as a whole. Yet Western Marxist critics have tended to place considerable emphasis on culture as a focal point for their theoretical and critical work. Write an essay that explains some of the reasons why Marxist critics would be particularly interested in culture. *Suggestion*: See chapter 4 of Anderson for a discussion of the Western

Marxist emphasis on culture; see Eagleton's *Ideology of the Aesthetic* for an extended reminder that the very idea of the aesthetic is a fundamental aspect of bourgeois ideology and thus a likely object of Marxist critique.

2. One of the major debates among Marxist theorists of culture in the twentieth century has involved the relative value of experimental form versus conventional realism in the literary expression of socialist ideas. Often called the "Brecht-Lukács debate," after major proponents of the respective positions, the controversy raised a number of crucial issues about Marxist aesthetics and about literature as a whole. Read some of the major statements made by its participants and summarize your conclusions regarding them. *Suggestion*: The volume edited by Taylor contains a number of the important statements in this debate.

3. Compare the positive reading of the potential of film by Benjamin to the negative reading of popular culture by Horkheimer and Adorno. Discuss the ways in which the power of these respective arguments might be influenced by the subsequent rise of television. How might the current rise of the Internet as a cultural force relate to these arguments?

4. Althusser's structuralist analysis of bourgeois ideology seems in many ways at odds with the Marxist tradition of strongly historicist analysis. Indeed, the tension between historicist approaches and Althusser's structuralist approach triggered an important debate among Marxist scholars in the 1970s. Research this debate and write an essay that assesses the points made by the two sides. *Suggestion*: See Thompson's *Poverty of Theory* for a major critique of Althusser. See Jameson's *Political Unconscious* (especially chapter 1) for an attempt to mediate between Althusser and more conventionally historicist Marxists such as Lukács.

5. The canon of Western literature from the Renaissance onward has been dominated by works that Marxist critics would describe as bourgeois in their orientation. Read a literary work written from a perspective opposed to bourgeois ideology and comment, using the insights of Marxist theory, on the ways in which this work differs from typical bourgeois literature. *Suggestion*: Some important literary works with a Marxist or socialist orientation include Robert Tressell, *The Ragged Trousered Philanthropists* (1955); Lewis Jones, *Cwmardy* (1937) and *We Live* (1939); Michael Gold, *Jews without Money* (1930); Jack Conroy, *The Disinherited* (1933); John Steinbeck, *The Grapes of Wrath* (1939); Richard Wright, *Native Son* (1940); and Meridel Le Sueur, *The Girl* (1978). Numerous British and American leftist novels are described in Booker, *The Modern British Novel of the Left* and *The Modern American Novel of the Left*. For a critical study of American leftist literature that offers many valuable suggestions about the special nature of leftist aesthetics, see Foley.

III. *Feminist Criticism and Theory (1–3 weeks)*

Feminist criticism and theory has been so influential in recent literary studies that it is indispensable to any survey of modern critical schools. In addition, the issues it raises create opportunities for dialogues involving race and class, as well as gender. French feminist theory has important connections with poststructuralist theory and Lacanian psychoanalysis, and it also provides key routes toward a more broadly conceived notion of gender studies. French feminism can be productively taught in conjunction with any of these approaches. The full version of this module includes several selections dealing with gender studies and queer theory; these selections can obviously be eliminated from the feminism module if they are taught in a separate module (included at the end of this chapter).

TEACHING TIP: The selections in this module naturally split into several submodules, including French feminism (Beauvoir, Cixous, Kristeva, Wittig), Anglo-American feminism (Wollstonecraft, Woolf, Gilbert and Gubar, Kolodny, Tompkins), and contemporary extensions of feminism (Smith, Christian, Anzaldúa, Bordo, Butler). Instructors should take these subdivisions into account in planning their courses.

	Suggested Readings	
1-week module	2-week module	3-week module
Woolf	Woolf	Wollstonecraft
Cixous	Beauvoir	Woolf
Kristeva	Gilbert & Gubar	Beauvoir
Barbara Smith	Kolodny	Gilbert & Gubar
Butler	Cixous	Kolodny
	Kristeva	Tompkins
	Barbara Smith	Cixous
	Christian	Kristeva
	Anzaldúa	Wittig
	Butler	Barbara Smith
		Christian
		Anzaldúa
		Bordo
		Butler

SUGGESTED READINGS AND DISCUSSION QUESTIONS

■ Mary Wollstonecraft, from *A Vindication of the Rights of Woman*
   1. Discuss the ways in which *A Vindication of the Rights of Woman*, written in the midst of the French Revolution, might have been influenced by that historic event.
   2. Wollstonecraft consistently uses slavery as a metaphor for the

condition of white, middle-class women. Discuss the implications of this usage.

3. Discuss the ways in which, according to Wollstonecraft, women are complicit in their own domination by men. In what ways is this complicity influenced by the social conditioning of women from early childhood on?

■ Virginia Woolf, from *A Room of One's Own*
1. In what ways does Woolf use her fable of Judith Shakespeare to suggest broader historical phenomena regarding the obstacles encountered by women who would seek to gain recognition as writers or artists?
2. Discuss the ways in which Woolf's treatment of gender in the fable of Shakespeare's sister also involves class and addresses the difficulties faced by working-class individuals who would seek to become writers or artists, regardless of their sex.

TEACHING TIP: It is helpful to note that Woolf's discussion of language and style (the "woman's sentence") in *A Room of One's Own* makes her a precursor of French feminism. On the other hand, her discussion of the social and economic restrictions that have limited the production of women writers makes her a precursor of Anglo-American feminism.

■ Simone de Beauvoir, from *The Second Sex*
1. Discuss Beauvoir's argument that Western tradition tends to depict the woman as a locus of mystery and otherness. In what way, according to Beauvoir, is this depiction useful to men?
2. What implications might Beauvoir's discussion have for our understanding of Western dualistic thinking in general?

TEACHING TIP: Though an important French feminist, Beauvoir, in her emphasis on stereotyping, is an important precursor of American feminist criticism, which began its rise to prominence in the late 1960s with studies of the stereotypical treatment of women in the "classics" of Western literature. The two most important early examples of this "stereotype" criticism were Ellmann and Millett.

■ Sandra M. Gilbert and Susan Gubar, from *The Madwoman in the Attic*
1. Discuss the ways in which, according to Gilbert and Gubar, conventional notions of literary tradition have typically shown a masculine bias that works to the detriment of women writers.
2. Explain the ways in which, according to Gilbert and Gubar, widespread social stereotypes about the behavior of women have been debilitating to women writers.
3. Discuss the strategies employed by women writers to overcome the special obstacles they have faced in their attempt to get their work published and critically accepted.

■ Annette Kolodny, "Dancing through the Minefield"
  1. Discuss Kolodny's notion of "playful pluralism" and the role she sees for it in feminist criticism.
  2. Discuss some of the ways in which, according to Kolodny, the experience of reading literary texts is mediated by prejudices and expectations that readers bring to the texts.
  3. In what ways, according to Kolodny, is the study of literature written by women crucial to the feminist project?

■ Jane Tompkins, "Me and My Shadow"
  1. In what ways does Tompkins's essay argue that personal, autobiographical criticism is particularly well suited to be a mode of feminine expression? Do you agree with this argument?
  2. How, according to Tompkins, is the decentering of the subject in poststructuralist thought antithetical to the goals of feminism?
  3. Summarize and comment on Tompkins's discussion of epistemology.

■ Hélène Cixous, "The Laugh of the Medusa"
  1. Describe the characteristics that for Cixous set *écriture féminine* (women's writing) apart from more conventional, masculine conceptions of language.
  2. Summarize the ways in which Cixous sees writing as central to the emancipation of women.
  3. Summarize the ways in which Cixous's thought is clearly poststructuralist. How does her work differ from that of important poststructuralist predecessors such as Jacques Derrida?

■ Julia Kristeva, from *Revolution in Poetic Language*
  1. Explain Kristeva's distinction between the semiotic and the symbolic.
  2. Compare Kristeva's notion of semiotic language with Cixous's notion of *écriture féminine*.
  3. Discuss the ways in which Kristeva's work suggests that literature and poetry might be especially valuable resources for feminist expression.

■ Monique Wittig, "One Is Not Born a Woman"
  1. Explain Wittig's distinction between the terms *women* and *woman*. Why does she see *woman* as an inherently negative category, even for feminists?
  2. Discuss Wittig's essentially Marxist notion that women, in order to escape oppression, must become and act as a class. Summarize Wittig's emphasis on the importance of women gaining the ability to constitute themselves as individual subjects. In what ways does this emphasis differ from traditional Marxist approaches?
  3. Why does Wittig believe that the true emancipation of women can

occur only after heterosexuality has been destroyed as the dominant paradigm of human sexuality?

TEACHING TIP: Wittig has also written several important novels that reinforce the points made in her critical and theoretical work. Instructors might want to emphasize this point or perhaps assign one of Wittig's novels as supplemental reading or as part of a research project. See the chapter on Wittig's novels (which focuses on *Les Guérillères* and *The Lesbian Body*) in Booker's *Techniques of Subversion*.

■ Barbara Smith, "Toward a Black Feminist Criticism"
1. Summarize and comment on Smith's critique of the approaches taken by previous critics to literature by black women, and particularly by black lesbians.
2. What are the basic principles that Smith suggests might be used by black feminist critics?
3. Smith suggests that literary critics can play important social and political roles and that in fact they have a responsibility to do so. Summarize her discussion of the social and political importance of literary critics. Do you agree with her argument?

■ Barbara Christian, "The Race for Theory"
1. For Christian, "theory" primarily means poststructuralist theory, especially as it has affected feminist criticism. But how might her critique also implicate trends in American literary studies that go back to New Criticism?
2. Christian appears to advocate a pluralist approach that would allow critics to adapt their methodologies to the text at hand. Compare and contrast her vision of pluralism with that of Kolodny in "Dancing through the Minefield."
3. Comment on Christian's argument that the turn to theory in literary studies might work to the disadvantage of third world writers and others outside the mainstream of white Western literature.

■ Gloria Anzaldúa, from *Borderlands/La Frontera*
1. In what ways does Anzaldúa's "mestiza" perspective both participate in and challenge the identity politics that have been central to much work in race and ethnicity studies?
2. Compare and contrast Anzaldúa's "mestiza" perspective with the concept of hybridity, as articulated by postcolonial critics (especially Bhabha).
3. In what ways does Anzaldúa's project resemble that of mainstream feminist theory and criticism. In what ways is it different?

■ Susan Bordo, from *Unbearable Weight*
1. Explain and comment on Bordo's argument that the human body is a product not merely of biology but also of social construction.

2. In what ways does Bordo's discussion of anorexia and bulimia illustrate her thesis concerning the social construction of the body?
3. What are the implications of Bordo's analysis for a feminist criticism that might oppose inimical social constructions of the female?

■ Judith Butler, from *Gender Trouble*
   1. In what ways does Butler's account of the social construction of individual identities challenge the identity politics common to Anglo-American feminist thought in the past few decades?
   2. How does Butler's discussion challenge the very notion of "woman" as it has conventionally been used in feminist theory and criticism?
   3. Summarize and comment on Butler's discussion of the ways in which socially constructed identities might be challenged by "subversive bodily acts."

TEACHING TIP: Butler's work has been particularly influential in the emerging gender studies and queer theory movements of recent years. Her work thus provides an excellent point of departure for discussing these studies within the feminism module.

KEY TERMS AND CONCEPTS

"The Angel in the House"	pluralism
canon	semiotic and symbolic
écriture féminine	sexuality
essentialism	social construction of gender
gender	stereotyping
identity politics	

ESSAY TOPICS

1. Summarize the arguments of the feminist theory and criticism you have read concerning the representation of women in the Western literary tradition.
2. Discuss the concern of feminist theory with language and style and with the prospect that women inherently express themselves in different modes and forms than do men.
3. What are some of the central findings and arguments of feminist critics who have concentrated on the study of literary works by women?
4. Summarize the arguments of various feminist critics concerning the distinction between sex as a biological category and gender as a socially constructed one.
5. In what ways does the rise of feminist theory and criticism in the past few decades grow out of the women's movement of the 1960s? What does this tell us about the intersection between literary studies and the larger social and historical world?

RESEARCH PROJECTS

1. Discuss some of the important differences between French and American feminist theory and criticism. *Suggestion*: Moi provides a useful survey of feminist theory that highlights these differences.

2. Do research and write an essay on the relationship between feminist theory and one other major school of theory and criticism (e.g., Marxism, psychoanalysis, postmodernism, poststructuralism).

3. Read Virginia Woolf's novel *Orlando* (1928). Discuss it using the feminist theory of Woolf herself, supplemented by the perspectives of other feminist theorists and critics you have read.

4. Survey the criticisms of mainstream white feminist theory and criticism by women of color (such as Christian, Anzaldúa, and Barbara Smith), who have called for more sensitivity to their specific situation and problems.

5. Read the selections in *NATC* by Rich, Sedgwick, and Zimmerman. Discuss the ways in which lesbian and queer theorists broaden the concerns of feminist theory and criticism.

IV. Poststructuralist Criticism and Theory (1–3 weeks)

Suggested Readings

1-week module	2-week module	3-week module
Barthes	Nietzsche	Nietzsche
"Death of the Author"	"On Truth and Lying"	"On Truth and Lying"
"From Work to Text"	Barthes	Saussure
de Man	"Death"	Barthes
"Semiology . . ."	"From Work to Text"	"Death of the Author"
Foucault	de Man	"From Work to Text"
Discipline and Punish	"Semiology and Rhetoric"	de Man
Derrida	"Return to Philology"	"Semiology and Rhetoric"
Of Grammatology	Foucault	"Return to Philology"
Dissemination	"What Is an Author?"	Foucault
	Discipline and Punish	"What Is an Author?"
	Derrida	*Discipline and Punish*
	Of Grammatology	*History of Sexuality*
	Dissemination	Derrida
	Barbara Johnson	*Of Grammatology*
	Bhabha	*Dissemination*
		Barbara Johnson
		Bloom
		Bhabha
		Baudrillard
		Deleuze & Guattari
		"Rhizome"

Poststructuralist criticism contains a variety of intellectually exciting ideas that often challenge the fundamental premises of conventional Western thought. A study of poststructuralist theory and criticism can thus create many opportunities for fruitful discussion of those premises. In addition, poststructuralist thought has been so influential in the past several decades that it has affected, in one way or another, virtually every aspect of intellectual life in the West. Note that many critics who are not specifically poststructuralist in their orientation have been influenced by poststructuralism (see particularly French feminists such as Cixous).

TEACHING TIP: In Anglo-American literary studies, deconstructive criticism was particularly prominent in the 1970s, and instructors who teach poststructuralism will want to be sure that they understand that phenomenon. Introductory discussions such as Culler's *On Deconstruction* and (especially) Leitch's *Deconstructive Criticism* can be particularly valuable reading in this regard. A study of poststructuralism offers students an opportunity to begin to understand these widespread influences.

SUGGESTED READINGS AND DISCUSSION QUESTIONS

■ Friedrich Nietzsche, "On Truth and Lying in a Non-Moral Sense"
  1. Nietzsche suggests that all language is ultimately metaphorical in nature. What does this tell us about the nature of literary texts and their importance as paradigms of language use in general?
  2. How does Nietzsche's thesis about the ultimate epistemological inaccessibility of truth challenge the premises of the Western philosophical tradition?
  3. How does Nietzsche's thesis about the "hardening" of metaphor into illusions that are taken for truths suggest a crucial epistemological function for literature? How does this function compare with the Russian formalist concept of defamiliarization?

■ Ferdinand de Saussure, from *Course in General Linguistics*
  1. Summarize Saussure's theory of the arbitrary nature of the sign and of the link between the signifier and the signified. How does this compare to Nietzsche's notion that all language begins in metaphor?
  2. Describe Saussure's concepts of *langue* and *parole*.

■ Roland Barthes, "The Death of the Author" and "From Work to Text"
  1. Explain what Barthes means by the *author*. Within this context, what is Barthes's concept of the *scriptor*?
  2. Describe Barthes's poststructuralist notion of intertextuality.
  3. What, for Barthes, distinguishes a "text" from the more traditional notion of the "work"?
  4. What are the implications of Barthes's notion of the text for the reading of literature?

■ Paul de Man, "Semiology and Rhetoric"
   1. What are the implications of de Man's vision of the instability of
      rhetoric for the interpretation of literary texts?
   2. In what ways does de Man's reading of Yeats's "Among School Chil-
      dren" suggest a challenge to the Aristotelian tradition of "either/or"
      logic?
   3. In what ways does de Man's essay suggest that literary texts are al-
      ways already engaged in their own deconstruction?

■ Michel Foucault, "What is an Author?"
   1. Explain Foucault's notion of the author-function. In what ways does
      this concept differ from traditional notions of authorship? In what
      ways does it resemble the concept of historical authorship examined
      by Barthes?
   2. Summarize Foucault's discussion of the special role played histori-
      cally by the concept of the author in the interpretation of literary
      texts.
   3. In what ways can Foucault's essay be read as a response to the em-
      phasis on writing in Derrida's thought?

TEACHING TIP: Foucault, like Derrida, is one of the most important
thinkers of poststructuralism. Therefore, instructors should make sure
that students gain some appreciation for the scope and importance of his
work. The chapter on Foucault in Booker's *Practical Introduction* provides a good overview of his career for instructors (or students) who feel
that they need a better understanding of his work. In addition, there is a
vast secondary literature on Foucault. *The Cambridge Companion to Foucault*, edited by Gutting, contains essays that are particularly helpful as an
introduction to various aspects of Foucault's work.

■ Michel Foucault, from *Discipline and Punish*
   1. Describe Foucault's vision of the way in which the modern prison
      functions as a representative manifestation of "normative" power in
      modern bourgeois society as a whole.
   2. Explain Foucault's notion that the "productive" techniques of power
      employed within modern carceral society actually exercise more ef-
      fective and thoroughgoing control of individual behavior than did
      the "repressive" techniques of earlier eras.
   3. In what ways does Foucault's notion of the carceral resemble Al-
      thusser's notion of ideology? In what ways is Foucault's notion dif-
      ferent?

■ Michel Foucault, from *The History of Sexuality*
   1. What is the "repressive hypothesis"? How does Foucault's critique
      of this hypothesis reflect his fundamental theory of the productive
      nature of power in modern bourgeois society?
   2. On what basis does Foucault believe the repressive hypothesis to be

an inaccurate description of the role played by sexuality in Victorian society?

3. Explain Foucault's notion that the functioning of sexuality in Victorian society produced not only discourse on sexuality but also a variety of forms of "perversion."

■ Jacques Derrida, from *Of Grammatology*
1. Explain Derrida's conceptualization of the "science" of grammatology.
2. What does Derrida mean by *logocentrism*?
3. Summarize and comment on Derrida's discussion of the "supplement" in this selection.
4. What does Derrida mean when he writes that "there is nothing outside the text"?

TEACHING TIP: However difficult, Derrida's work is indispensable to understanding the development of poststructuralism, and particularly of deconstruction. In addition to the introductions to deconstruction by Leitch (*Deconstructive Criticism*) and Culler (*On Deconstruction*), instructors might want to consult Norris for useful comments on Derrida's work.

■ Jacques Derrida, from *Dissemination*
1. Why, according to Plato, is writing dangerous and misleading? How does Derrida refute this argument?
2. Describe Derrida's exploration of the contradictory meanings of the Greek word *pharmakon*. How does this exploration, according to Derrida, undermine the logic on which Plato's original argument was based?
3. Explain and comment on Derrida's treatment in this selection of the opposition between presence and absence.
4. What are the implications of Derrida's discussion in terms of the strict distinction, accepted by formalist critics, between literary and nonliterary language?

■ Barbara Johnson, from "Melville's Fist"
1. Discuss the ways in which, according to Johnson, this story deconstructs the simple polar oppositions that, at first glance, it seems to support and rely on.
2. Summarize and comment on Johnson's figuration of this story as an allegory of reading and writing.
3. Discuss the ways in which, according to Johnson, Melville's story turns on itself, undermining any attempt to produce an authoritative reading of it.

■ Harold Bloom, from *The Anxiety of Influence*
1. Explain and comment on Bloom's vision of the devolution of poetry since the time of Milton.

2. Explain and comment on Bloom's idea that in today's postmodern era, literary tradition is valuable because it stifles the weak and represses the strong.
3. Explain and critique Bloom's notion of misprision.

■ Homi K. Bhabha, "The Commitment to Theory"
1. Bhabha espouses a belief that "theory" can be a valuable tool for postcolonial critics. On the evidence of this essay, what kinds of theory does he himself seem to draw on?
2. Bhabha seeks, in this essay, to refute the charge that the application of Western theory to postcolonial culture is a potential form of cultural imperialism that runs counter to the economic and political interests of the formerly colonized world. Is he successful in this argument? In what ways might Bhabha's argument be criticized?
3. Explain and comment on the crucial notion of hybridity that informs Bhabha's argument in this essay (and in his work elsewhere).

TEACHING TIP: Bhabha's essay addresses an extremely important debate over the status of theory in postcolonial studies. For a direct critique of Bhabha's work (which argues that Bhabha's own theorization loses sight of political reality), see JanMohamed. For a cogent discussion of the dangers of theorization in postcolonial studies, see San Juan.

■ Jean Baudrillard, from *The Precession of Simulacra*
1. Explain Baudrillard's use of the notion of the simulacrum. In what ways does this use particularly pertain to the postmodern condition?
2. Discuss the ways in which Baudrillard's discussion of modern consumer society criticizes not only capitalism but also colonialism.
3. What aspects of our contemporary world seem to bear out Baudrillard's analysis of the precession of simulacra in the postmodern world? What aspects might dispute his findings?

■ Gilles Deleuze and Félix Guattari, from "Rhizome" (A *Thousand Plateaus*)
1. Discuss the importance and various ramifications of the central "rhizome" metaphor in this essay.
2. What do Deleuze and Guattari mean by *representational thought* in the Western philosophical tradition?
3. Describe their critique of this representational thought. What is postmodern about it?
4. What, according to Deleuze and Guattari, are the implications of representational thought for our view of the individual subject?

KEY TERMS AND CONCEPTS

archaeology
the author function
carceral society
deconstruction
genealogy
grammatology
hybridity
intertextuality
logocentrism

metaphysics
the Panopticon
polar oppositions
the repressive hypothesis
rhetoric
simulacra/simulation
technologies of the self
tropology
the will to knowledge

ESSAY TOPICS

1. What differences do you see between the focus of Foucault's work and Derrida's?
2. What, in your view, are the most important strengths and weaknesses of poststructuralism?
3. What, in your view, are the principal implications of poststructuralism for the study of literature?
4. What, in your view, are the principal implications of poststructuralism in areas that go beyond the study of literature?

RESEARCH PROJECTS

1. Discuss the ways in which Foucault's genealogical and archaeological methods of historical research and analysis challenge some of the basic premises of Western scientific historiography. *Suggestion*: It might be helpful to read Foucault's historical work (e.g., *Discipline and Punish* or *The History of Sexuality*) in more detail. See Poster and also the collection of essays edited by Goldstein.
2. Discuss the relationship between structuralism and poststructuralism, including the ways in which the latter challenges key premises of the former. *Suggestion*: Some of the early essays of Derrida (including "Structure, Sign, and Play" and the opening chapter of *Of Grammatology*) might provide a useful beginning point for this project.
3. Research and comment on the importance of Nietzsche as a forerunner of poststructuralist thinkers such as Foucault and Derrida. *Suggestion*: Megill might be a good place to start in researching this project. See also the essays in the collection edited by Allison.
4. Derrida, in particular, has often been criticized for turning away from social reality and toward a self-indulgent concern with playful textuality. Do you believe that this criticism is justified? How might Derrida's work in fact inspire more overtly political critics? *Research hints*: A good place to start might be Ryan's discussion of potential points of contact between Derrida and Marx. See also Derrida's own engagement with Marx in *Specters of Marx*.

5. In the 1970s, deconstruction became extremely popular among American critics who were seeking an alternative to New Criticism. Later reflection, however, has often made it appear that the seemingly radical ideas underlying deconstruction are not, in fact, all that different from basic New Critical premises. Research this issue and write an essay that comments on the differences and similarities between deconstruction and New Criticism. *Suggestion*: See Cain's discussion of American deconstruction and its relationship with New Criticism.

V. Ethnicity and Race Studies (1–3 weeks)

Ethnicity and race studies has been one of the most exciting and productive fields in contemporary literary scholarship, and serious critical attention is now being paid not only to African American, black British, and other black literature, but also to Australian and Canadian indigenous literatures and Native American, Hispanic American, Asian American, and other ethnic literatures. This field is closely related to postcolonial studies, and the following full module includes a number of works of postcolonial theory and criticism. Those works can, of course, be omitted if the course contains a separate postcolonial module.

Suggested Readings		
1-week module	2-week module	3-week module
Du Bois	Du Bois	Du Bois
Hughes	Hughes	Hughes
Barbara Smith	Hurston	Hurston
Anzaldúa	"White Publishers"	"White Publishers"
	Barbara Smith	Barbara Smith
	Baker	Baker
	Gates	Gates
	Anzaldúa	hooks
	Vizenor	Christian
	Said	Anzaldúa
		Allen
		Vizenor
		Achebe
		Said

SUGGESTED READINGS AND DISCUSSION QUESTIONS

■ W. E. B. Du Bois, "Criteria of Negro Art"

1. Summarize Du Bois's description of the white "culture industry" and of the ways in which that industry contributes to the stereotyping of African Americans, denying them equal access to venues of self-expression and self-representation.

2. Summarize Du Bois's vision of the role of the artist in the African American struggle for emancipation.

3. Discuss Du Bois's conclusion that "all art is propaganda." How does this notion differ from conventional white American visions of art, especially as promulgated in formalist criticism and theory?

- Langston Hughes, "The Negro Artist and the Racial Mountain"
  1. Discuss some of the ways in which Hughes's argument suggests an interrelationship between race and class in American society.
  2. In what ways does Hughes suggest that African American art might provide a powerful weapon in the struggle against white ideological domination?
  3. Discuss Hughes's emphasis on the importance of the production of "racial art" by African American artists.

TEACHING TIP: It might be valuable to emphasize the participation of Hughes in the Harlem Renaissance. On the intersection of the Harlem Renaissance and modernism, see Hutchinson. On the political engagement of the members of the Harlem Renaissance, see Maxwell.

- Zora Neale Hurston, "What White Publishers Won't Print"
  1. What sorts of literature not currently being published by white publishers does Hurston hope to see in the future?
  2. Why, according to Hurston, have such works not been published in the past?
  3. What, according to Hurston, might be accomplished by the publication of such works?

TEACHING TIP: Hurston, like Hughes, was closely associated with the Harlem Renaissance, which provides a fruitful context within which to discuss her work. Her work as an anthropologist also adds important new perspectives.

- Barbara Smith, "Toward a Black Feminist Criticism"
  1. Summarize and comment on Smith's critique of the approaches taken by previous critics to literature by black women, and particularly by black lesbians.
  2. What are the basic principles that Smith suggests might be used by black feminist critics?
  3. Smith suggests that literary critics can play important social and political roles and that in fact they have a responsibility to do so. Summarize her discussion of the social and political importance of literary critics. Do you agree with her argument?

- Houston A. Baker Jr., from *Blues, Ideology, and Afro-American Literature*
  1. Explain Baker's conception of the "blues matrix" as a crucial element of African American culture.

2. Summarize the principal theoretical approaches that inform Baker's vision of the blues matrix. *Suggestion*: Note that this concept is informed not just by race and ethnicity studies but also by the insights of cultural studies, which itself has strong Marxist underpinnings.
3. Explain Baker's conclusion that works of art have no "intrinsic aesthetic value." How does this notion reinforce his emphasis on the importance of the blues matrix? How does it support the serious study of popular culture as a whole?

■ Henry Louis Gates Jr., "Talking Black"
1. Summarize Gates's description of the way in which achieving literacy and producing literature was, for Africans and African Americans, a key to being regarded as human beings by white Western society. What does this legacy suggest about the cultural importance of African and African American literature?
2. Summarize and comment on Gates's advocacy of the use of theory by critics of African American culture.
3. What, according to Gates, must critics and theorists do to put theory to the most effective use in supporting the development of an African American cultural tradition?

■ bell hooks, "Postmodern Blackness"
1. Summarize hooks's critique of postmodernist discourses as "exclusionary." In what ways have African American women, in particular, been excluded by these discourses?
2. Discuss the ways in which, for hooks, postmodernism offers potential opportunities for African American writers and intellectuals.
3. Discuss the role of identity in hooks's elaboration of the relationship between postmodernism and African American cultural and intellectual life.

■ Barbara Christian, "The Race for Theory"
1. For Christian, "theory" primarily means poststructuralist theory, especially as it has affected feminist criticism. But how might her critique also implicate trends in American literary studies that go back to New Criticism?
2. Christian seems to advocate a pluralist approach that would allow critics to adapt their methodologies to the text at hand. Compare and contrast her vision of pluralism with that of Kolodny in "Dancing through the Minefield."
3. Summarize Christian's argument that the turn to theory in literary studies might work to the disadvantage of third world writers and others outside the mainstream of white Western literature.

■ Gloria Anzaldúa, from *Borderlands/La Frontera*
1. In what ways does Anzaldúa's "mestiza" perspective both participate in and challenge the identity politics that have been central to much work in race and ethnicity studies?

2. Compare and contrast Anzaldúa's "mestiza" perspective with the concept of hybridity, as articulated by postcolonial critics (especially Bhabha).
3. In what ways does Anzaldúa's project resemble that of mainstream feminist theory and criticism? In what ways is it different?

■ Paula Gunn Allen, "Kochinnenako in Academe"
1. Summarize and comment on the critique of Western universalism that underlies much of Allen's discussion.
2. Explain and comment on Allen's delineation of a "tribal-feminist" style of interpretation.
3. In what ways does Allen's essay suggest common ground between feminist theorists and critics and theorists and critics who work from a postcolonial perspective? In what ways might this suggestion of common ground be challenged?

■ Gerald Vizenor, from *Manifest Manners*
1. Summarize and comment on Vizenor's discussion of the stereotyping of Native Americans. In what ways does this phenomenon resemble that described by Said in *Orientalism*?
2. What does Vizenor mean by a *postindian*?
3. What forms of "survivance," or resistance to cultural domination, are practiced by Vizenor's postindians?
4. What are Vizenor's theoretical sources?

■ Chinua Achebe, "An Image of Africa"
1. Briefly summarize the reasons why Achebe concludes that *Heart of Darkness* is a racist text.
2. Do you agree with Achebe's argument and conclusions?
3. In what ways might Achebe's essay be taken as much as a criticism of certain styles of reading and teaching as of *Heart of Darkness*? *Suggestion*: Note that Achebe himself has for some time regularly taught *Heart of Darkness* as a key text in his own courses on the African novel at Bard College. Thus, he does not oppose teaching the book; he merely believes that it should not be taught without addressing such issues as racism and colonialism.
4. Given the canonical status of *Heart of Darkness,* what does Achebe's essay imply about the nature of canonicity and the importance of multicultural concerns in literary studies? *Suggestion*: One can, of course, argue that Conrad's attitude was typical of its time; but Achebe's point is really that Conrad's text was still being promoted as a work of great literature many years later, when such attitudes had become generally unacceptable.

TEACHING TIPS: Achebe's essay triggered considerable debate in Conrad studies, ultimately sparking not only increased attention to racism and colonialism as issues in Conrad's text but also the growth of postcolonial studies as a whole. For a response to Achebe, see Hawkins. For essays that essentially support Achebe's position, see Singh and Parrinder. On this issue, see also Booker (*Practical Introduction*, 219–25).

■ Edward W. Said, from *Orientalism*
   1. Describe the motivations behind and basic characteristics of the discourse of Orientalism.
   2. Though Said's analysis focuses primarily on nineteenth-century texts, his conclusions have far-reaching implications that remain relevant at the beginning of the twenty-first century. Describe the contemporary relevance of Said's ideas for ethnic and postcolonial studies, and for scholarly work as a whole.
   3. Discuss Said's use of the Foucauldian notion of discourse to describe the legacy of colonialist tendencies in Western thought.

TEACHING TIP: As what many regard as the founding text in the field of colonial discourse analysis, *Orientalism* was one of the most influential works of criticism and theory to be published in the last quarter of the twentieth century. Instructors with relatively little background in postcolonial studies might want to study *Orientalism* in more detail before teaching Said's work as an example of the analysis of racist discourses. The discussion of Said in Moore-Gilbert provides a useful overview. MacKenzie challenges Said's work in some ways but is still influenced by it, providing a good example of the kinds of productive debate that have been triggered by Said's work in recent decades.

KEY TERMS AND CONCEPTS

colonial discourse analysis	oral culture
colonialism	Orientalism
ethnicity	racism
the Harlem Renaissance	slave narratives
hybridity	stereotyping
identity politics	universalism
ideology	women of color
neocolonialism	

ESSAY TOPICS

   1. Why is it important that texts by nonwhite and non-Western writers be read and analyzed with special critical approaches that might differ from those used to read and analyze texts by white Western writers?
   2. In what ways might the traditional exclusion of nonwhite writers from the U.S. canon have produced a distorted view not only of American literary history but of American history as a whole?

3. Compare the projects of race and ethnicity critics and theorists with those of feminist critics and theorists.

4. Discuss the use of at least one other theoretical approach (Marxist, feminist, poststructuralist, etc.) by the race and ethnicity critics in the selections you have read.

5. Discuss some of the ways in which the insights of race and ethnicity criticism might affect our reading of texts by white writers.

RESEARCH PROJECTS

1. Read a novel or other major literary work by an African American or other ethnic author. Write an essay summarizing and commenting on aspects of the work that might not be understood without the perspective of critical approaches that focus on questions of race and ethnicity. *Suggestion*: Toni Morrison's *Beloved* (1987) might be a good choice for this project.

2. Many of the essays in *NATC* suggest important points of intersection between ethnicity and race studies and critical approaches based on other social categories, such as class and gender. Looking at the work in *NATC* of such authors as Christian, Barbara Smith, hooks, Anzaldúa, Allen, Vizenor, and Fanon, comment on the problems and opportunities presented by these points of intersection among race/ethnicity, class, and gender.

3. African American critics such as Gates have consistently argued the value of Western literary theory for the analysis of African American culture. At the same time, Gates grants that critics of African American culture need to adapt theory to the special situation of that culture. Choose a major school of criticism studied in this course and comment on the ways in which it might need to be adapted to be applicable to African American or another ethnic culture.

4. Read some of the poetry or other literature produced by members of the Harlem Renaissance. Comment on the ways in which these writers were engaged in projects that clearly went beyond race and ethnicity to encompass issues such as the modernist quest for new forms of literary expression and the Marxist desire for social justice. *Suggestion*: On the intersection of the Harlem Renaissance and modernism, see Hutchinson. On the Marxist inclinations of the members of the Harlem Renaissance, see Maxwell.

5. Compare the selections in *NATC* on the criticism and theory of ethnic culture with those dealing with postcolonial culture. Write an essay that comments on the ways in which the concerns of critics and theorists of American ethnic culture are similar to those of critics and theorists of postcolonial culture. In what ways are the concerns of these two groups different?

Additional or Alternative Modules

I. Psychoanalytic Criticism and Theory (1–3 weeks)

Beginning with the pioneering work of Sigmund Freud at the end of the nineteenth century, psychoanalysis has become one of the most influential intellectual phenomena of our time. Ideas associated with psychoanalysis continue to play a major role in the development of new modes of literary criticism. The study of psychoanalytic criticism is thus valuable in its own right, while also providing important background information for the study of a variety of other approaches, especially feminist and reader-response criticism.

TEACHING TIP: Because of Freud's central importance as a modern intellectual figure, many students will have at least some familiarity with his basic ideas. However, an introductory lecture covering some of these major ideas (the tripartite structure of the psyche, the Oedipal drama, etc.) can be extremely useful for a unit on psychoanalytic and psychological criticism and theory. In addition to the *NATC* headnote on Freud, instructors might want to prepare for such a lecture by consulting a succinct summary, such as the chapter on psychoanalytic criticism in Booker (*Practical Introduction*). For a good introductory survey of the application of psychoanalytic theory to literature, see Wright. Instructors might also

---

Suggested Readings

1-week module	2-week module	3-week module
Freud	Freud	Freud
Interpretation of Dreams	*Interpretation of Dreams*	*Interpretation of Dreams*
Jung	"The 'Uncanny' "	"The 'Uncanny' "
Lacan	Jung	"Fetishism"
"Mirror Stage"	Bloom	Jung
"Agency of the Letter"	Gilbert & Gubar	Frye
	Lacan	Bloom
	"Mirror Stage"	Gilbert & Gubar
	"Agency of the Letter"	Lacan
	"Signification of the	"Mirror Stage"
	Phallus"	"Agency of the Letter"
	Foucault	"Signification of the
	History of Sexuality	Phallus"
		Foucault
		History of Sexuality
		Cixous
		Kristeva
		Mulvey

want to emphasize the broad impact of Freud's ideas, which have influenced a wide range of thinkers represented in *NATC*, including Jameson, Deleuze and Guattari, Davis, Sedgwick, Butler, Tompkins, and Fanon.

SUGGESTED READINGS AND DISCUSSION QUESTIONS

■ Sigmund Freud, from *The Interpretation of Dreams*
   1. Explain Freud's notion of the dream-work.
   2. Explain the process of displacement and condensation that Freud sees as central to the construction of the dream-work. How might these processes parallel the process of constructing a work of literature?

■ Sigmund Freud, "The 'Uncanny' "
   1. Briefly describe the experience Freud refers to as "uncanny."
   2. Summarize and comment on Freud's conclusions concerning the source of uncanny feelings.
   3. In this essay, Freud concludes that writers can produce uncanny feelings because they are able to control the return of the repressed in literature. What might this conclusion imply about Freud's general notion of the source of artistic creativity?
   4. In what ways does Freud's focus on literature in this essay suggest the applicability of psychoanalysis to the interpretation of literature in general?

TEACHING TIP: Instructors might want to note that this essay has been particularly important to poststructuralist critics and theorists. See, in particular, Harold Bloom's use of this essay in *The Anxiety of Influence*.

■ Sigmund Freud, "Fetishism"
   1. What does Freud mean by *fetishism*?
   2. What, according to Freud, is the source of fetishism?
   3. Compare Freud's notion of fetishism with Marx's discussion of commodity fetishism.

■ Carl Gustav Jung, "On the Relation of Analytical Psychology to Poetry"
   1. Explain Jung's notions of the collective unconscious and archetypes. What roles, according to Jung, do these notions play in artistic creativity?
   2. Explain and comment on Jung's distinction between "introverted" and "extraverted" forms of artistic creation.
   3. In what ways does Jung's essay challenge and criticize potentially impoverishing forms of psychoanalytic interpretation of literary texts?

■ Northrop Frye, "The Archetypes of Literature"
   1. Describe the ways in which Frye's notion of archetypes draws on concepts from Jungian psychoanalysis.

2. What, exactly, does Frye mean by a *literary archetype*? What might be some of the objections to Frye's hypothesis that all literary genres are derived from the quest-myth?

3. In what ways is Frye's attitude, as expressed in this essay, reminiscent of American New Criticism? In what ways does Frye suggest important limitations in formalist approaches such as New Criticism?

■ Harold Bloom, from *The Anxiety of Influence*
1. Explain and comment on Bloom's vision of the devolution of poetry since the time of Milton.
2. Explain and comment on Bloom's idea that in the today's postmodern era, literary tradition is valuable because it stifles the weak and represses the strong.
3. Explain and critique Bloom's notion of misprision.

■ Sandra M. Gilbert and Susan Gubar, from *The Madwoman in the Attic*
1. In what ways, according to Gilbert and Gubar, does "anxiety" operate in special ways for women writers?
2. Compare the discussion of the anxiety of authorship by Gilbert and Gubar with Bloom's discussion of the anxiety of influence.
3. What, according to Gilbert and Gubar, is the historical connection between women writers and madness?

■ Jacques Lacan, "The Mirror Stage"
1. Explain what Lacan means by the *mirror stage*.
2. How does Lacan's formulation of the notion of the mirror stage relate to Freud's discussion of the Oedipal drama? To Kristeva's concept of the semiotic?
3. How might Lacan's emphasis on the mirror stage be applied to our understanding of literature, and in particular to the emphasis of many kinds of criticism and theory on the organic wholeness of the work of art?

TEACHING TIP: A consideration of Lacan's immensely influential work is indispensable for understanding how psychoanalysis has been applied to the study of literature and culture in recent decades. However, there is no getting around the fact that Lacan's writing will be extremely difficult for most students (and, for that matter, instructors) to read. For that reason, an introductory lecture describing some of Lacan's major ideas (the Symbolic, Imaginary, and Real orders; the vision of castration as an acceptance of the rules of the Symbolic order of language) is highly recommended. In addition to the headnote in *NATC*, instructors preparing such a lecture might want to consult a brief summary of Lacan's ideas, such as that contained in Booker (*Practical Introduction*, 35–37) or Wright (107–22). Perhaps the most accessible book-length introduction to Lacan's work is Benvenuto and Kennedy. Ragland-Sullivan is also useful.

Instructors should note not only Lacan's distinctive application of structuralist methods to psychoanalysis but also his important influence on such movements as French feminism.

■ Jacques Lacan, from "The Agency of the Letter in the Unconscious"
 1. Summarize and comment on Lacan's suggestion that language and its structures are prior to and constitutive of the individual subject.
 2. Explain and comment on Lacan's notion of the signifying chain.
 3. What distinction does Lacan make between metaphor and metonymy?

■ Jacques Lacan, "The Signification of the Phallus"
 1. Explain Lacan's conception of the phallus.
 2. In what ways does Lacan's conception of the phallus as signifier suggest that language functions as a paradigm of the workings of the human psyche?
 3. Comment on Lacan's conception of desire. In what ways does his analysis show that human desire can never ultimately be fulfilled?

■ Michel Foucault, from *The History of Sexuality*
 1. What is the "repressive hypothesis"? On what basis does Foucault believe the repressive hypothesis to be an inaccurate description of the role played by sexuality in Victorian society?
 2. Explain Foucault's notion that the functioning of sexuality in Victorian society produced not only discourse on sexuality but also a variety of forms of "perversion."

TEACHING TIP: Instructors might want to provide a broad overview of Foucault's multivolume "History of Sexuality" project when teaching this selection. This overview might also provide an opportunity to emphasize Foucault's importance to gender studies and queer theory, as well as his critique of psychoanalysis.

■ Hélène Cixous, "The Laugh of the Medusa"
 1. Describe the characteristics that for Cixous set *écriture féminine* (women's writing) apart from more conventional, masculine conceptions of language.
 2. Summarize the ways in which Cixous sees writing as central to an project for the emancipation of women.
 3. Summarize and comment on Cixous's engagement with psychoanalysis, particularly Lacanian psychoanalysis.

■ Julia Kristeva, from *Revolution in Poetic Language*
 1. Explain Kristeva's distinction between the semiotic and the symbolic. How do these concepts relate to Lacanian psychoanalysis?
 2. Compare Kristeva's notion of semiotic language with Cixous's notion of *écriture féminine*.

3. Discuss the ways in which Kristeva's work suggests that literature and poetry might be especially valuable resources for feminist expression.

■ Laura Mulvey, "Visual Pleasure and Narrative Cinema"
1. Discuss Mulvey's vision of the two contradictory aspects (separation and identification) of the experience of visual pleasure in the cinema.
2. Summarize and comment on Mulvey's discussion of the role of the female star in the experience of visual pleasure in Hollywood cinema.
3. Discuss the ways in which Mulvey, while using the tools of Lacanian psychoanalysis, also challenges many typical psychoanalytic assumptions.

KEY TERMS AND CONCEPTS

archetype	*jouissance*
castration	mirror stage
collective unconscious	Oedipal drama
condensation	phallus
displacement	pleasure principle
dream-work	the repressive hypothesis
écriture féminine	repression
ego	sublimation
fetishism	superego
the gaze	the uncanny
id	unconscious
introvert/extrovert	

ESSAY TOPICS

1. What, in your view, are the principal strengths and weaknesses of psychoanalysis as a technique for the interpretation of literature?
2. What do you see as the principal differences between Lacanian and Freudian psychoanalysis?
3. What, from a feminist point of view, might be some of the major objections to either Freudian or Lacanian psychoanalysis?
4. In what ways might psychoanalytic theory be particularly applicable to film theory?

RESEARCH PROJECTS

1. Read a substantial example of myth/archetype criticism. Write an essay commenting on the use of Jungian concepts in that criticism. *Suggestion*: Bodkin is still the classic example of such criticism.
2. Read vol. 1 of Foucault's *History of Sexuality*. Write an essay commenting on Foucault's dialogue with Freudian psychoanalysis in that volume.

3. Do some reading on Norman Holland's use of psychoanalytic concepts to develop his own distinctive kind of reader-response criticism. Write an essay that summarizes and comments on Holland's approach. *Suggestion*: A succinct introduction to Holland's work can be found in a handbook such as Booker's *Practical Introduction* (47–49). A more extensive introduction can be found in Freund (112–33). For Holland's own work, see *Poems in Persons* and *5 Readers Reading*. See also Holland's essay "Unity Identity Text Self."

4. Research the relationship between the work of Lacan and that of French feminists such as Cixous, Kristeva, and Irigaray. Write an essay that summarizes and comments on this relationship. *Suggestion*: See the discussion of this topic in Moi.

5. Beginning with the essay by Mulvey, do further research on the use of Lacanian psychoanalysis in film studies. Write an essay that summarizes and comments on this use. *Suggestion*: The leading figure in Lacanian film studies is probably Slavoj Žižek.

II. Structuralist Criticism and Theory (1–2 weeks)

Structuralist methodology was extremely important in European intellectual life in the middle part of the twentieth century, providing influential approaches not only to literary criticism but also to anthropology, psychology, and a variety of other disciplines. By the time structuralism began to become widely known in the English-speaking world, in the late 1960s, it was already being challenged in Europe by poststructuralism. Structuralist and poststructuralist approaches can be effectively taught together.

TEACHING TIP: Instructors who feel that they need a better general grounding in structuralist literary criticism and theory might want to consult Culler's *Structuralist Poetics*, perhaps the best general introduction to the topic. Note also that a number of figures included in *NATC* were important forerunners of structuralism, from Aristotle to Aquinas to Marx and Freud.

SUGGESTED READINGS AND DISCUSSION QUESTIONS

■ Ferdinand de Saussure, from *Course in General Linguistics*
   1. Summarize Saussure's theory of the arbitrary nature of the sign, and the link between the signifier and the signified.
   2. Explain Saussure's concepts of *langue* and *parole*.
   3. What does Saussure mean by synchronic and diachronic analysis?

■ Roman Jakobson, from "Linguistics and Poetics"
   1. Summarize and comment on Jakobson's discussion of the "poetic function" in language.

Suggested Readings

1-week module	2-week module
Saussure	Saussure
Jakobson	Jakobson
"Linguistics and Poetics"	"Linguistics and Poetics"
"Two Aspects of Language"	"Two Aspects of Language"
Lacan	Frye
"Agency of the Phallus"	White
Althusser	Lévi-Strauss
"Ideology"	Austin
Todorov	Lacan
	"Agency of the Letter"
	Althusser
	"Ideology"
	Todorov
	Deleuze & Guattari
	"Rhizome"

---

2. Summarize and comment on the communication model used by Jakobson to describe the workings of language.
3. Explain Jakobson's concept of metalanguage and summarize the role it plays in his discussion.

■ Roman Jakobson, from "Two Aspects of Language and Two Types of Aphasic Disturbances"
   1. How does Jacobson use the symptoms of aphasia to draw conclusions about the basic workings of language?
   2. Explain and comment on Jacobson's distinction between metaphor and metonymy.
   3. Why, according to Jacobson, is metaphor the characteristic mode of poetry and metonymy the characteristic mode of prose?

■ Northrop Frye, "The Archetypes of Literature"
   1. Though Frye's approach may not, strictly speaking, be a structuralist one, it clearly has much in common with structuralist approaches. Discuss some of the ways in which Frye's approach in this essay might be considered structuralist.
   2. In what ways is Frye's attitude, as expressed in this essay, reminiscent of American New Criticism? In what ways does Frye suggest important limitations in formalist approaches such as New Criticism?
   3. What, exactly, does Frye mean by a *literary archetype*? What might be some of the objections to Frye's hypothesis that all literary genres are derived from the quest-myth?

■ Hayden White, "The Historical Text as Literary Artifact"
1. Explain and comment on White's contention that the classics of historical writing should be regarded as essentially literary works.
2. Explain and comment on White's notion of emplotment and of the way in which history can be emplotted in certain basic forms.
3. In what ways does White's vision of history draw on the work of specific literary theorists?
4. What are some of the implications of White's work for literary theory and for the ways in which we understand the historical context of literature?

■ Claude Lévi-Strauss, "A Writing Lesson" (*Tristes Tropiques*)
1. Summarize and comment on Lévi-Strauss's conclusions concerning the role of writing in society and world history.
2. Lévi-Strauss concludes that his introduction of writing to the Nambikwara culture could lead to increased bureaucratization and decreased freedom in that society. Derrida (in *Of Grammatology*) has criticized this conclusion as a paradigmatic example of the "metaphysics of presence," arguing instead that one could see the introduction of writing as a moment of potential liberation. Comment on these conflicting interpretations.
3. Lévi-Strauss seems especially fascinated by the elements of violence that inform the native cultures he is observing. What might this fascination tell us about his work and about anthropology in general?

TEACHING TIP: Because this selection does not necessarily make clear the structuralist nature of Lévi-Strauss's project, instructors might want to emphasize his structuralism in their classroom presentations. See, for example, the chapter on Lévi-Strauss in Kurzweil.

■ J. L. Austin, "Performative Utterances"
1. In what ways does Austin's elaboration of speech act theory both resemble and diverge from the linguistic project of Saussure?
2. Explain and comment on Austin's distinction between "statements" and "performatives."
3. Summarize and comment on Austin's elaboration of the rhetorical aspects of performative language.

■ Jacques Lacan, from "The Agency of the Letter in the Unconscious"
1. Summarize and comment on Lacan's suggestion that language and its structures are prior to and constitutive of the individual subject.
2. Explain and comment on Lacan's notion that the unconscious is structured like language.
3. What distinction does Lacan make between metaphor and metonymy?

- Louis Althusser, from "Ideology and Ideological State Apparatuses"
  1. Explain Althusser's concept of the Ideological State Apparatus (ISA).
  2. Discuss Althusser's notion of interpellation. What does it suggest about the difficulty of resistance to official ideology in a capitalist society?
  3. In what ways in Althusser's understanding of the concept of ideology and the construction of the subject structuralist in nature?

- Tzvetan Todorov, "Structural Analysis of Narrative"
  1. Summarize and comment on Todorov's analysis of the narrative structure of the tales in the *Decameron*.
  2. In what ways does Todorov's analysis of narrative draw on models and ideas derived from linguistics?
  3. In what ways does Todorov's approach differ from that of the New Critics? In what ways does it resemble New Criticism and other formalist methods?

- Gilles Deleuze and Félix Guattari, from "Rhizome" (*A Thousand Plateaus*)
  1. Discuss the importance and various ramifications of the central "rhizome" metaphor in this essay.
  2. What do Deleuze and Guattari mean by *representational thought* in the Western philosophical tradition?
  3. What aspects of this essay can be taken as a critique of structuralism?
  4. What, according to Deleuze and Guattari, are the implications of representational thought for our view of the individual subject?

KEY TERMS AND CONCEPTS

archetype	*parole*
convention	poetics
diachronic	semiotics
Ideological State Apparatus (ISA)	sign
interpellation	signifier
intertextuality	signified
langue	synchronic
linguistics	tropology
narratology	

ESSAY TOPICS

1. Summarize the basic premises of structuralism and explain why this methodology could be applied to so many different fields.
2. In what ways does structuralism resemble New Criticism? In what ways does it differ from New Criticism?
3. What do you see as the principal strengths and weaknesses of structuralism?

4. Choose any one of the selections on structuralist approaches and write a critique of it.

RESEARCH PROJECTS

1. Research the relationship between the Prague School structuralists and Russian formalism. Write an essay summarizing this relationship and commenting on its significance. *Suggestion*: Holub contains a succinct description of this relationship that should serve as a good starting point for this project.
2. Discuss the structuralist concept of intertextuality. How does it differ from poststructuralist figurations of this same concept?
3. Read the essay "The Idea of Enlightenment" in *Dialectic of Enlightenment*, by Horkheimer and Adorno. Write an essay that compares and contrasts the treatment of Enlightenment science by Horkheimer and Adorno to the treatment of writing by Lévi-Strauss in "A Writing Lesson."
4. Read Todorov's *Mikhail Bakhtin* for an extended view of the work of Bakhtin through the optic of structuralism. Then do some further reading, in both Bakhtin's work and other works about Bakhtin. Write an essay describing the aspects of Bakhtin's work that are emphasized by Todorov's structuralist reading. Then suggest aspects of Bakhtin's work that do not fit in well with Todorov's approach. *Suggestion*: The best general introduction to the work of Bakhtin is probably the book by Morson and Emerson.
5. Do some additional research and write an essay tracing the historical impact of structuralism on Western thought in a variety of disciplines. *Suggestion*: Culler's *Structuralist Poetics* is probably the best introduction to the use of structuralism in analyzing literature. See the two volumes by Dosse for a history of structuralism; Kurzweil might be helpful in this regard as well.

III. Cultural Studies (1–3 weeks)

Cultural studies represents a broad and diverse array of approaches that have in common the perception that the traditional study of literature needs to be extended to include a broader consideration of culture as a whole. Often this perception leads to studies of film, television, and other elements of popular culture. At other times, cultural studies retains a focus on works of "high" art, but pays serious attention to the impact of material and ideological forces on the production, circulation, and reception of this art. Thus cultural studies has much in common with Marxist, feminist, postcolonial, and other forms of criticism that emphasize the social and historical conditioning of culture. In addition, much recent work in cultural studies has been significantly influenced by postmodernism, poststructuralism, and other recent theoretical developments.

TEACHING TIP: Marxism has provided an especially important theoretical source for cultural studies, particularly British cultural studies. If the cultural studies. If the cultural studies module is taught without a separate module on Marxist theory and criticism (including especially the selections by Benjamin, Gramsci, Williams, and Horkheimer and Adorno), then these selections should be included in the cultural studies module as background, with perhaps an additional week of coverage. For further information on the Marxist heritage of British cultural studies, see Dworkin.

For a broad introduction to the varieties of critical and theoretical activity encompassed by cultural studies, see the essays in the volume edited by Grossberg, Nelson, and Treichler.

Suggested Readings	
1-week module	2-week module
Barthes	Barthes
Mythologies	*Mythologies*
Bourdieu	Bourdieu
Hebdige	Ohmann
Hall	Hebdige
Mulvey	Hall
Bordo	Haraway
	Mulvey
	Baker
	Baudrillard
	Moulthrop
	Butler
	Bordo
	Davis

SUGGESTED READINGS AND DISCUSSION QUESTIONS

■ Roland Barthes, from *Mythologies*
 1. In what ways, according to Barthes, does advertising tend to mythologize commodities? How does this process relate to Marx's discussion of the fetishism of the commodity?
 2. In what ways does Barthes's discussion of Einstein's brain suggest the general manner in which myth functions in the modern secular world?
 3. In what ways does Barthes's analysis of the function of photographs of candidates in electoral campaigns suggest the subtle (but powerful) workings of ideology in the contemporary world?

TEACHING TIP: Barthes's work provides a convenient opportunity to emphasize the impact of poststructuralist thought on cultural studies. On this topic, see Leitch's *Cultural Criticism*.

■ Pierre Bourdieu, from *Distinction*
1. Discuss the ways in which, in the broad realm of the aesthetic, Bourdieu's argument supports the Marxist notion that in any given era, the dominant ideas of a society reflect the point of view of the ruling class.
2. Bourdieu argues that the distinction between the aesthetic and the nonaesthetic is a false one. Comment on this argument and compare it to the formalist notion of a strict separation between the work of art and the social work outside that work.
3. Bourdieu ends his introduction by arguing that art, by its very nature, tends to legitimate social differences. Comment on this argument and its implications for the study of art and literature.

■ Richard Ohmann, from "The Shaping of a Canon"
1. Summarize and comment on Ohmann's conclusions regarding the role of hardback bestsellers in contemporary American culture.
2. Summarize and comment on Ohmann's conclusions regarding the role played by large publishing companies and influential media outlets (such as the *New York Times Book Review*) in the acceptance of new books as "literature."
3. Summarize and comment on Ohmann's conclusions regarding the role of class (particularly the "professional-managerial" class) in the potential canonization of specific works.
4. Compare and contrast Ohmann's conclusions with those reached by Horkeimer and Adorno in their commentary on the "culture industry."

■ Dick Hebdige, from *Subculture*
1. Summarize Hebdige's discussion of the term *culture*.
2. Discuss the ways in which, according to Hebdige's Marxist analysis, the dominant culture in any society at any given time reflects the ideology of the ruling class of that society.
3. Hebdige argues that "there is an ideological dimension to every signification." How might this notion affect our methods of reading and interpreting literary and cultural texts?

■ Stuart Hall, "Cultural Studies and Its Theoretical Legacies"
1. Summarize Hall's discussion of the importance of the work of Gramsci to the development of his ideas and the growth of British cultural studies as a whole.
2. Discuss Hall's description of the crucial, though complex, influence of Marxist theory on the development of cultural studies. How have issues of gender and race modified and enriched the fundamental (essentially Marxist) emphasis on class that underlies British cultural studies?
3. Discuss Hall's notion of "intellectual work" as the principal project of cultural studies.

- Donna Haraway, "A Manifesto for Cyborgs"
  1. Discuss Haraway's elaboration of the "informatics of domination."
  2. Describe some of the major characteristics of the "cyborg," according to Haraway.
  3. The subtitle of Haraway's essay identifies its stance as socialist feminist. In what ways does her essay reflect that political perspective?
  4. In what ways does Haraway's essay reflect a postmodern sensibility?

TEACHING TIP: For some illuminating insights into Haraway's somewhat difficult essay, see the interview of Haraway by Ross and Penley.

- Laura Mulvey, "Visual Pleasure and Narrative Cinema"
  1. Discuss Mulvey's vision of the two contradictory aspects (separation and identification) of the experience of visual pleasure in the cinema.
  2. Summarize and comment on Mulvey's discussion of the role of the female star in the experience of visual pleasure in Hollywood cinema.

- Houston A. Baker Jr., from *Blues, Ideology, and Afro-American Literature*
  1. Explain Baker's conception of the blues matrix as a crucial element of African American culture.
  2. Summarize the principal theoretical resources that inform Baker's vision of the blues matrix.
  3. Explain Baker's conclusion that works of art have no "intrinsic aesthetic value." How does this notion reinforce his emphasis on the importance of the blues matrix? How does it support the serious study of popular culture as a whole?

- Jean Baudrillard, from *The Precession of Simulacra*
  1. Explain Baudrillard's use of the notion of the simulacrum. In what ways does this use particularly pertain to the postmodern condition?
  2. Discuss the ways in which Baudrillard's discussion of modern consumer society criticizes not only capitalism but also colonialism.
  3. What aspects of our contemporary world seem to bear out Baudrillard's analysis of the precession of simulacra in the postmodern world? What aspects might dispute his findings?

- Stuart Moulthrop, "You Say You Want a Revolution"
  1. Briefly define the concepts of hypertext and hyperreality.
  2. Summarize and comment on Moulthrop's discussion of the potential social, cultural, and political impact of hypertext.
  3. In what ways does the rapid rise of the Internet since Moulthrop's essay was published in 1991 bear out his ideas about hypertext? How has the Internet expanded beyond what Moulthrop anticipated?

■ Judith Butler, from *Gender Trouble*

1. In what ways does Butler's account of the social construction of individual identities challenge the identity politics common to Anglo-American feminist thought in the past few decades?
2. How does Butler's discussion challenge the very notion of "woman" as it has conventionally been used in feminist theory and criticism?
3. Summarize and comment on Butler's discussion of the ways in which socially constructed identities might be challenged by "subversive bodily acts."

■ Susan Bordo, from *Unbearable Weight*

1. Explain and comment on Bordo's argument that the human body is a product not merely of biology but also of social construction.
2. In what ways does Bordo's discussion of anorexia and bulimia illustrate her thesis concerning the social construction of the body?
3. What are the implications of Bordo's analysis for a feminist critical practice that might oppose inimical social constructions of the female?

■ Lennard J. Davis, from *Visualizing the Disabled Body*

1. Summarize and comment on Davis's review of the representation of disability in the Western literary and cultural tradition.
2. Describe and comment on the role played by the relationship between wholeness and fragmentation in Davis's essay.
3. In what ways does Davis's discussion of the opposition between normalcy and "abnormality" parallel similar discussions in gender studies and in race and ethnicity studies?

KEY TERMS AND CONCEPTS

aura	docile body
canon	fragmented body
carceral society	hegemony
commodification	Ideological State Apparatus (ISA)
cultural materialism	ideology
culture	informatics of domination
culture industry	interpellation
culture wars	media culture
cyborg	popular culture

ESSAY TOPICS

1. What are some of the implications of expanding the coverage of literary studies to include a broader coverage of cultural texts?
2. In what ways do the cultural studies selections you have read suggest the applicability of literary theory to other cultural texts? In what ways does literary theory need to be modified to be applied in this broader context?

3. In what ways do the cultural studies texts you have read suggest the importance of class as a category for understanding modern culture?

4. What aspects of cultural studies are reminiscent of the findings of feminism, race and ethnicity studies, and gender studies?

5. How might the insights of cultural studies change our approach to the study of literary texts?

RESEARCH PROJECTS

1. Both Hall and Hebdige indicate the strong influence of the Marxist tradition on British cultural studies. Research this phenomenon further and comment on it, paying attention to reasons why Marxism may have been less influential in U.S. cultural studies.

2. Read one of the major works of British cultural studies. Then write an essay summarizing and commenting on this work as an example of cultural studies. *Suggestion*: Hebdige, Thompson (*The Making of the English Working Class,*) and Hoggart might be good candidates for this project. See also Dworkin for more background on British cultural studies.

3. The cultural studies movement has been influenced by Marxism, feminism and gender studies, and race and ethnicity studies in obvious and important ways. Write an essay examining the ways in which cultural studies also shows the influence of poststructuralism.

4. In many ways, the inclusive premises of cultural studies directly contradict the project of the New Critics and many others to identify and promulgate a canon of "great works" of literature. Do some research on contemporary debates over the canon and comment on this issue in an essay. *Suggestion*: In addition to the selection by Ohmann in *NATC*, valuable works dealing with the debate over the canon and canonicity include the collection edited by Fiedler and Baker; Lauter; Harold Bloom, *The Western Canon*; and Guillory.

5. The cultural studies movement has been at the heart of the recent "culture wars" that have taken the form of sometimes heated debates over the nature and purpose of literary scholarship and teaching. Research these culture wars and write an essay describing your conclusions concerning them. *Research hints*: Useful volumes in this debate include Allan Bloom; Levine; Gates, *Loose Canons*; and Graff, *Beyond the Culture Wars*.

IV. Phenomenological, Hermeneutic, and Reader-Response Criticism and Theory (1–2 weeks)

The category of phenomenological, hermeneutic, and reader-response criticism includes an array of approaches united by a central focus on the experience of human perception of reality, with the reading of literary texts envisioned as a special example of that perception. This kind of criticism has a long history that goes back to the concern with understanding sacred texts in the ancient Christian and Jewish traditions. Such approaches to interpretation were also particularly important in the medieval period (e.g., see in *NATC* the theories of Moses Maimonides, Aquinas, and Dante). In contemporary times, much of that philosophical background has also influenced the development of poststructuralist and other contemporary theoretical movements. For brief chapters on phenomenological, hermeneutic, and reader-response theory in a U.S. context, see Leitch, *American Criticism*.

Suggested Readings	
1-week module	2-week module
Hirsch	Schleiermacher
Heidegger	Hirsch
Poulet	Heidegger
Iser	Kenneth Burke
Fish	Poulet
	Sartre
	Jauss
	Iser
	Fish
	Knapp & Michaels

SUGGESTED READINGS AND DISCUSSION QUESTIONS

■ Friedrich Schleiermacher, from *Hermeneutics*
  1. What, according to Schleiermacher, constitutes "good" interpretation?
  2. Summarize and comment on Schleiermacher's categorization of various types of interpretation.
  3. Summarize and comment on Schleiermacher's discussion of "misunderstanding" in interpretation.

■ E. D. Hirsch Jr., "Objective Interpretation"
  1. Summarize and comment on Hirsch's insistence that the meaning of a text must coincide with the intention of the author. Contrast Hirsch's conclusion with the rejection of authorial intention by Wimsatt and Beardsley.
  2. Explain and comment on Hirsch's distinction between meaning and significance in a literary text.
  3. Summarize Hirsch's engagement with European philosophers of phenomenology such as Husserl and Heidegger.
  4. Explain and comment on Hirsch's concept of historical "horizon."

■ Martin Heidegger, "Language"
1. Summarize and comment on Heidegger's notion that language is as primordial as human consciousness, so that language speaks the subject and constructs the world.
2. In what ways does Heidegger's theory of language undermine conventional Western notions of the centered subject?
3. Comment on Heidegger's reading of the poem in this selection.

■ Kenneth Burke, "Kinds of Criticism"
1. What kinds of criticism, per Burke's scheme, would be associated with phenomenological and hermeneutic criticism? With reader-response criticism?
2. Describe and comment on Burke's notion of the "Criticism of Criticism."
3. Discuss Burke's distinction between "genetic" and "implicational" types of extrinsic criticism. What critical schools might be included in these two categories, respectively?

■ Georges Poulet, "Phenomenology of Reading"
1. Summarize and comment on Poulet's argument that books represent a unique category of objects.
2. Explain Poulet's vision of the reading process as a mingling of the minds of the reader and author.
3. In what ways does Poulet's vision of the reading process conflict with structuralist and poststructuralist reading practices?

■ Jean-Paul Sartre, "Why Write?" (*What is Literature?*)
1. What answers does Sartre ultimately propose to the question posed in the title of this selection?
2. What, according to Sartre, is the role of the reader in bringing to life the literary object? Contrast this role with the one proposed by Poulet.

■ Hans Robert Jauss, from "Literary History as a Challenge to Literary Theory"
1. In what ways is Jauss's attempt to historicize the reception of literary texts opposed to New Criticism and other formalist approaches to literature?
2. Explain and comment on the distinction made by Jauss between his model of literary history and more conventional models.
3. Explain and comment on the notion of the horizon of expectations as used by Jauss in this essay.

TEACHING TIP: For an accessible introduction to the German reception theory represented by the work of Jauss and Iser, see Holub.

■ Wolfgang Iser, "Interaction between Text and Reader"
  1. Summarize and comment on the role played by textual "gaps" or "blanks" in Iser's description of the reading process.
  2. Explain and comment on Iser's notion of the repertoire of a literary text.
  3. Contrast Iser's reader-response approach to that put forth by Fish via the notion of interpretive communities.

TEACHING TIP: For an accessible introduction to the German reception theory represented by the work of Jauss and Iser, see Holub.

■ Stanley Fish, "Interpreting the *Variorum*"
  1. Summarize and comment on Fish's critique of formalist criticism.
  2. Fish's approach depends on descriptions of the activities of "the reader." Who, exactly, is this "reader" and how does Fish know what he or she will do when encountering a specific text?
  3. Explain Fish's notion of interpretive communities. How are these communities, for Fish, constitutive of meaning in the literary text?

TEACHING TIP: For an accessible introduction to reader-response theory as a whole, see Freund. See also the essays collected in the volume edited by Tompkins.

■ Steven Knapp and Walter Benn Michaels, "Against Theory"
  1. Explain what Knapp and Michaels mean by *theory*. Comment on the implications of this definition.
  2. Summarize and comment on the critique of Hirsch's theory of meaning by Knapp and Michaels. What objections might be raised to the simple equation between meaning and intention that Knapp and Michaels propose?
  3. Summarize and comment on Knapp and Michael's discussion of the notion of belief. Comment on their critique of Fish in this regard.

TEACHING TIP: See Jameson's *Postmodernism* (181–88) for an interesting response to this essay.

KEY TERMS AND CONCEPTS

gaps (in the text)	interpretive community
the Geneva School	meaning
the hermeneutic circle	phenomenology
hermeneutics	reception theory
horizon	

ESSAY TOPICS

1. What, in your view, are the major strengths and weaknesses of German reception theory, as represented by the work of Jauss and Iser?

2. Compare and contrast the reader-response approaches is Iser and Fish.

3. Suggest ways in which reader-response theory might be adapted to theater or film criticism.

4. How might the insights of phenomenology suggest an important role for literature in helping us to understand the world outside of literature?

5. What, in your view, are some of the strengths and weaknesses of hermeneutics, based on the selections from Schleiermacher and Hirsch?

RESEARCH PROJECTS

1. Discuss the ways in which the phenomenology of Heidegger can be seen as an important background for poststructuralism. *Suggestion*: Megill might be a good place to start in researching this project.

2. Read the discussion of phenomenology, hermeneutics, and reception theory in Eagleton's *Literary Theory* (54–90). Write an essay describing his suggestion that all of these approaches are centrally informed by bourgeois ideology. What do you think of Eagleton's analysis?

3. Read a substantial example of phenomenological criticism and write an essay that comments on this example and the ways in which it matches or does not match your expectations based on your understanding of phenomenological theory. *Suggestion*: Perhaps the most important example of U.S. phenomenological criticism is the early Geneva School work of J. Hillis Miller, as in his *Poets of Reality*.

4. In the early 1980s, Fish and Iser engaged in a spirited debate concerning the relative merits of their views of reader-response theory. Research this debate and write an essay that summarizes it and expresses your own conclusions regarding the relative merits of the two sides. *Suggestion*: This exchange began with Fish's "Why No One's Afraid of Wolfgang Iser" and continued with Iser's rejoinder in "Talk Like Whales." For brief summaries of the debate, see Freund (148–51) and Holub (101–6).

5. Do some reading on Norman Holland's use of psychoanalytic concepts to develop his own distinctive kind of reader-response criticism. Write an essay that summarizes and comments on Holland's approach. *Suggestion*: A succinct introduction to Holland's work can be found in a handbook such as Booker's *Practical Introduction* (47–49). A more extensive introduction can be found in Freund (112–33). For Holland's own work, see *Poems in Persons* and *5 Readers Reading*, as well as his essay "Unity Identity Text Self."

V. *Postmodern Criticism and Theory (1–2 weeks)*

The exact nature of postmodernism is still intensely debated, but it seems clear that the term describes a wide array of late-twentieth-century cultural productions, a range of contemporary modes of criticism and thought, and a distinctive historical period of postindustrial, media-saturated societies. To a large extent, similar issues are at stake in postmodern and poststructuralist studies, and these two modules can be productively taught together (though each can be understood separately). Note that the term *postmodern theory* has two common meanings, "poststructuralist theory" or a theory rooted in diagnoses of late capitalist consumer society.

Suggested Readings

1-week module	2-week module
Lyotard	Lyotard
Habermas	Baudrillard
"Modernity"	Habermas
Jameson	"Modernity"
"Postmodernism"	Jameson
hooks	"Postmodernism"
Deleuze & Guattari	Anzaldúa
"Rhizome"	Vizenor
	Haraway
	hooks
	Moulthrop
	Deleuze & Guattari
	"Rhizome"

Suggested Readings and Discussion Questions

■ Jean-François Lyotard, "Defining the Postmodern"
  1. Summarize and comment on Lyotard's distinction between modernist and postmodernist architecture.
  2. Summarize and comment on Lyotard's discussion of the status of the idea of progress in the postmodern era.
  3. Summarize and comment on Lyotard's notion that the postmodern era is a time for analyzing and reflecting on the past. In what ways is his vision here a poststructuralist one?

TEACHING TIP: Lyotard is one of the leading theorists of postmodernism. The brief selection in *NATC* does not make entirely clear that Lyotard is best known for his idea, expressed in *The Postmodern Condition*, that postmodernism is marked by "incredulity toward metanarratives," where *metanarratives* are totalizing theories of the workings of history, society, and epistemological inquiry. Instructors might want to familiarize themselves with Lyotard's argument in that book before teaching his work. Lyotard's work also has much in common with that of other poststructuralist thinkers, such as Derrida and Foucault. See, for example, Carroll.

■ Jean Baudrillard, from *The Precession of Simulacra*
1. Explain Baudrillard's use of the notion of the simulacrum. In what ways does this use particularly pertain to the postmodern condition?
2. Discuss the ways in which Baudrillard's discussion of modern consumer society criticizes not only capitalism but also colonialism.
3. What aspects of our contemporary world seem to bear out Baudrillard's analysis of the precession of simulacra in the postmodern world? What aspects might dispute his findings?

■ Jürgen Habermas, "Modernity—An Incomplete Project"
1. What does Habermas mean by *modernity*? In what sense, according to Habermas, is the project of modernity incomplete? How might this vision affect our understanding of postmodernism?
2. Discuss Habermas's notion of the fragmentation of modern bourgeois society into separate, seemingly autonomous spheres of activity. What are the implications of this fragmentation?
3. In what sense does Habermas believe supposedly radical thinkers such as Foucault and Derrida to be "neoconservatives"?

TEACHING TIP: It is a good idea to place Habermas's critique of modernity within the context of the work of Frankfurt School predecessors, such as Horkheimer and Adorno.

■ Fredric Jameson, "Postmodernism and Consumer Society"
1. Summarize some of the key characteristics of postmodernist culture as described by Jameson in this essay.
2. Discuss Jameson's use of Lacan's figuration of schizophrenia as a metaphor for postmodern textuality and postmodern experience as a whole.
3. Summarize and comment on Jameson's key conclusion that postmodernism replicates the logic of consumer capitalism.

TEACHING TIP: Jameson is probably the most important of the many Marxist thinkers and critics who have addressed the phenomenon of postmodernism, generally from a critical perspective that sees postmodernism as the cultural equivalent of capitalism in its global, consumerist phase. Instructors might want to consult Jameson's book on the subject, *Postmodernism*, before teaching this module. Jameson draws on a characterization of global capitalism that can be found in Ernest Mandel's *Late Capitalism*. For other Marxist commentaries on postmodernism, see Harvey and Callinicos.

■ Gloria Anzaldúa, from *Borderlands/La Frontera*
1. In what ways does Anzaldúa's "mestiza" perspective both participate in and challenge the identity politics that have been central to much work in race and ethnicity studies?
2. In what ways does Anzaldúa's challenging of fixed boundaries par-

ticipate in poststructuralism? in postmodernism? In what ways does it differ from either of these movements?

■ Gerald Vizenor, from *Manifest Manners*

1. Summarize and comment on Vizenor's discussion of the stereotyping of Native Americans. In what ways does this phenomenon resemble that described by Said in *Orientalism*?
2. What does Vizenor mean by a *postindian*?
3. What forms of "survivance," or resistance to cultural domination, are practiced by Vizenor's postindians?
4. What are Vizenor's theoretical sources?

■ Donna Haraway, "A Manifesto for Cyborgs"

1. Describe some of the major characteristics of the "cyborg," according to Haraway.
2. The subtitle of Haraway's essay identifies its stance as socialist feminist. In what ways does her essay reflect that political perspective?
3. What, according to Haraway, are the main features of postmodern society?

TEACHING TIP: For some illuminating insights into Haraway's difficult essay, see the interview of Haraway by Ross and Penley.

■ bell hooks, "Postmodern Blackness"

1. How does hooks define *postmodernism*?
2. Summarize hooks's critique of postmodernist discourses as "exclusionary." In what ways have African American women, in particular, been excluded by these discourses?
3. Discuss the ways in which, for hooks, postmodernism offers potential opportunities for African American writers and intellectuals.
4. Discuss the role of identity in hooks's elaboration of the relationship between postmodernism and African American cultural and intellectual life.

■ Stuart Moulthrop, "You Say You Want a Revolution"

1. Briefly define the concepts of hypertext and hyperreality. In what ways are these concepts postmodernist ones?
2. Summarize and comment on Moulthrop's discussion of the potential social, cultural, and political impact of hypertext.
3. In what ways does the rapid rise of the Internet since Moulthrop's essay was published in 1991 bear out his ideas about hypertext? How has the Internet expanded beyond what Moulthrop anticipated?

■ Gilles Deleuze and Félix Guattari, from "Rhizome" (*A Thousand Plateaus*)

1. Discuss the importance and various ramifications of the central "rhizome" metaphor in this essay.

2. What do Deleuze and Guattari mean by *representational thought* in the Western philosophical tradition?
3. Describe their critique of this representational thought. What is postmodern about it?
4. What, according to Deleuze and Guattari, are the implications of representational thought for our view of the individual subject?

KEY TERMS AND CONCEPTS

consumer capitalism	metanarrative
cyborg	modernity
fragmentation	popular culture
hypertext	postmodernism
informatics of domination	simulacra
late capitalism	society of spectacle
media culture	

ESSAY TOPICS

1. Based on your own experience with contemporary culture, what aspects of that culture might be considered postmodern?
2. Based on your reading in this class, what similarities do you see between poststructuralism and postmodernism? What differences do you see?
3. What aspects of postmodern culture seem to you particularly valuable? What aspects seem problematic?
4. Comment on the parallels you see between postmodernism and the rise of feminist criticism, gender studies, and race and ethnicity studies as important discourses of literary theory and criticism.

RESEARCH PROJECTS

1. In the introduction to *Postmodernism*, Jameson suggests that the cyberpunk fiction of William Gibson may be the supreme literary expression of postmodernism. Jameson then expresses his regret that he does not discuss Gibson's work in his book. Read Gibson's *Neuromancer* (1984) and write an essay that comments on the book as a paradigmatic postmodernist work.
2. One of the most debated topics surrounding postmodernist literature is its engagement, or lack of engagement, with history. Write an essay that addresses this debate, making reference to participants in the debate and referring to specific works of postmodernist literature to illustrate your own conclusions concerning this issue. *Suggestion*: A central discussion of postmodernist engagement with history appears in Hutcheon. Jameson's *Postmodernism* contains an important argument that postmodernist art is disengaged from history.
3. The intersection between postmodernism and feminism has drawn considerable critical commentary. Research the debate surrounding

this issue and write an essay that summarizes the debate and your own conclusions concerning it. *Suggestion*: The essays in the collection edited by Nicholson provide a good entry point into this issue.

4. Marxist theorists and critics have been particularly concerned with the implications of postmodernism. Summarize some of the Marxist commentary on postmodernism and comment on the reasons why Marxist thinkers would find this such a crucial topic. *Suggestion*: For detailed Marxist readings of postmodernism, see Jameson, *Postmodernism*; Harvey, and Callinicos.

5. Much commentary surrounding postmodernism has involved attempts to differentiate that movement from modernism. Research the debate on this issue and write an essay that summarizes some of its most important points. *Suggestion*: The appendix to Booker's *Vargas Llosa* summarizes much of this debate. The essays contained in the collection edited by Brooker might also prove a valuable starting point for this project, as might the volumes by Fokkema and Huyssen. Hassan is an especially valuable essay.

VI. *Postcolonial Criticism and Theory (1–2 weeks)*

Postcolonial studies emerged in the late twentieth century as a vibrant field of scholarship. The field has much in common with race and ethnicity studies, though specific issues concerning colonialism and its aftermath take a special form in postcolonial studies proper. This module offers an opportunity to introduce students to ideas, cultures, and literary texts with which they might otherwise remain unfamiliar.

TEACHING TIP: The burgeoning field of postcolonial studies includes a wide range of cultural phenomena from around the world. Instructors unfamiliar with this field might want to acquaint themselves with some general discussions such as those by Boehmer, Moore-Gilbert, Gandhi, Walder, and Ashcroft, Griffiths, and Tiffin. Several anthologies of useful essays have been published, including those edited by Mongia, by Williams and Chrisman, and by Ashcroft, Griffiths, and Tiffin. Convenient introductions to important bodies of postcolonial literature can be found in studies such as Booker, *The African Novel in English*, and Booker and Juraga. For important critiques of the tendency of postcolonial theory toward poststructuralist textualism and away from political reality, see Ahmad and San Juan. See also the bibliographic essay in *NATC*.

SUGGESTED READINGS AND DISCUSSION QUESTIONS

■ Frantz Fanon, from "The Pitfalls of National Consciousness" (*The Wretched of the Earth*)

1. In what ways, for Fanon, is national consciousness a useful tool in the anticolonial struggle?

Suggested Readings	
1-week module	2-week module
Fanon	Fanon
"Pitfalls"	"Pitfalls"
Achebe	"On National Culture"
Said	Achebe
Bhabha	Said
	Bhabha
	Spivak
	Gates
	Ngugi et al.

2. What are the "pitfalls" of this consciousness, especially in the post-colonial era?
3. Describe Fanon's characterization of the colonial and postcolonial bourgeoisie.

■ Frantz Fanon, from "On National Culture" (*The Wretched of the Earth*)
1. How does Fanon define *national culture*?
2. What, according to Fanon, is the role of nationalism and national culture in the fight against colonial domination?
3. What, according to Fanon, are the principal pitfalls of a focus on nationalism as a mode of anticolonial resistance?
4. Summarize and comment on Fanon's discussion of the "native intellectual."

TEACHING TIP: Fanon is probably the most important third world anticolonial thinker of the twentieth century, and his work has been immensely influential not only for other critics and theorists but for numerous postcolonial novelists, especially in Africa. Radical postcolonial novelists, such as Kenya's Ngugi wa Thiong'o and Senegal's Ousmane Sembène, have been strongly influenced by his work, particularly *The Wretched of the Earth*.

■ Chinua Achebe, "An Image of Africa"
1. Briefly summarize the reasons why Achebe concludes that *Heart of Darkness* is a racist text.
2. Do you agree with Achebe's argument and conclusions?
3. In what ways might Achebe's essay be taken as much a criticism of certain styles of reading and teaching as of *Heart of Darkness*? *Suggestion*: Note that Achebe himself has for some time regularly taught *Heart of Darkness* as a key text in his own courses on the African novel at Bard College. Thus, Achebe believes that the book can be productively taught, but not without addressing such issues as racism and colonialism.

4. Given the canonical status of *Heart of Darkness*, what does Achebe's essay imply about the nature of canonicity and the importance of multicultural concerns in literary studies? *Suggestion*: One can, of course, argue that Conrad's attitude was typical of its time; but Achebe's point is really that Conrad's text was still being promoted as a work of great literature in the 1970s, when such attitudes had become generally unacceptable.

TEACHING TIPS: Achebe's essay triggered considerable debate in Conrad studies, ultimately sparking not only increased attention to racism and colonialism as issues in Conrad's text but also the growth of postcolonial studies as a whole. For a response to Achebe, see Hawkins. For essays that essentially support Achebe's position, see Singh and Parrinder. On this issue, see also Booker (*Practical Introduction*, 219–25).

■ Edward W. Said, from *Orientalism*
1. Discuss Said's use of the Foucauldian notion of discourse to describe the legacy of colonialist tendencies in Western thought and to define Orientalism as an institution.
2. Describe the motivations behind and basic characteristics of the discourse of Orientalism.
3. Though Said's analysis focuses primarily on nineteenth-century texts, his conclusions have far-reaching implications that remain relevant at the beginning of the twenty-first century. Describe the contemporary relevance of Said's ideas for ethnic and postcolonial studies, and for scholarly work more generally.

TEACHING TIP: As what many regard as the founding text in the field of colonial discourse analysis, *Orientalism* was one of the most influential works of criticism and theory to be published in the last quarter of the twentieth century. Instructors with relatively little background in postcolonial studies might want to study *Orientalism* in more detail before teaching Said's work as an example of the analysis of colonialist discourses. They might also want to discuss the influence of Foucault on this work. In the later *Culture and Imperialism*, Said extends his analysis to consider the postcolonial response to colonialist discourses. The discussion of Said in Moore-Gilbert provides a useful overview. MacKenzie challenges Said's work in some ways but is still influenced by it, providing a good example of the kinds of productive debate that have been triggered by Said's work in recent decades.

■ Homi K. Bhabha, "The Commitment to Theory"
1. Bhabha espouses a belief that "theory" can be a valuable tool for postcolonial critics. On the evidence of this essay, what kinds of theory does he himself seem to draw on?
2. Bhabha seeks, in this essay, to refute the charge that the application of Western theory to postcolonial culture is a potential form of cultural imperialism that runs counter to the economic and political

interests of the formerly colonized world. Is he successful in this argument? In what ways might Bhabha's argument be criticized?

3. Explain and comment on the crucial notion of hybridity that informs Bhabha's argument in this essay (and in his work elsewhere).

TEACHING TIP: Bhabha's essay addresses an extremely important debate over the status of theory in postcolonial studies. For a direct critique of Bhabha's work (which argues that Bhabha's own theorization loses sight of political reality), see the essay by JanMohamed.

■ Gayatri Chakravorty Spivak, from *A Critique of Postcolonial Reason*

1. What does Spivak mean by a *subaltern*? In what sense is the subaltern denied speech in the colonial situation?

2. How does Spivak's discussion of the status of the subaltern woman intersect with the concerns of Western feminism?

3. Comment on Spivak's complex engagement with Western theory in this essay.

■ Henry Louis Gates Jr., "Talking Black"

1. Summarize Gates's description of the way in which achieving literacy and producing literature was, for Africans and African Americans, a key to being regarded as human beings by white Western society. What does this legacy suggest about the cultural importance of African and African American literature?

2. Summarize and comment on Gate's advocacy of the use of theory by critics of African American culture.

3. What, according to Gates, must critics and theorists do to put theory to the most effective use in supporting the development of an African American cultural tradition?

TEACHING TIP: Gates's discussion in this essay is reminiscent of the so-called language debate in postcolonial studies, and particularly of the argument over whether African writers should write in English, French, and other former colonial languages or in African vernacular languages. For a brief summary of this debate, see Booker (*African Novel in English* 14–17). For a cogent argument in support of the use of African vernacular languages, see Ngugi, *Decolonising the Mind*. For an argument that African writers can use English effectively, see Achebe, "The African Writer and the English Language."

■ Ngugi wa Thiong'o, Taban lo Liyong, and Henry Owuor-Anyumba, "On the Abolition of the English Department."

1. What, according to this essay, is the role of literature and language in both the colonial and neocolonial domination of Africa by the West?

2. In what ways does this essay suggest an important role for language and literature in the African project to develop viable postcolonial cultural identities that escape the legacy of that domination?

3. Discuss the emphasis on oral culture that is reflected in this essay.
4. In what ways does this essay anticipate Ngugi's later turn away from English and toward Gikuyu as the principal language for his own writing?

TEACHING TIP: For a more extended treatment of Ngugi's views on the topics addressed in this essay, see his *Decolonising the Mind*.

KEY TERMS AND CONCEPTS

colonialism
cultural imperialism
decolonization
hybridity
imperialism
nationalism

national literature
neocolonialism
oral vs. written culture
Orientalism
postcolonial culture
vernacular language

ESSAY TOPICS

1. In what ways do the concerns of postcolonial criticism resemble those of race and ethnicity studies?
2. Summarize some of the pitfalls of which Western readers need to be aware when approaching the study of postcolonial cultures.
3. What aspects of contemporary culture seem to bear out Said's concern about the persistence of Orientalism even in the present day?
4. How might a study of postcolonial cultures enhance our understanding of Western culture as well?

RESEARCH PROJECTS

1. Read a British novel set in Africa (perhaps Joseph Conrad's *Heart of Darkness* [1902] or Joyce Cary's *Mister Johnson* [1939]). Then read an African novel (perhaps Chinua Achebe's *Things Fall Apart* [1958] or Tsitsi Dangarembga's *Nervous Conditions* [1989]). Compare the two, drawing conclusions about the difference in cultural point of view between them. *Suggestion*: The introductory chapter of Booker's *African Novel in English* contains a succinct introduction to the ways in which African novels differ from Western ones, while at the same time engaging them in productive dialogue.
2. Radical African writers such as Kenya's Ngugi wa Thiong'o and Senegal's Ousmane Sembène have been crucially influenced by the theoretical work of Frantz Fanon. Read a novel by Ngugi or Sembène and comment on the ways on which it reflects the influence of Fanon. *Suggestion*: Ngugi's *Devil on the Cross* (1982) and Sembène's *Xala* (1973) should be good choices for this project.
3. Read some of the recent texts criticizing postcolonial studies as immersed in theoretical abstractions and thus divorced from the social and political realities of the formerly colonized world. Summarize

the arguments of these critiques and draw your own conclusions regarding their validity. *Suggestion*: See Ahmad, Brennan, Dirlik, and San Juan for some of these critiques.

4. Said's crucial work in *Orientalism* suggests that Western intellectuals and scholars were complicit in the colonial project. Achebe's critique, in "An Image of Africa," of the study and teaching of *Heart of Darkness* suggests that literary critics today often continue colonialist legacies. Write an essay describing the ways in which literary scholarship might help perpetuate colonialist stereotypes. Try to draw conclusions about the lessons to be learned from this phenomenon by would-be critics of postcolonial literature. *Suggestion*: See Viswanathan for a particularly suggestive study of the role of literary studies in the colonial domination of India by England.

5. Do some reading on the role of gender in postcolonial studies and write an essay summarizing your conclusions from this research. *Suggestion*: See the work of Spivak, McClintock, Stoler, Stratton, and Trinh. Also see the essays in the collection edited by McClintock.

VII. Gender Studies and Queer Theory (1–2 weeks)

The insights of feminist criticism have provided some of the most important energies in Western literary studies in recent decades. Lately, driven particularly by the insights of gay and lesbian studies, feminist studies has expanded to include a broader consideration of the cultural roles of gender and of "queer" sexualities.

TEACHING TIP: This module excludes basic works of feminist criticism that ground the broader field of gender studies. If this module is taught in a course without a separate module on feminist criticism, instructors should consider adding some feminist selections, including those by Woolf, Beauvoir, Cixous, Kolodny, Gilbert and Gubar, and Anzaldúa.

Suggested Readings	
1-week module	2-week module
Foucault	Foucault
History of Sexuality	*History of Sexuality*
Rich	Rich
Sedgwick	Zimmerman
Butler	Barbara Smith
	Wittig
	Sedgwick
	Bordo
	Butler

Suggested Readings and Discussion Questions

■ Michel Foucault, from *The History of Sexuality*
1. What is the "repressive hypothesis"? How does Foucault's critique of this hypothesis reflect his notion that sexuality is an important locus of knowledge/power in modern society?
2. On what basis does Foucault believe the repressive hypothesis to be an inaccurate description of the role played by sexuality in Victorian society?
3. Explain Foucault's notion that the functioning of sexuality in Victorian society produced not only discourse on sexuality but also a variety of forms of "perversion."

TEACHING TIP: Instructors might want to present a broad overview of Foucault's multivolume "History of Sexuality" project when teaching this selection, at the same time discussing the importance of Foucault's work—which, among other things, provides a link between poststructuralism and gender studies—to the growth of gender studies.

■ Adrienne Rich, from "Compulsory Heterosexuality and Lesbian Existence"
1. Summarize and comment on Rich's discussion of "compulsory heterosexuality."
2. Explain Rich's key concepts of "lesbian experience" and the "lesbian continuum."
3. In what ways does Rich's essay suggest that literature and culture might play key roles in overcoming the tradition of compulsory heterosexuality?

■ Bonnie Zimmerman, "What Has Never Been"
1. What, according to Zimmerman, have been the principal tasks of early lesbian criticism?
2. In what ways, according to Zimmerman, is lesbian criticism an important movement for all feminists?
3. Describe the lesbian literary tradition discussed by Zimmerman.

■ Barbara Smith, "Toward a Black Feminist Criticism"
1. Summarize and comment on Smith's critique of the approaches taken by previous critics to literature by black women, and particularly by black lesbians.
2. Summarize and comment on the principles that Smith suggests might be used by black feminist critics.

■ Monique Wittig, "One Is Not Born a Woman"
1. Explain Wittig's distinction between the terms *women* and *woman*. Why does she see *woman* as an inherently negative category, even for feminists?

2. Explain Wittig's Marxist notion that women, in order to escape oppression, must become and act as a class. Summarize Wittig's emphasis on the importance of women gaining the ability to constitute themselves as individual subjects. In what ways does this emphasis differ from more traditional Marxist approaches?
3. Why does Wittig believe that the true emancipation of women can occur only after heterosexuality has been destroyed as the dominant paradigm of human sexuality?

■ Eve Kosofsky Sedgwick, from *Between Men* and from *Epistemology of the Closet*
1. Summarize Sedgwick's attempt to differentiate among the terms *sex, gender,* and *sexuality.* How might the distinctions made in queer theory and in feminist theory be different?
2. How, according to Sedgwick, might the very concept of gender be biased toward heterosexual assumptions?
3. Explain the distinction made by Sedgwick between homosexual and homosocial behavior. How and why does this distinction function differently for men than for women?

■ Susan Bordo, from *Unbearable Weight*
1. Explain and comment on Bordo's argument that the human body is a product not merely of biology but also of social construction.
2. In what ways does Bordo's discussion of anorexia and bulimia illustrate her thesis concerning the social construction of the body?
3. What are the implications of Bordo's analysis for a feminist criticism that might oppose inimical social constructions of the female?

■ Judith Butler, from *Gender Trouble*
1. In what ways does Butler's vision of the social construction of individual identities challenge the identity politics common to Anglo-American feminist thought in the past few decades?
2. How does Butler's discussion challenge the very notion of "woman" as it has conventionally been used in feminist theory and criticism?
3. Summarize and comment on Butler's discussion of the ways in which socially constructed identities might be challenged by "subversive bodily acts."

TEACHING TIP: Because gender studies has recently been such an influential area of theoretical inquiry, instructors might find it valuable to read the entire text of *Gender Trouble* before teaching the Butler selections. Instructors might also usefully compare Butler's treatment of "subversive bodily acts" to Toby Miller's discussion of the "parody politics" practiced by Australian gay activists. Among other things, Miller's overtly Foucauldian perspective usefully supplements Butler's own engagement with Foucault.

KEY TERMS AND CONCEPTS

canon	queer theory
compulsory heterosexuality	sex
essentialism	sexuality
gender	social construction of gender
homophobia	stereotyping
identity politics	the subject
perversions	

ESSAY TOPICS

1. In what ways does the understanding of gender in gender studies and queer theory resemble and differ from that in feminist theory and criticism?
2. In what ways have gender studies and queer theory built on the insights of poststructuralism, postmodernism, and other theoretical schools?
3. What new insights into culture are provided by gender studies and queer theory that might not be available via other approaches, including feminist criticism?
4. What do you see as the principal strengths and weaknesses of gender studies and queer theory as a means of understanding culture?

RESEARCH PROJECTS

1. Lesbian critics have often been critical of feminist critics for ignoring the lesbian perspective. Research this debate and comment on its key issues.
2. Read one or more substantial works of gay or lesbian literature, perhaps from those mentioned in Zimmerman's essay. Then write an essay commenting on the ways in which this work, read from the perspective of gender studies and queer theory, expresses attitudes and insights that might not be found in conventional canonical literature.
3. Foucault's work has been crucial in inspiring the project of gender studies, even though he has often been criticized for maintaining a resolutely masculine (though gay) point of view. Research the complex relationship between Foucault and feminism and write an essay that comments on your findings. *Suggestion:* Sawicki and the collection edited by Diamond and Quinby provide useful starting points for researching this topic.
4. Gay and lesbian studies have formed a crucial part of gender studies and queer theory in recent years. Yet the perspectives of gays and of lesbians are not necessarily the same. Research this issue and write an essay that comments on differences and similarities between these viewpoints.
5. Comment on the role of the body in gender studies and queer theory. Write an essay that explores this role and considers the ways in which it resembles the role played by the body in feminist studies. In what ways is it different?

CHAPTER 4

Sample Course: Theory, Criticism, and Literary Forms

Most undergraduate students in courses on literary theory and criticism are more accustomed to studying literature itself than the theory and criticism of literature. Therefore, they often find it easiest to approach theory and criticism through a framework that is determined by literature, relating theory and criticism either to specific literary movements or to specific literary genres. The modules in this chapter can be used to construct a syllabus that is based on either or both of these approaches.

Course Modules
A. Theory, Criticism, and Literary Movements
    1.   Classicism (1–3 weeks)
    II.   Romanticism (1–3 weeks)
    III.   Romanticism (1–3 weeks)
    IV.   Modernism (1–3 weeks)
    V.   Postmodernism (1–3 weeks)

B. Theory, Criticism, and Literary Genres
    I.   Poetry (1–3 weeks)
    II.   Drama (1–3 weeks)
    III.   The Novel (1–3 weeks)
    IV.   Film and Popular Culture (1–3 weeks)

Course Modules

A. Theory, Criticism, and Literary Movements

In many cases, the relationship between literature and literary theory and criticism is most easily understood within the context of specific literary movements that reflect the historical events and ideas that also inform the theory and criticism of the same period. These modules, focusing on specific literary movements, will help students understand this relationship in a number of individual cases, while at the same time they gain a greater understanding of the symbiosis between literature and theory and criticism. In order to leave time for instructors to introduce the various literary movements (and to assign sample literary readings representative of the movements), the course modules in this segment include slightly fewer readings from *NATC* than do most others in the manual.

I. Classicism (1–3 weeks)

The classical literature (as well as the theory and criticism) of the ancient Greeks and Romans has for centuries provided a model against which many aspects of Western culture have been measured. In part, the term *classicism* refers to the themes and aesthetic principles that over time have come to be associated with this classical art. However, classicism in literature (and in theory and criticism) also encompasses a broader category of writers, theorists, and critics who have defined their work in relation to the Greek and Roman classics, often through direct imitation. In the twentieth century, classicism has to some extent come to mean an objective adherence to precise, abstract, geometric form in direct opposition to the Romantic emphasis on emotion and passion. Many modernist writers, such as T. S. Eliot, can thus be seen as attempting a return to classicism in their rejection of Romanticism. (T. E. Hulme's essay "Romanticism and Classicism" is perhaps the central expression of this notion of classicism.) Historically, however, classicism beyond the Greek and Roman period itself emerges most prominently in an overt program of imitation of the classics that begins in the Renaissance and culminates in the French classicism and English neoclassicism of the seventeenth and eighteenth centuries, drawing on such ancient statements as Aristotle's *Poetics* and Horace's *Arts Poetica* to define what is being imitated. In the latter sense, classicism is clearly related to the historical phenomenon of the Enlightenment, with its emphasis on rational, scientific thought and principles. The selections in *NATC* from Corneille and Pope well represent French classicism and English neoclassicism.

For more details on teaching Greek and Roman theory and criticism, see the module on classical theory and criticism in chapter 2 of this manual. For overviews of Greek and Roman theory and criticism, see Russell and the first volume of *The Cambridge History of Literary Criticism,* edited by George Kennedy. See Greenberg for an introduction to Corneille within the context of French classicism. For a good introduction to neo-classicism in the arts, see Irwin.

	Suggested Readings	
1-week module	2-week module	3-week module
Aristotle	Aristotle	Plato
Poetics	*Poetics*	*Republic* VII & X
Corneille	Horace	Aristotle
	Corneille	*Poetics*
	Pope	Horace
		Longinus
		Corneille
		Pope
		Nietzsche
		Birth of Tragedy

TEACHING TIP: The module on classicism can be effectively enriched through supplemental readings of literary texts. This project might include a comparative reading of a classic work of Greek drama (such as Sophocles' *Oedipus the King*) and a French classicist or English neoclassicist work, such as one of the plays of Corneille. In the latter category, *Horace* (1639) well represents Corneille's classicism, though the deviations from classical principles in *Le Cid* (1636), generally regarded as Corneille's greatest play, might produce effective discussion.

Suggested Readings and Discussion Questions

■ Plato, from *The Republic,* Books VII and X
  Discussion questions—see chapter 2.

■ Aristotle, *Poetics*
  Discussion questions—see chapter 2.

■ Horace, *Ars Poetica*
  Discussion questions—see chapter 2.

■ Longinus, from *On Sublimity*
  Discussion questions—see chapter 2.

■ Pierre Corneille, "Of the Three Unities of Action, Time, and Place"
  Discussion questions—see chapter 2.

■ Alexander Pope, *An Essay on Criticism*
  Discussion questions—see chapter 2.

■ Friedrich Nietzsche, from *The Birth of Tragedy*
   Discussion questions—see chapter 2.

TEACHING TIP: Though certainly not a classicist himself, Nietzsche's selection represents an important late-nineteenth-century reaction to the Greek classics and indicates the ongoing importance of those classics to Western thought.

KEY TERMS AND CONCEPTS

catharsis	neoclassicism
classicism	rhetoric
decorum	the sublime
idealism	the three unities
mimesis	trope

ESSAY TOPICS

1. Briefly summarize your understanding of the basic aesthetic principles characteristic of classicism in literature.
2. How do French classicism and English neoclassicism relate to the classicism of the Greeks and Romans?

II. Romanticism (1–3 weeks)

Romanticism was a broad literary, cultural, and philosophical movement that arose in Western Europe at the end of the eighteenth century, partly spurred by the French Revolution; it was largely a reaction to the rationalist tendencies of the Enlightenment and the formalist tendencies of neoclassicism. As a result, Romanticism can be taught very effectively in dialogue with classicism. Romanticism involves an emphasis on the beauty of nature, a celebration of individual creativity, and a privileging of passion and emotion over reason and intellection. In Germany, Romanticism (epitomized by the work of writers and critics such as Goethe and Schiller) grew largely out of the *Sturm und Drang* movement of the eighteenth century, itself influenced by such thinkers as the Swiss-born Jean-Jacques Rousseau. In English literature, the beginning of Romanticism is often located in the publication of Wordsworth and Coleridge's *Lyrical Ballads* in 1798, though writers such as William Blake were producing Romantic poetry even before that date. Both German and English Romanticism were influential in early-nineteenth-century America, particularly on the Transcendentalist movement, epitomized by the work of Emerson. Abrams's *The Mirror and the Lamp* is probably the most definitive single work on the basic inclinations of Romantic thought, especially in England.

Many Romantic ideas (such as the emphasis on innovation and creativity in art) have remained influential and will strike many students simply as common sense. Instructors should thus strive to historicize the movement and to emphasize that those ideas arose in a specific context and in response to specific stimuli. This approach will help students understand the historical nature of aesthetic thought, challenging the naive assumption that aesthetic values somehow transcend history.

Suggested Readings		
1-week module	2-week module	3-week module
Wordsworth	Schiller	Schiller
Coleridge	Wordsworth	de Staël
Emerson	Coleridge	Wordsworth
	Shelley	Coleridge
	Emerson	Peacock
		Shelley
		Emerson
		Poe

TEACHING TIP: The module on Romanticism can be effectively enriched through a reading of some works of Romantic literature. Some instructors might want to choose to introduce some of the poems of such figures as Wordsworth and Coleridge in conjunction with their critical writings. For example, Wordsworth's "Tintern Abbey" (1798) and "Ode: Intimations of Immortality" (1807) and Coleridge's "Rime of the Ancient Mariner" (1798) and "Kubla Khan" (1816) should work well for this purpose. Instructors who want to introduce a more extensive work might find that Goethe's *Sorrows of Young Werther* (1774), the protagonist of which is the prototype of the Romantic hero, works well as an introduction to certain aspects of Romanticism.

SUGGESTED READINGS AND DISCUSSION QUESTIONS

■ Friedrich von Schiller, from *On the Aesthetic Education of Man*
Discussion questions—see chapter 2.

■ Germaine Necker de Staël, from "Essay on Fictions" and from "On Literature Considered in Its Relationship to Social Institutions"
Discussion questions—see chapter 2.

■ William Wordsworth, Preface to the Second Edition of *Lyrical Ballads*
Discussion questions—see chapter 2.

■ Samuel Taylor Coleridge, from *Biographia Literaria* and *The Statesman's Manual*
Discussion questions—see chapter 2.

■ Thomas Love Peacock, "The Four Ages of Poetry"
Discussion questions—see chapter 2.

■ Percy Bysshe Shelley, from *A Defence of Poetry*
  Discussion questions—see chapter 2.

■ Ralph Waldo Emerson, from "The American Scholar" and "The Poet"
  Discussion questions—see chapter 2.

■ Edgar Allan Poe, "The Philosophy of Composition"
  Discussion questions—see chapter 2.

TEACHING TIP: Poe's selection might be taught in conjunction with a brief discussion of his own literary production, offering instructors an opportunity to introduce the use of the fantastic and the supernatural in Romantic literature. (Other key examples include Goethe's *Faust* [1808, 1832], the tales of E. T. A. Hoffmann, and Mary Shelley's *Frankenstein* [1818].)

KEY TERMS AND CONCEPTS

beauty	the sublime
Lyrical Ballads	symbol
Romanticism	Transcendentalism

ESSAY TOPICS

1. Briefly summarize your understanding of the basic characteristics of Romanticism in literature.
2. Compare and contrast German Romanticism with English Romanticism.
3. Describe and comment on the relationship between English Romanticism and American Transcendentalism.
4. Compare and contrast Romantic theory with the theory of classicism.

III. Realism (1–3 weeks)

Perhaps even more than Romanticism, literary realism has had such a pervasive influence that it will seem to many students merely common-sensical. Instructors should thus endeavor to make clear the status of realism as a historical phenomenon that arose under a particular set of political, economic, and social circumstances. For example, instructors should emphasize the close connection between the evolution of literary realism and the development of the novel as a genre. Therefore, this module can be very effectively taught in conjunction with the module below on the novel. See Watt for the definitive description of the impact of a realist aesthetic on the novel's rise to literary prominence in the eighteenth century, especially in England. Watt's special emphasis on the novel as the representative genre of an emergent middle class brought to power in Europe by the spread of capitalism is essential to any proper understanding of realism. Also important in this regard is Marxist criticism of literary realism, especially the work of György Lukács; see *The Historical Novel* and *Studies in European Realism* (in addition to the Lukács selection in *NATC*).

Suggested Readings		
1-week module	2-week module	3-week module
Lukács	James	James
	Lukács	Lukács
		Howe

TEACHING TIP: While the entries in *NATC* do not emphasize naturalism, some instructors might want to introduce that movement in conjunction with the discussion of realism. Lukács's work (especially the two-part essay "Narration vs. Description") is again crucial for an understanding of the difference between naturalism and realism. The novels of Émile Zola (e.g., *Germinal* [1885]) are the logical choice for representative readings in naturalism, though instructors might want to consider a relatively brief and still highly representative work such as Frank Norris's *McTeague* (1899).

SUGGESTED READINGS AND DISCUSSION QUESTIONS

■ Henry James, "The Art of Fiction"
  Discussion questions—see chapter 2.

■ György Lukács, "Realism in the Balance"
  Discussion questions—see chapter 2.

TEACHING TIP: The selection from Lukács opposes realism to expressionism, a form of modernist art. It thus provides an effective link to the module on modernism below. In particular, though this essay engages in a specific debate with Ernst Bloch over the merits of literary expressionism, it also participates in a general defense of realism and critique of modernism that represented Lukács's contribution to what is often called the "Brecht-Lukács debate," Brecht being a leading defender of modernism on the Left. For more on this important argument, see Lunn and the essays collected in the volume edited by Taylor.

Instructors who feel they need a better understanding of expressionism might consult Sheppard's essay or Nicholls's chapter on expressionism.

■ Irving Howe, "History and the Novel."
  1. Discuss Howe's notions of historical stoppage and historical flow as they relate to the representation of historical context in the novel.

2. Discuss Howe's critique of the notion that the best literature represents "eternal" themes rather than specific historical experiences.
3. In what ways does Howe's discussion imply that the novel, as a genre, has a particularly close relationship with history?

TEACHING TIPS: Howe was a leading figure among a group of critics and theorists collectively known as the New York Intellectuals. For more on that group, see the chapter on them in Leitch's *American Literary Criticism*, or see Wald's book-length study.

KEY TERMS AND CONCEPTS

historical novel
naturalism
realism
romance
socialist realism

ESSAY TOPICS

1. Briefly summarize your understanding of the basic characteristics of realism in literature.
2. Explain why realism rose to prominence at the particular time that it did.
3. Explain why the novel is the dominant genre of literary realism and why realism has long been the dominant mode of the novel.

IV. Modernism (1–3 weeks)

While the exact nature and implications of modernism are still being debated, most theorists and critics, in retrospect, agree that certain distinct tendencies in Western culture at the beginning of the twentieth century can be considered part of a single broad cultural movement, informed by a strong tendency toward innovation and experimentation and driven by a sense of cultural crisis that rendered the artistic approaches of the past largely obsolete. This large and diverse movement is referred to as *modernism*. See Spears, Fokkema, and the essays by Beebe for some typical surveys of the modernist movement. For a broad general discussion of modernism in the arts, see Nicholls. For a discussion of modernism within the context of other modern artistic movements, such as postmodernism and the avant-garde, see Calinescu. For further discussions of modernism in relation to postmodernism, see Fokkema, Huyssen, and Hassan.

Modernism can be taught effectively in dialogue not just with postmodernism but with all the other movements included in this course. The selection from Mallarmé can serve to remind students of the impact of French symbolism on modernism, while the selections from Wilde suggests the influence of nineteenth-century aestheticism. Because modernist writers often defined their project in direct opposition to the conventions of literary realism, modernism can very effectively be taught in dialogue with realism. Many theorists of modernism (and many modernists, such as T. S. Eliot) have seen the movement as a turn toward classicism and away from Romanticism (see the two essays by Beebe for a succinct expression of this view). Other critics, such as Frank Kermode and Monroe Spears, have seen modernism, with its emphasis on innovation, as an extension of Romanticism.

There is a vast (and sometimes contradictory) literature on modernism. For discussions of the movement from a variety of perspectives, see (in addition to the sources cited above) the volumes edited by Brooker, by Bradbury and McFarlane, and by Chefdor, Quinones, and Wachtel.

Suggested Readings		
1-week module	2-week module	3-week module
Mallarmé	Mallarmé	Mallarmé
Benjamin	Eliot	Wilde
	Benjamin	"Critic as Artist"
	Ransom	Eliot
		Woolf
		Ransom
		Benjamin

TEACHING TIP: While most literary works regarded as modernist were produced between 1900 and 1930, the rise of modernist literature to a central position in the Western canon occurred only in the 1950s, in part because of the political climate of the cold war: complex, sophisticated works could be compared to the works of Soviet socialist realism to make the latter appear primitive and simplistic. A discussion of this phenomenon (see Huyssen) can help students appreciate the historicity of aesthetic criteria and the contingency of canons.

TEACHING TIP: While the selections from Eliot and Ransom do not focus on modernist literature per se, they do offer instructors an opportunity to discuss the close relationship between the canonization of modernist literature and the institutionalization of New Criticism as the dominant mode of literary criticism in America. The New Critics were great promoters of modernist literature, whose complexities responded well to the New Critical emphasis on close reading; in turn, the sophisticated techniques of New Criticism provided a framework within which at least some aspects of modernist literature could be better understood. As Alan Wilde points out, "modernist literature is by now virtually inextricable from the shape modernist criticism has imposed upon it" (20). A discussion of this close relationship might provide instructors with a good opportunity to address the relationship between literature and criticism in general. See also the concluding chapter to Booker's *"Ulysses," Capitalism, and Colonialism.*

TEACHING TIP: A modernist poem, such as T. S. Eliot's *The Waste Land,* (1922) should provide an excellent supplement to this module, though instructors should emphasize to students that modernist artists did not all share Eliot's conservative attitudes. Of course, James Joyce's *Ulysses* (1922) is the most often mentioned exemplar of literary modernism, though its length would make it an unwieldy supplement to this module. Some of the novels of Virginia Woolf (particularly *Mrs. Dalloway* [1925] and *To the Lighthouse* [1927]) are also exemplary.

SUGGESTED READINGS AND DISCUSSION QUESTIONS

■ Stéphane Mallarmé, "Crise de vers"
  1. In what ways can Mallarmé's elaboration of a "crisis" in poetry be seen as a harbinger of the later coming of modernism?
  2. Summarize and comment on Mallarmé's critique of realism and Romanticism.
  3. Summarize and comment on Mallarmé's distinction between the ordinary language of the "mob" and the language of poetry.

■ Oscar Wilde, from "The Critic as Artist"
  1. Summarize and comment on Wilde's argument that form and technique are the most important aspects of poetry and thus the most important concerns of the literary critic.
  2. Summarize and comment on Wilde's treatment of history as a possible concern of literary critics.
  3. In what ways does Wilde's attitude reflect the nineteenth-century "art for art's sake" movement?
  4. In what ways does Wilde's attitude in this essay prefigure certain aspects of modernism?

TEACHING TIP: Primarily because of the influence of the New Critics, modernist literature was long felt to emphasize form and technique over content and to attempt an escape from history into aesthetics. Much recent scholarship on modernism and on major modernist artists challenges this view, however. See, for example, Jameson's view of modernism, in *Postmodernism* and elsewhere, as a protest against the growing global hegemony of capitalism.

■ T. S. Eliot, "Tradition and the Individual Talent" and "The Metaphysical Poets"
  Discussion questions—see chapter 2.

- Virginia Woolf, from *A Room of One's Own*
  Discussion questions—see chapter 2.

TEACHING TIP: While Woolf's selection does not deal directly with modernist literature, it does express some of the important ideas of a major modernist artist. It also suggests the way in which new attitudes toward gender (including increased opportunities for women writers) were a part of the modernist phenomenon. On the prominence of women writers in modernism, see Gilbert and Gubar's *No Man's Land,* especially vol. 1.

- John Crowe Ransom, "Criticism, Inc."
  Discussion questions—see chapter 2.

- Walter Benjamin, "The Work of Art in the Age of Mechanical Reproduction"
  Discussion questions—see chapter 2.

KEY TERMS AND CONCEPTS

epic theater
modernism
modernity
New Criticism

SUGGESTED ESSAY TOPICS

1. Briefly summarize your understanding of the basic characteristics of modernism in literature.
2. In what ways can modernism be seen as posing a direct challenge to the conventions of literary realism?
3. In what ways does modernism respond to and participate in the historical context in which it arose?

V. *Postmodernism (1–3 weeks)*

The term *postmodernism* refers to a broad complex of cultural phenomena that arose in the late twentieth century. The name reflects postmodernism's historical position after modernism and the tendency to define it in relation to modernism, though the precise relationship between the two movements remains open to debate. For a discussion of postmodernism within the context of other modern artistic movements, such as modernism and the avant-garde, see Calinescu. For further discussions of postmodernism in relation to modernism, see Fokkema, Huyssen, and Hassan.

The exact nature of postmodernism is still intensely debated, but it seems clear that the term describes a wide array of late-twentieth-century cultural productions, a range of contemporary styles of criticism and thought, and a distinctive historical period of postindustrial, media-saturated societies. See the section on postmodern criticism and theory in chapter 3.

	Suggested Readings	
1-week module	2-week module	3-week module
Lyotard	Lyotard	Lyotard
Habermas	Baudrillard	Baudrillard
"Modernity"	Habermas	Habermas
Jameson	"Modernity"	"Modernity"
"Postmodernism"	Jameson	Jameson
	"Postmodernism"	"Postmodernism"
	Deleuze & Guattari	Deleuze & Guattari
	"Rhizome"	"Rhizome"
	hooks	Anzaldúa
		Haraway
		hooks
		Moulthrop

SUGGESTED READINGS AND DISCUSSION QUESTIONS

■ Jean-François Lyotard, "Defining the Postmodern"
  Discussion questions—see chapter 3.

TEACHING TIP: Lyotard is one of the leading theorists of postmodernism. The brief selection in *NATC* does not make entirely clear that Lyotard is best known for his idea, expressed in *The Postmodern Condition*, that postmodernism is marked by "incredulity toward metanarratives," where *metanarratives* are totalizing theories of the workings of history, society, and epistemological inquiry. Instructors might want to familiarize themselves with Lyotard's argument in that book before teaching his work. Lyotard's work also has much in common with that of other poststructuralist thinkers, such as Derrida and Foucault. See, for example, Carroll.

■ Jean Baudrillard, from *The Precession of Simulacra*
  Discussion questions—see chapter 3.

■ Jürgen Habermas, "Modernity—An Incomplete Project"
  Discussion questions—see chapter 3.

■ Fredric Jameson, "Postmodernism and Consumer Society"
  Discussion questions—see chapter 3.

TEACHING TIP: Jameson is probably the most important of the many Marxist thinkers and critics who have addressed the phenomenon of postmodernism, generally from a critical perspective that sees postmodernism as the cultural equivalent of capitalism in its global, consumerist phase. Instructors might want to consult Jameson's book on the subject, *Postmodernism*, before teaching this module. Jameson's book draws on a characterization of global capitalism that can be found in Ernest Mandel's *Late Capitalism*. For other Marxist commentaries on postmodernism, see Harvey and Callinicos.

■ Gilles Deleuze and Félix Guattari, from "Rhizome" (*A Thousand Plateaus*)
   Discussion questions—see chapter 3.

■ Gloria Anzaldúa, from *Borderlands/La Frontera*
   Discussion questions—see chapter 3.

■ Donna Haraway, "A Manifesto for Cyborgs"
   Discussion questions—see chapter 3.

■ bell hooks, "Postmodern Blackness"
   Discussion questions—see chapter 3.

■ Stuart Moulthrop, "You Say You Want a Revolution"
   Discussion questions—see chapter 3.

KEY TERMS AND CONCEPTS

consumer capitalism	modernity
fragmentation	popular culture
late capitalism	simulacra
media culture	

ESSAY TOPICS

1. Briefly summarize your understanding of the basic characteristics of postmodernism in literature.
2. How do these characteristics of postmodernism reflect the late-twentieth-century context in which the phenomenon occurs?
3. Briefly summarize your understanding of the relationship between modernism and postmodernism in literature.

B. Theory, Criticism, and Literary Genres

The notion of genre has long provided one of the most convenient frameworks within which to categorize, and thereby better understand, different kinds of literature. Recent trends in genre theory and criticism have emphasized that genres are not merely formal constructs: they arise under specific historical circumstances and express particular ideological leanings. Thus Fredric Jameson emphasizes, in *The Political Unconscious*, that "genres are essentially literary *institutions*, or social contracts between a writer and a specific public, whose function is to specify the proper use of a particular cultural artifact" (106). Jameson concludes that "a genre is essentially a socio-symbolic message, or in other terms, that form is immanently and intrinsically an ideology in its own right" (141). Also influential is the work of Mikhail Bakhtin, who has elaborated, in *The Dialogic Imagination,* a view connecting genres to specific sociopolitical views of the world, with the novel functioning as a special, highly dialogic genre that can express multiple sociopolitical points of view by incorporating multiple genres into a single work. Given this starting point, one can easily see particular genres as corresponding to particular theoretical and critical approaches, especially since most works of literary criticism through the centuries have addressed literary works in specific genres. Genre thus provides a convenient framework for presenting theory and criticism to students who are accustomed to thinking in terms of literature and literary forms. For a standard, more formalist, discussion of genre theory, see Fowler.

TEACHING TIP: Many students may be confused by the somewhat loose usage of the term *genre* in literary studies. Thus, the novel is typically referred to as a genre—but a broader category, such as fiction, is sometimes also described as a genre, as may be a narrower subcategory, such as the realist novel. For a course of this type, it is probably best not to worry too much about technicalities; simply acknowledge that the term has this range of application.

I. Poetry (1–3 weeks)

Poetry is probably the most ancient of literary forms, though it continues to function (and to evolve) in the present day. While virtually all the selections in NATC have some relevance to various forms of poetry, some entries direct address poetry and the forms and techniques that might render it most effective as a genre. This module includes many of those entries, a number of which were written by well-known poets who were, at least in part, reflecting on their own poetic practice.

TEACHING TIP: Of all the genres discussed here, poetry offers special teaching opportunities because many poems are brief and can easily be read and discussed within a class period. Instructors should take advantage of this fact to introduce samples of poetry in conjunction with the selections from NATC listed below.

SELECTED READINGS AND DISCUSSION QUESTIONS

■ Horace, *Ars Poetica*
  Discussion questions—see chapter 2.

	Suggested Readings	
1-week module	2-week module	3-week module
Horace	Horace	Horace
Sidney	Dante	Dante
Shelley	Sidney	Ronsard
	Coleridge	Sidney
	Shelley	Wordsworth
	Eliot	Coleridge
		Peacock
		Shelley
		Eliot
		Brooks

■ Dante Alighieri, from *Il Convivio* and the Letter to Can Grande
  Discussion questions—see chapter 2.

■ Pierre de Ronsard, "A Brief on the Art of French Poetry"
  Discussion questions—see chapter 2.

■ Sir Philip Sidney, *An Apology for Poetry*
  Discussion questions—see chapter 2.

■ William Wordsworth, Preface to the Second Edition of *Lyrical Ballads*
  Discussion questions—see chapter 2.

■ Samuel Taylor Coleridge, from *Biographia Literaria* and *The States-man's Manual*
  Discussion questions—see chapter 2.

■ Thomas Love Peacock, "The Four Ages of Poetry"
  Discussion questions—see chapter 2.

■ Percy Bysshe Shelley, from *A Defence of Poetry*
  Discussion questions—see chapter 2.

TEACHING TIP: Shelley's "defence" was written largely as a response to Peacock's "Four Ages of Poetry," so these two selections can be taught very effectively in dialogue with one another.

■ T. S. Eliot, "Tradition and the Individual Talent" and "The Metaphysical Poets"
  Discussion questions—see chapter 2.

■ Cleanth Brooks, "The Heresy of Paraphrase" (*The Well Wrought Urn*)
  Discussion questions—see chapter 2.

TEACHING TIP: The selection from Brooks offers an excellent opportunity to discuss New Criticism within the context of genre and, in particular, to emphasize that the close-reading strategies of the New Critics were
more effective for poetry than for other genres.

KEY TERMS AND CONCEPTS

decorum	modernism
epic	Romanticism
lyric	versification
metaphysical poetry	

ESSAY TOPICS

1. Briefly describe your understanding of the basic characteristics of
   classical poetry.
2. Briefly describe your understanding of the basic characteristics
   of Romantic poetry.
3. Briefly describe your understanding of the basic characteristics of
   modernist poetry.

II. Drama (1–3 weeks)

As perhaps the central genre of both classical Greek literature and English Renaissance literature, drama plays an especially important role in
the history of Western literature. Similarly, drama theory and criticism
have been crucial to the development of literary theory and criticism as a
whole. For a selection of some of the leading statements of dramatic theory and criticism, see the volumes edited by Barrett Clark and by Sidnell
et al.

Suggested Readings		
1-week module	2-week module	3-week module
Aristotle	Aristotle	Aristotle
Poetics	*Poetics*	*Poetics*
Corneille	Corneille	Behn
	Dryden	Corneille
	Samuel Johnson	Dryden
	Shakespeare	Samuel Johnson
	Nietzsche	*Shakespeare*
		Nietzsche
		Birth of Tragedy

Suggested Readings and Discussion Questions

■ Aristotle, *Poetics*
Discussion questions—see chapter 2.

TEACHING TIP: Instructors should emphasize the crucial historical role of Aristotle's comments on tragedy as a model against which so much later dramatic theory defined itself.

■ Aphra Behn, "Epistle to the Reader" from *The Dutch Lover* and Preface to *The Lucky Chance*
Discussion questions—see chapter 2.

■ Pierre Corneille, "Of the Three Unities of Action, Time, and Place"
Discussion questions—see chapter 2.

■ John Dryden, various selections
Discussion questions—see chapter 2.

■ Samuel Johnson, from *Shakespeare*
Discussion questions—see chapter 2.

TEACHING TIP: This selection from Johnson indicates the central role played by Shakespeare in Western (especially Anglo-American) drama theory and criticism since the Renaissance. Note, for example, the central role of Shakespeare in the recent rise of New Historicism (though the selection in *NATC* from Greenblatt, a Shakespeare scholar who is probably the most important New Historicist critic, does not display that centrality).

■ Friedrich Nietzsche, from *The Birth of Tragedy*
Discussion questions—see chapter 2.

III. The Novel (1–3 weeks)

The novel has been the dominant literary genre in Western culture since the nineteenth century. As such, it has been central to the later evolution of literary theory and criticism. But the novel is a particularly flexible and loosely defined genre that resists theoretical description. In the twentieth century, Mikhail Bakhtin's work, which focuses on the form's diversity and flexibility, has provided perhaps the most influential single formulation of genre theory on the novel. Bakhtin's *Dialogic Imagination* provides important formulations of the stylistic features of the novel, as well as descriptions of the close connection between the novel and its historical and social contexts. Because the novel gained dominance as part of a complex of broader historical phenomenon (including the rise of capitalism), Marxist studies of the novel have also been particularly prominent. Notable here is the work of György Lukács, who consistently emphasized the value of the realistic novel in furthering Marxist ends.

The novel's rapid ascension at a particular historical moment has also meant that some of the most important theoretical attempts to describe the genre's basic characteristics have focused on its origins. Watt's classic study is still the definitive description of the impact of a realist aesthetic on the rise of the novel to literary prominence in the eighteenth century, especially in England. Watt's special emphasis on the novel as the representative genre of the new bourgeois class brought to power in Europe by the rise of capitalism is essential to any proper understanding of either realism or the novel. However, several recent studies have extended and refined Watt's analysis. McKeon's more dialectical analysis extends Watt's discussion by paying more attention to the roots of the novel before the eighteenth century and to the persistence of those prior forms in the eighteenth century. Hunter considers a much broader variety of texts and cultural phenomena than did Watt; Davis explores the relationship between the novel and nonfiction forms such as journalism, viewing the novel as a consolidation of journalism, history, and literature that arose out of anxieties over fictionality and as a response to censorship. Doody draws on Bakhtin and other sources to trace the origins of the novel to ancient literary sources, including such texts as the *Satyricon* of Petronius and *The Golden Ass* of Apuleius. Finally, see Spencer for an attempt to rectify Watt's lack of attention to women novelists and Azim for a discussion of the important role played by colonialism in providing material for novels and in stimulating the novelistic imaginations of both writers and readers.

	Suggested Readings	
1-week module	2-week module	3-week module
Bakhtin	Samuel Johnson	Samuel Johnson
Lukács	*Rambler*	*Rambler*
	Rasselas	*Rasselas*
	James	de Staël
	Bakhtin	James
	Lukács	Bakhtin
		Lukács
		Howe

TEACHING TIP: Unfortunately, novels by their nature are time-consuming to read, so in a course of this kind students cannot complete a wide variety of them. One or two representative novels (including perhaps a realistic novel by a writer such as Honoré de Balzac or Charles Dickens and perhaps a modernist novel by a writer such as Virginia Woolf or William Faulkner) might, however, be effectively used as a supplement to this module. Instructors who wish to introduce multicultural issues might also want to consider assigning a novel by an African American writer, such as Richard Wright or Toni Morrison, or by a postcolonial writer, such as Chinua Achebe or Ngugi wa Thiong'o.

Suggested Readings and Discussion Questions

■ Samuel Johnson, from *The Rambler* and *Rasselas*
Discussion questions—see chapter 2.

■ Germaine Necker de Staël, from "Essay on Fictions" and from "On Literature Considered in Its Relationship to Social Institutions"
Discussion questions—see chapter 2.

■ Henry James, "The Art of Fiction"
Discussion questions—see chapter 2.

■ Mikhail M. Bakhtin, from "Discourse in the Novel"
Discussion questions—see chapter 2.

■ György Lukács, "Realism in the Balance"
Discussion questions—see chapter 2.

TEACHING TIP: Lukács's *Historical Novel* is an exemplary study of one particular subgenre of the novel in its historical context in the eighteenth and nineteenth centuries. For a somewhat similar study of the bildungsroman, see Moretti.

■ Irving Howe, "History and the Novel"
   1. Discuss Howe's notions of historical stoppage and historical flow as they relate to the representation of historical context in the novel.
   2. Discuss Howe's critique of the notion that the best literature represents "eternal" themes rather than specific historical experiences.
   3. In what ways does Howe's discussion imply that the novel, as a genre, has a particularly close relationship with history?

TEACHING TIPS: Howe was a leading figure among a group of critics and theorists collectively known as the New York Intellectuals. For more on that group, see the chapter on them in Leitch's *American Literary Criticism*, or see Wald's book-length study.

Key Terms and Concepts

bildungsroman
dialogism
heteroglossia
historical novel
realism

ESSAY TOPICS

1. Based on your readings from *NATC*, how would you describe the basic characteristics of the novel as a genre?
2. Suggest some reasons why the novel, as a genre, might be linked particularly closely to its historical context.
3. Suggest some reasons why the novel, as a genre, rose to prominence in the period from the eighteenth century onward.

IV. Film and Popular Culture (1–3 weeks)

In recent decades, the broad phenomenon of cultural criticism has extended literary theory and criticism to include studies of film, television, and other cultural forms. As part of this larger phenomenon, film studies has become a particularly rich area of academic and scholarly work. Film theory and criticism grows out of literary theory and criticism in a number of direct and obvious ways. Instructors might want to emphasize these links to students, so that they will not feel that they are suddenly in alien territory. At the same time, the distinctive aspects of film (and other forms of popular culture)—ranging from its visual and sound elements to the production of individual films within the institution of the film industry—should also be emphasized. Instructors who feel that they need more background in film theory might begin by consulting Andrew. Corrigan, intended primarily as an undergraduate textbook, provides an especially accessible discussion of the relationship between literature and film (and between literary criticism and film criticism). For more details on cultural criticism, see the module on that movement above, in chapter 3.

Suggested Readings		
1-week module	2-week module	3-week module
Benjamin	Benjamin	Benjamin
Horkheimer & Adorno	Horkheimer & Adorno	Horkheimer & Adorno
Mulvey	Gramsci	Gramsci
	Mulvey	Mulvey
		Hebdige
		Baker

TEACHING TIP: To provide a focal point for discussing film theory and criticism, it is probably worthwhile to arrange that the class view a film. Any number of films could be used for this purpose, of course, though an especially good choice might be one that lavishly uses the resources of cinema, such as Orson Welles's *Citizen Kane* (1941). Welles's film also has many modernist characteristics and thus might help students enrich their understanding of modernism. Some instructors might prefer a film in the classic Hollywood style (such as *Casablanca* [1942]), as more representative of film as a cultural phenomenon.

SUGGESTED READINGS AND DISCUSSION QUESTIONS

■ Walter Benjamin, "The Work of Art in the Age of Mechanical Reproduction"
   Discussion questions—see chapter 3.

■ Max Horkheimer and Theodor Adorno, from "The Culture Industry: Enlightenment as Mass Deception" (*Dialectics of Enlightenment*)
   Discussion questions—see chapter 3.

TEACHING TIP: The selection from Benjamin, with its positive figuration of the emancipatory potential of film, can be taught in opposition to the Horkheimer and Adorno essay to suggest what have essentially been the two poles in studies of popular culture in recent decades.

■ Antonio Gramsci, from *The Prison Notebooks*
   Discussion questions—see chapter 3.

TEACHING TIP: Though this selection does not deal with film or popular culture per se, Gramsci's work forms a crucial theoretical background to the development of film studies and cultural studies as a whole.

■ Laura Mulvey, "Visual Pleasure and Narrative Cinema"
   Discussion questions—see chapter 3.

TEACHING TIP: The selection from Mulvey, like the selection below from Hebdige, gives instructors the opportunity to introduce and discuss the important British cultural studies movement. For more on the background of this movement, see the selection in *NATC* from Hall, which some instructors might wish to assign in this module. For a book-length study, see Dworkin. Note that the selection from Mulvey also offers an opportunity to discuss the importance of feminism and gender studies in film theory and criticism. Much feminist film theory draws strongly on psychoanalytic theory (especially Lacanian psychoanalysis), and instructors who wish to emphasize this topic might want to assign a selection from Lacan in *NATC*, perhaps "The Mirror Stage."

■ Dick Hebdige, from *Subculture*
   Discussion questions—see chapter 3.

■ Houston A. Baker Jr., from *Blues, Ideology, and Afro-American Literature*
   Discussion questions—see chapter 3.

KEY TERMS AND CONCEPTS

aura   hegemony
commodification   ideology
cultural studies   popular culture
culture industry

ESSAY TOPICS

1. Describe some of the ways in which the insights and techniques of literary criticism can be applied directly to film studies.

2. Describe some of the ways in which film studies offers special problems and opportunities that require and enable approaches that go beyond or differ from those typical of literary criticism.

3. Discuss the ways in which the obvious role of economics in the film industry underscores the importance of analyses that go beyond formalist studies of films themselves.

4. How does the inherently collective nature of film production problematize conventional notions of authorship?

CHAPTER 5

Sample Course: Major Topics in Literary Theory and Criticism

Literary theory and criticism can be grouped into certain broad topical categories that indicate the central concerns of literary study, and an introductory survey of literary theory and criticism can be effectively structured around such topics. This chapter includes suggestions for organizing such a course, using *NATC* as the principal text. The primary course modules in this chapter address some of the basic topical concerns of literary studies. Possible additional or alternative modules are also suggested; these include additional basic categories, as well as issues that have been at the center of debates in literary studies in recent years. A va-

Course Modules
- I. Literature and Language (1–4 weeks)
- II. Literature and the Human Mind (1–4 weeks)
- III. Literature, Ideology, and Society (1–4 weeks)
- IV. Literature, Gender, and Sexuality (1–4 weeks)
- V. Literature and Culture (1–4 weeks)
- VI. Literature in Multicultural Context (1–4 weeks)
- VII. Interpretation/Reading Theory (1–3 weeks)
- VIII. National Literatures and Vernaculars (1–3 weeks)
- IX. Literary Tradition and the Canon (1–3 weeks)
- X. The Institution and History of Academic Literary Studies (1–3 weeks)
- XI. Postmodernity (1–2 weeks)

riety of introductory and advanced courses can be constructed using these modules.

Course Modules

I. Literature and Language (1–4 weeks)

Language is obviously the stuff that literature is made on. It is thus not surprising that many approaches to the study of literature have focused on the study of literary language. They have often involved formalist assumptions that literary language is a special case, functioning according to principles completely distinct from those that govern the use of everyday language. But many other theorists have considered literary language to be continuous with other linguistic use, seeing the careful study of language in literature as providing insights into language in general. Such theorists have often viewed literature as a sort of laboratory for conducting various experiments with language, whose results have broad implications for our understanding of all language use. See the modules on formalism, structuralism, and poststructuralism in chapter 3 for more details on those approaches to the study of language in literature.

Suggested Readings			
1-week module	2-week module	3-week module	4-week module
Eichenbaum	Plato	Gorgias	Gorgias
Brooks	*Phaedrus*	Plato	Plato
Bakhtin	Hugh of St. Victor	*Phaedrus*	*Phaedrus*
Derrida	Saussure	Hugh of St. Victor	Augustine
Dissemination	Eichenbaum	Wordsworth	Hugh of St. Victor
	Brooks	Saussure	Aquinas
	Bakhtin	Jakobson	du Bellay
	Derrida	Eichenbaum	Lessing
	Dissemination	Ransom	Wordsworth
	De Man	Brooks	Saussure
	"Semiology and	Bakhtin	Jakobson
	Rhetoric"	Derrida	Eichenbaum
		Dissemination	Ransom
		De Man	Brooks
		"Semiology and	Bakhtin
		Rhetoric"	Derrida
		Cixous	*Dissemination*
			De Man
			"Semiology and
			Rhetoric"
			Cixous

TEACHING TIP: The module on literature and language might be use-fully supplemented by discussions of literary language and of the ways in which it does, or does not, differ from the language of the everyday world. One useful drill that is often used in this respect is to choose a poem, such as William Carlos Williams's "The Red Wheelbarrow" (1923) that seems to be written in relatively ordinary language and to discuss the ways in which this language functions distinctively because it appears in a poem. Conversely, some instructors find it useful to excerpt a passage from a text such as a newspaper article, reformat it as a poem, and then present it to the class, asking them to discuss it as a poem.

SUGGESTED READINGS AND DISCUSSION QUESTIONS

■ Gorgias, from *Encomium of Helen*
   Discussion questions—see chapter 2.

■ Plato, from *Phaedrus*
   Discussion questions—see chapter 2.

TEACHING TIP: These selections from Gorgias and Plato together indi-cate some of the controversies and concerns that have surrounded language throughout Western history. Introducing students to these con-troversies, previously unknown to many of them, can effectively lead them to think about language in more sophisticated ways.

■ Augustine, from *On Christian Doctrine* and *The Trinity*
   Discussion questions—see chapter 2.

TEACHING TIP: The concern with language and sign theory that informs the selections from Augustine, Hugh of St. Victor, and Aquinas usefully rein-forces the classical debates over figurative language, thereby helping to make students aware that important theoretical concerns underlie our approach to language and literature. They also help demonstrate that fundamental ideas about the nature and function of language can change over time.

■ Hugh of St. Victor, from *The Didascalicon*
   Discussion questions—see chapter 2.

■ Thomas Aquinas, from *Summa Theologica*
   Discussion questions—see chapter 2.

■ Joachim du Bellay, from *The Defence and Illustration of the French Lan-guage*
   Discussion questions—see chapter 2.

TEACHING TIP: Du Bellay's discussion of the French language can help introduce important issues surrounding the use of national and vernacular languages in writing literature. Similar concerns underlie a number of other selections in *NATC*, including those by Dante, Giraldi, Ronsard, Corneille, Emerson, and Ngugi et al. Instructors may want to introduce one or more of these additional selections in conjunction with the selection from du Bellay. See the module on national literatures and vernaculars, below.

■ Gotthold Ephraim Lessing, from *Laocoön*
   Discussion questions—see chapter 2.

■ William Wordsworth, Preface to the Second Edition of *Lyrical Ballads*
   Discussion questions—see chapter 2.

TEACHING TIP: Wordsworth's belief that ordinary language should be used to construct poetry can serve as an effective focal point for discussing the differences between ordinary language and literary language.

■ Ferdinand de Saussure, from *Course in General Linguistics*
   Discussion questions—see chapter 2.

TEACHING TIP: Saussure's studies in linguistics provide a bridge to structuralism and poststructuralism in literary studies and many other fields. His work can thus be effectively taught as a unit with the writings of thinkers such as Jakobson, Barthes, and de Man.

■ Roman Jakobson, from "Linguistics and Poetics"
   Discussion questions—see chapter 2.

11. Boris Eichenbaum, "The Theory of the 'Formal Method' "
   Discussion questions—see chapter 2.

■ John Crowe Ransom, "Criticism, Inc."
   Discussion questions—see chapter 2.

■ Cleanth Brooks, "The Heresy of Paraphrase" (*The Well Wrought Ura*) and "The Formalist Critics"
   Discussion questions—see chapter 2.

■ Mikhail M. Bakhtin, from "Discourse in the Novel"
   Discussion questions—see chapter 2.

■ Jacques Derrida, from *Dissemination*
   Discussion questions—see chapter 3.

TEACHING TIP: This selection is particularly useful for the dialogue it establishes with the excerpt from Plato's *Phaedrus*. Instructors who wish, in the interest of time, to read less Derrida (and thus forgo the dialogue with Plato) might consider using instead the excerpt from *Of Grammatology*.

■ Paul de Man, "Semiology and Rhetoric"
  Discussion questions—see chapter 2.

■ Hélène Cixous, "The Laugh of the Medusa"
  Discussion questions—see chapter 2.

TEACHING TIP: Cixous's essay enables instructors to introduce the importance of poststructuralist language theory to French feminism. In this regard, some instructors might also wish to include the selection from Kristeva.

KEY TERMS AND CONCEPTS

deconstruction	rhetoric
dialogism	Russian formalism
formalism	semiology
linguistics	sign theory
New Criticism	structuralism
poststructuralism	

ESSAY TOPICS

1. What is rhetoric and what role does it play in the study of literature?
2. What are vernacular languages and what role does the concept of vernacular language play in the history of literature and literary studies?
3. What is formalism?
4. Compare and contrast the basic concerns, assumptions, and methodologies of Russian formalism and American New Criticism.
5. What basic assumptions does New Criticism make concerning the nature of literary language?
6. What is structuralism?
7. Describe some of the ways in which structuralist approaches can be used for the study of literature.
8. Compare and contrast different accounts of language among poststructuralists.

II. Literature and the Human Mind (1–4 weeks)

As numerous theorists and critics have pointed out, literature comes to life when it is encountered by human beings who read it, interpret it, and experience its emotional impact. Many critics, in fact, have argued that the study of literature should focus on this encounter and that literature can be best understood by examining how the human mind experiences and interprets it.

Such approaches have typically been informed either by Freudian psychoanalysis or by reader-response theories that themselves often relied heavily on phenomenological and hermeneutic philosophy. For more details on these approaches, see the modules in chapter 3 on psychological and psychoanalytic theory and criticism and on phenomenological, hermeneutic, and reader-response criticism. For a good introduction to psychological and psychoanalytic approaches, see Wright. For an introductory discussion of reader-response criticism, see Freund.

Suggested Readings

1-week module	2-week module	3-week module	4-week module
Freud	Aristotle	Aristotle	Aristotle
"The 'Uncanny'"	*Poetics*	*Poetics*	*Poetics*
Jung	Freud	Macrobius	Longinus
Lacan	*Interpretation of*	Freud	Macrobius
"Mirror Stage"	*Dreams*	*Interpretation of*	Kant
Iser	"The 'Uncanny'"	*Dreams*	Freud
Fish	Jung	"The 'Uncanny'"	*Interpretation of*
	Lacan	"Fetishism"	*Dreams*
	"Mirror Stage"	Jung	"The 'Uncanny'"
	Kristeva	Frye	"Fetishism"
	Mulvey	Bloom	Jung
	Poulet	Lacan	Frye
	Iser	"Mirror Stage"	Bloom
	Fish	"Agency of the	Lacan
		Letter"	"Mirror Stage"
		Kristeva	"Agency of the
		Mulvey	Letter"
		Poulet	"Signification of
		Iser	the Phallus"
		Fish	Foucault
			History of Sexuality
			Kristeva
			Mulvey
			Poulet
			Jauss
			Iser
			Fish

Suggested Readings and Discussion Questions

■ Aristotle, *Poetics*
  Discussion questions—see chapter 2.

TEACHING TIP: Though Aristotle might not immediately come to mind in connection with this module, his emphasis on catharsis in some ways makes him the forerunner of all theories based on reader or audience response. Including Aristotle in this context thus offers a number of opportunities for discussions of the history of response theory. The selections from Longinus and Macrobius below offer similar opportunities for comparing response theories from different historical periods.

■ Longinus, from *On Sublimity*
  Discussion questions—see chapter 2.

■ Macrobius, from *Commentary on the Dream of Scipio*
  Discussion questions—see chapter 3.

TEACHING TIP: Macrobius's comments can be particularly aptly compared with Freud's later work on the interpretation of dreams.

■ Immanuel Kant, from *Critique of Judgment*
  Discussion questions—see chapter 2.

TEACHING TIP: Kant's focus on the beautiful and the sublime can easily be seen as concentrating on the impact of artworks on the human mind. For a discussion of the ways in which Kant's aesthetics were integral to emerging modern theories of the subject, see the chapter on Kant in Eagleton's *Ideology of the Aesthetic*.

■ Sigmund Freud, from *The Interpretation of Dreams*
  Discussion questions—see chapter 3.

■ Sigmund Freud, "The 'Uncanny' "
  Discussion questions—see chapter 3.

■ Sigmund Freud, "Fetishism"
  Discussion questions—see chapter 3.

■ Carl Gustav Jung, "On the Relation of Analytical Psychology to Poetry"
  Discussion questions—see chapter 3.

■ Northrop Frye, "The Archetypes of Literature"
  Discussion questions—see chapter 3.

■ Harold Bloom, from *The Anxiety of Influence*
  Discussion questions—see chapter 3.

■ Jacques Lacan, "The Mirror Stage"
    Discussion questions—see chapter 3.

■ Jacques Lacan, from "The Agency of the Letter in the Unconscious"
    Discussion questions—see chapter 3.

■ Jacques Lacan, "The Signification of the Phallus"
    Discussion questions—see chapter 3.

■ Michel Foucault, from *The History of Sexuality*
    Discussion questions—see chapter 3.

■ Julia Kristeva, from *Revolution in Poetic Language*
    Discussion questions—see chapter 3.

■ Laura Mulvey, "Visual Pleasure and Narrative Cinema"
    Discussion questions—see chapter 3.

■ Georges Poulet, "Phenomenology of Reading"
    Discussion questions—see chapter 3.

■ Hans Robert Jauss, from "Literary History as a Challenge to Literary Theory"
    Discussion questions—see chapter 3.

TEACHING TIP: The selections from Jauss, Iser, and Fish represent reader-response theory. Some instructors may wish to teach this theory alongside a selection to which reader-response theory is diametrically opposed, such as Wimsatt and Beardsley, "The Affective Fallacy."

■ Wolfgang Iser, "Interaction between Text and Reader"
    Discussion questions—see chapter 3.

■ Stanley Fish, "Interpreting the *Variorum*"
    Discussion questions—see chapter 3.

TEACHING TIP: It might be worth mentioning to students, within the context of this module, the reader-response theories of Norman Holland, which rely crucially on psychoanalytic conceptions. A succinct introduction to Holland's work can be found in a handbook such as Booker's *Practical Introduction* (47–49). A more extensive introduction can be found in Freund (112–33). For Holland's own work, see *Poems in Persons* and *5 Readers Reading*. See also Holland's essay "Unity Identity Text Self."

Key Terms and Concepts

archetype
collective unconscious
condensation
displacement
dream-work
hermeneutics

myth criticism
phenomenology
psychoanalysis
reader-response criticism
reception theory

Essay Topics

1. What, in your view, are the principal strengths and weaknesses of psychoanalysis as a technique for the interpretation of literature?
2. What do you see as the some of the principal differences between Lacanian and Freudian psychoanalytic theory? *Suggestion*: Undergraduate students will need to approach this question at a rather rudimentary level, emphasizing such aspects as the influence of structuralism on Lacan.
3. What, in your view, are the major strengths and weaknesses of reception theory, as represented by the work of Jauss and Iser?
4. Compare and contrast the reader-response approaches of Iser and Fish.
5. Suggest ways in which reader-response theory might be adapted to the criticism of drama or to film studies.

III. *Literature, Ideology, and Society (1–4 weeks)*

An increased attention to the political, social, and historical contexts of literature has been one of the most vital and important trends in the literary theory and criticism of recent decades. Much of that attention has been focused on such issues as sexuality, gender, race, ethnicity, and colonialism, which are treated in modules IV and V of this chapter. The current module focuses primarily on Marxist analyses of ideology and of the ways in which literature and literary theory and criticism are inevitably informed by specific ideological inclinations. That this module is dominated by Marxist theory and criticism is not surprising, given that Marxist theorists and critics have led the way in understanding the relationship between literature and the social world. However, it also includes the work of such critics as Foucault, Bourdieu, and Barbara Herrnstein Smith, who, working from non-Marxist perspectives, have also pointed toward the ideological underpinnings of society and its cultural products. Instructors who seek more guidance in teaching this module should see the module on Marxist theory and criticism in chapter 3, above. For a succinct introduction to the Marxist critique of ideology, see McLellan's *Ideology*. For a good Marxist historical survey of the ideological implications of various aesthetic philosophies, see Eagleton's *Ideology of the Aesthetic*.

Suggested Readings and Discussion Questions

■ Theóphile Gautier, from Preface to *Mademoiselle Maupin*
Discussion questions—see chapter 2.

TEACHING TIP: The selection from Gautier, with its insistence on art for art's sake, serves as a useful counterview against which to read the other selections in this module, which stress the interrelationship between art and the social world. Some instructors might wish to use one or more of the selections from formalist criticism (see chapter 3) for this purpose instead of or in addition to Gautier.

Suggested Readings

1-week module	2-week module	3-week module	4-week module
Marx & Engels	Marx & Engels	Marx & Engels	Gautier
German Ideology	*German Ideology*	*German Ideology*	Marx
Communist	*Communist*	*Communist*	Preface to
Manifesto	*Manifesto*	*Manifesto*	*Critique*
Gramsci	Lukács	Lukács	*Manuscripts of 1844*
Horkheimer &	Gramsci	Gramsci	*Grundrisse*
Adorno	Benjamin	Benjamin	Marx & Engels
Althusser	Horkheimer &	Horkheimer &	*German Ideology*
"Ideology"	Adorno	Adorno	*Communist*
	Althusser	Wilson	*Manifesto*
	"Ideology"	Althusser	Lukács
	Williams	"Ideology"	Gramsci
	Jameson	Williams	Benjamin
	Political	Habermas	Horkheimer &
	Unconscious	"Modernity"	Adorno
	Bourdieu	Jameson	Wilson
		Political	Howe
		Unconscious	Althusser
		Foucault	"Ideology"
		Discipline and	Williams
		Punish	Habermas
		Bourdieu	"Modernity"
		B. Herrnstein	Jameson
		Smith	*Political*
		Ohmann	*Unconscious*
			"Postmodernism"
			Foucault
			Discipline and
			Punish
			Bourdieu
			B. Herrnstein Smith
			Ohmann

■ Karl Marx, from Preface to *A Contribution to the Critique of Political Economy* and *Economic and Philosophic Manuscripts of 1844*
   Discussion questions—see chapter 3.

■ Karl Marx, from *The Grundrisse*
   Discussion questions—see chapter 3.

■ Karl Marx and Friedrich Engels, from *The German Ideology*
   Discussion questions—see chapter 3.

■ Karl Marx and Friedrich Engels, from *The Communist Manifesto*
   Discussion questions—see chapter 3.

■ György Lukács, "Realism in the Balance"
   Discussion questions—see chapter 3.

■ Antonio Gramsci, from *Prison Notebooks*
   Discussion questions—see chapter 3.

■ Walter Benjamin, "The Work of Art in the Age of Mechanical Reproduction"
   Discussion questions—see chapter 3.

■ Max Horkheimer and Theodor Adorno, from "The Culture Industry: Enlightenment as Mass Deception" (*Dialectic of Enlightenment*)
   Discussion questions—see chapter 3.

■ Edmund Wilson, "Marxism and Literature"
   Discussion questions—see chapter 3.

■ Irving Howe, "History and the Novel"
   Discussion questions—see chapter 4.

■ Louis Althusser, from "Ideology and Ideological State Apparatuses"
   Discussion questions—see chapter 3.

■ Raymond Williams, from *Marxism and Literature*
   Discussion questions—see chapter 3.

TEACHING TIP: Williams played a central role in the postwar British New Left and in the rise of the British cultural studies movement after the war. For more background on Williams's work, see the collection edited by Eagleton. For more on Williams's cultural and intellectual context in postwar Britain, see Dworkin. See also the module below on literature and culture.

■ Jürgen Habermas, "Modernity—An Incomplete Project"
   Discussion questions—see chapter 3.

■ Fredric Jameson, from *The Political Unconscious*
  Discussion questions—see chapter 3.

■ Fredric Jameson, "Postmodernism and Consumer Society"
  Discussion questions—see chapter 3.

■ Michel Foucault, from *Discipline and Punish*
  Discussion questions—see chapter 3.

TEACHING TIP: Though Foucault's approach is not itself Marxist, his notion of the psychological techniques of power at work in modern carceral societies has much in common with Althusser's elaboration of the ideological domination at the heart of bourgeois society. Note that Althusser was Foucault's teacher in college. On Foucault and Marxism, see Poster and Smart.

■ Pierre Bourdieu, from *Distinction*
  Discussion questions—see chapter 3.

■ Barbara Herrnstein Smith, from *Contingencies of Value*
  1. How do Smith's conclusions challenge the traditional notion of literary canons?
  2. Discuss the implications of Smith's notion of the contingency of value for New Criticism and other kinds of formalist criticism.
  3. In what ways does Smith's essay reinforce the recent critical interest in cultural products beyond conventionally canonical works of literature, including works of popular culture, works by women, works by gay and lesbian writers, works by nonwhite writers, works by third world writers, and so on?

TEACHING TIP: This selection does not specifically focus on "ideology," though it does insist that aesthetic judgments are conditioned by contextual forces rather than by abstract and universal standards. This selection, like the ones from Foucault and Bourdieu, thus usefully supplements the Marxist selections in this module. It should be noted, however, that both Foucault and Bourdieu engage the Marxist tradition more directly than does Smith.

■ Richard Ohmann, from "The Shaping of a Canon"
  Discussion questions—see chapter 3.

KEY TERMS AND CONCEPTS

aura	hegemony
canon	Ideological State Apparatus (ISA)
carceral society	ideology
class consciousness	interpellation
the Frankfurt School	

Essay Topics

1. Referring to specific selections in this module (such as Marx's Preface or Althusser's "Ideology"), briefly define ideology.
2. Referring to specific selections in this module, briefly explain the role played by class in the production, consumption, and criticism of literature and culture.
3. Compare Althusser's concept of the ISA to Gramsci's notion of hegemony
4. Compare and contrast the selections from Bourdieu and Barbara Herrnstein Smith concerning the contextual nature of aesthetic judgments.

IV. Literature, Gender, and Sexuality (1–4 weeks)

Gender and sexuality have reached prominence as concerns of literary theorists and critics since the women's movement of the 1960s called attention to them. The work of feminist theorists and critics, as well as of other theorists and critics concerned with gender and sexuality, has revealed problematic assumptions about gender and sexuality in central works of the Western literary canon. In addition, they have given serious critical attention to the works of women, gays, lesbians, and others who have been marginalized and denied entry into the canon because of their sex or sexuality. For additional details on these issues, see the modules on feminism and on gender studies in chapter 3 of this manual.

Suggested Readings			
1-week module	2-week module	3-week module	4-week module
Woolf	Woolf	Wollstonecraft	Christine de Pizan
Cixous	Beauvoir	Woolf	Wollstonecraft
Sedgwick	Gilbert & Gubar	Beauvoir	Woolf
Butler	Kolodny	Gilbert & Gubar	Beauvoir
	Cixous	Kolodny	Gilbert & Gubar
	Kristeva	Cixous	Kolodny
	Barbara Smith	Kristeva	Cixous
	Sedgwick	Zimmerman	Kristeva
	Butler	Barbara Smith	Zimmerman
		Wittig	Barbara Smith
		Foucault	Wittig
		History of Sexuality	Foucault
			History of Sexuality
		Sedgwick	Sedgwick
		Butler	Christian
			Anzaldúa
			Bordo
			Butler

Suggested Readings and Discussion Questions

- Christine de Pizan, from *The Book of the City of Ladies*
  Discussion questions—see chapter 2.

- Mary Wollstonecraft, from *A Vindication of the Rights of Woman*
  Discussion questions—see chapter 2.

- Virginia Woolf, from *A Room of One's Own*
  Discussion questions—see chapter 3.

- Simone de Beauvoir, from *The Second Sex*
  Discussion questions—see chapter 3.

- Sandra M. Gilbert and Susan Gubar, from *The Madwoman in the Attic*
  Discussion questions—see chapter 3.

- Annette Kolodny, "Dancing through the Minefield"
  Discussion questions—see chapter 3.

- Hélène Cixous, "The Laugh of the Medusa"
  Discussion questions—see chapter 3.

- Julia Kristeva, from *Revolution in Poetic Language*
  Discussion questions—see chapter 3.

- Bonnie Zimmerman, "What Has Never Been"
  Discussion questions—see chapter 3.

- Barbara Smith, "Toward a Black Feminist Criticism"
  Discussion questions—see chapter 3.

- Monique Wittig, "One Is Not Born a Woman"
  Discussion questions—see chapter 3.

- Michel Foucault, from *The History of Sexuality*
  Discussion questions—see chapter 3.

- Eve Kosofsky Sedgwick, from *Between Men* and from *Epistemology of the Closet*
  Discussion questions—see chapter 3.

- Barbara Christian, "The Race for Theory"
  Discussion questions—see chapter 3.

- Gloria Anzaldúa, from *Borderlands/La Frontera*
  Discussion questions—see chapter 3.

■ Susan Bordo, from *Unbearable Weight*
  Discussion questions—see chapter 3.

■ Judith Butler, from *Gender Trouble*
  Discussion questions—see chapter 3.

KEY TERMS AND CONCEPTS

androgyny	homophobia
bisexuality	queer theory
écriture féminine	semiotic and symbolic
essentialism	sexuality
feminism	the social construction of gender
gender	stereotyping
gender studies	the subject

ESSAY TOPICS

1. Summarize and comment on the findings of selected feminist critics on the representation of women in the canonical works of Western literature.
2. Summarize and comment on the findings of selected feminist critics on literature written by women.
3. Compare and contrast the approaches taken by French feminist critics and Anglo-American feminist critics.
4. In what ways do the findings of gender studies go beyond, and in some cases challenge, the findings of feminist theory and criticism?
5. In what ways do the findings of feminism and gender studies affect our understanding of the literary canon?

V. *Literature and Culture (1–4 weeks)*

In one of the most vibrant trends in literary studies of recent years, "literary texts" have been extended to encompass a broader array of cultural products, including film, television, music, and other forms of popular culture. In addition, studies of literature have expanded to examine how literature functions within a larger cultural context that includes a range of cultural products. Finally, by bringing into consideration broad ideological contexts, such extension has inevitably led to significant meditations on the nature of literary studies and of the institutional frameworks within which those studies are conducted.

This phenomenon in large part falls under the broad rubric of "cultural studies," and instructors should consult the cultural studies module in chapter 3 for additional details. Much of this work has involved an increased understanding of the social, political, and ideological implications of literary texts, and many of the selections in the module above on literature, ideology, and society provide crucial background to the development of cultural studies. As a result, there is some necessary overlap between these two modules, though that overlap has been minimized here. Instructors should carefully coordinate these two modules, ensuring in particular that the selections above from Gramsci, Benjamin, and Horkheimer and Adorno are taught in conjunction with the module on literature and culture.

TEACHING TIP: While the cultural studies movement itself arose in the second half of the twentieth century, it is clearly rooted in a long history of theoretical and critical meditations on the role of literature in society, ranging from the anxieties of Plato to the reliance of Arnold on literature and culture as a counterbalance to the increasing confusion and fragmentation of modern society. It therefore might be useful to examine some of these precursors in conjunction with more recent works of cultural theory and criticism. One could, for example, establish dialogues between Plato's concerns over the misleading nature of literature and Marxist concerns over the ideological manipulation of readers by bourgeois literature—or between Vico's and Peacock's mappings of the changing functions of literature in society.

Suggested Readings

1-week module	2-week module	3-week module	4-week module
Arnold	Plato	Plato	Plato
Ransom	*Republic* VII & X	*Republic* VII & X	*Republic* VII & X
Eagleton	Arnold	Hugh of St. Victor	Hugh of St. Victor
Barthes	Ransom	Shelley	Sidney
Mythologies	Eagleton	Arnold	Vico
Ohmann	Graff	Ransom	Peacock
	Barthes	Eagleton	Shelley
	Mythologies	Graff	Arnold
	Ohmann	Barthes	Ransom
	Mulvey	*Mythologies*	Eagleton
	Baker	Ohmann	Graff
	Moulthrop	Hebdige	Barthes
		Mulvey	*Mythologies*
		Baker	Ohmann
		Moulthrop	Hebdige
		Davis	Hall
			Haraway
			Mulvey
			Baker
			Moulthrop
			Davis

Suggested Readings and Discussion Questions

▪ Plato, from *Republic*, Books VII and X
  Discussion questions—see chapter 2.

▪ Hugh of St. Victor, from *The Didascalicon*
  Discussion questions—see chapter 2.

▪ Sir Philip Sidney, *An Apology for Poetry*
  Discussion questions—see chapter 2.

▪ Giambattista Vico, from *The New Science*
  Discussion questions—see chapter 2.

▪ Thomas Love Peacock, "The Four Ages of Poetry"
  Discussion questions—see chapter 2.

▪ Percy Bysshe Shelley, from *A Defence of Poetry*
  Discussion questions—see chapter 2.

TEACHING TIP: Shelley's "defence" was written largely as a response to Peacock's "Four Ages of Poetry," so these two selections can be taught very effectively in dialogue with one another.

▪ Matthew Arnold, "The Function of Criticism at the Present Time" and from "Sweetness and Light" (*Culture and Anarchy*)
  Discussion questions—see chapter 2.

▪ John Crowe Ransom, "Criticism, Inc."
  Discussion questions—see chapter 3.

TEACHING TIP: The Ransom selection, with its focus on the professionalization of literary studies, provides a good introduction to this aspect of New Criticism, as well as to debates about professionalization that are still raging today. Instructors might want to consult Robbins for a cogent overview of this subject.

▪ Terry Eagleton, from *Literary Theory*
  Discussion questions—see chapter 3.

▪ Gerald Graff, "Taking Cover in Coverage"
  1. In what ways, according to Graff, does the compartmentalization of literary studies in the current university system limit our ability to understand literature to the fullest?
  2. In what ways can Graff's essay be interpreted as a defense of "theory"?

3. In what ways can Graff's recommendation to "teach the conflicts" be seen as a form of pluralism? What might be some of the difficulties with this seemingly commonsense approach?

■ Roland Barthes, from *Mythologies*
  Discussion questions—see chapter 3.

■ Richard Ohmann, from "The Shaping of a Canon"
  Discussion questions—see chapter 3.

■ Dick Hebdige, from *Subculture*
  Discussion questions—see chapter 3.

TEACHING TIP: The selections from Hebdige, Hall, and Mulvey should be introduced within the context of the British cultural studies movement. For more on this movement, see Dworkin.

■ Stuart Hall, "Cultural Studies and Its Theoretical Legacies"
  Discussion questions—see chapter 3.

■ Donna Haraway, "A Manifesto for Cyborgs"
  Discussion questions—see chapter 3.

■ Laura Mulvey, "Visual Pleasure and Narrative Cinema"
  Discussion questions—see chapter 3.

■ Houston A. Baker Jr., from *Blues, Ideology, and Afro-American Literature*
  Discussion questions—see chapter 3.

■ Stuart Moulthrop, "You Say You Want a Revolution"
  Discussion questions—see chapter 3.

TEACHING TIP: Though the rapid expansion of the Internet in the late 1990s rendered some of the specifics of Moulthrop's discussion obsolete, his essay nonetheless offers instructors the opportunity to introduce the crucial subject of the Internet and to discuss its contemporary and future impact on culture.

■ Lennard J. Davis, from *Visualizing the Disabled Body*
  Discussion questions—see chapter 3.

KEY TERMS AND CONCEPTS

canon	hegemony
commodification	ideology
cultural materialism	media culture
culture	popular culture
culture wars	professionalization

ESSAY TOPICS

1. What are some of the implications of extending literary theory and criticism to encompass film, television, and other products of popular culture?
2. In what ways do the cultural studies selections you have read suggest the applicability of literary theory to other cultural texts? In what ways does literary theory need to be modified to be applied in these broader contexts?
3. What parallels do you see between the extension of literary studies to include a broader array of cultural phenomena and the extension of literary studies in feminist criticism, race and ethnicity studies, gender studies, and postcolonial studies to include a broader array of literary texts?
4. In what ways do the obvious economic motivations that lie behind most products of popular culture affect how we study and understand them?
5. How might the insights of cultural studies change our approach to the study of literary texts?

VI. *Literature in Multicultural Context (1–4 weeks)*

Much recent literary theory and criticism has called attention to the fact that Western canonical literature has been produced largely by white, male writers. At the same time, postcolonial studies and studies of literature produced by nonwhite Western writers have demonstrated that literary products emerging from different cultural perspectives can reflect entirely different aesthetic premises than those embodied in the standards of Western canonical literature. This module is designed to indicate the insights of race and ethnicity studies on the multiplicity of culture; it also introduces the insights of postcolonial studies on the value of studying literature from formerly colonized nations around the world. See the modules on ethnicity and race studies and on postcolonial studies in chapter 3 for additional details.

SUGGESTED READINGS AND DISCUSSION QUESTIONS

■ W. E. B. Du Bois, "Criteria of Negro Art"
Discussion questions—see chapter 3.

■ Langston Hughes, "The Negro Artist and the Racial Mountain"
Discussion questions—see chapter 3.

TEACHING TIP: It might be valuable to emphasize the participation of Hughes in the Harlem Renaissance. On the intersection of the Harlem Renaissance and modernism, see Hutchinson.

■ Zora Neale Hurston, "What White Publishers Won't Print"
Discussion questions—see chapter 3.

| *Suggested Readings* | | | |
1-week module	2-week module	3-week module	4-week module
Du Bois	Du Bois	Du Bois	Du Bois
Anzaldúa	Hughes	Hughes	Hughes
Allen	Barbara Smith	Hurston	Hurston
Said	Gates	"White Publishers"	"White Publishers"
Ngugi et al.	Anzaldúa	Barbara Smith	Barbara Smith
	Allen	Baker	Baker
	Fanon	Gates	Gates
	"Pitfalls"	Anzaldúa	hooks
	Said	Allen	Christian
	Ngugi et al.	Vizenor	Anzaldúa
		Fanon	Allen
		"Pitfalls"	Vizenor
		Said	Fanon
		Bhabha	"Pitfalls"
		Ngugi et al.	"On National
		Deleuze & Guattari	Culture"
		Kafka	Achebe
			Said
			Bhabha
			Spivak
			Ngugi et al.
			Deleuze & Guattari
			Kafka

■ Barbara Smith, "Toward a Black Feminist Criticism"
  Discussion questions—see chapter 3.

■ Houston A. Baker Jr., from *Blues, Ideology, and Afro-American Literature*
  Discussion questions—see chapter 3.

■ Henry Louis Gates Jr., "Talking Black"
  Discussion questions—see chapter 3.

■ bell hooks, "Postmodern Blackness"
  Discussion questions—see chapter 3.

■ Barbara Christian, "The Race for Theory"
  Discussion questions—see chapter 3.

■ Gloria Anzaldúa, from *Borderlands/La Frontera*
  Discussion questions—see chapter 3.

■ Paula Gunn Allen, "Kochinnenako in Academe"
Discussion questions—see chapter 3.

■ Gerald Vizenor, from *Manifest Manners*
Discussion questions—see chapter 3.

■ Frantz Fanon, from "The Pitfalls of National Consciousness" (*The Wretched of the Earth*)
Discussion questions—see chapter 3.

■ Frantz Fanon, from "On National Culture" (*The Wretched of the Earth*)
Discussion questions—chapter 3.

■ Chinua Achebe, "An Image of Africa"
Discussion questions—see chapter 3.

■ Edward W. Said, from *Orientalism*
Discussion questions—see chapter 3.

TEACHING TIP: As what many regard as the founding text in the field of colonial discourse analysis, *Orientalism* was one of the most influential works of criticism and theory to be published in the last quarter of the twentieth century. Instructors with relatively little background in post-colonial studies might want to study *Orientalism* in more detail before teaching Said's work as an example of the analysis of racist discourses. The discussion of Said in Moore-Gilbert provides a useful overview. MacKenzie challenges Said's work in some ways, but is still influenced by it, providing a good example of the kinds of productive debate that have been triggered by Said's work in recent decades.

■ Homi K. Bhabha, "The Commitment to Theory"
Discussion questions—see chapter 3.

■ Gayatri Chakravorty Spivak, from *A Critique of Postcolonial Reason*
Discussion questions—see chapter 3.

■ Ngugi wa Thiong'o, Taban lo Liyong and Henry Owuor-Anyumba, "On the Abolition of the English Department"
Discussion questions—see chapter 3.

■ Gilles Deleuze and Félix Guattari, from *Kafka: Toward a Minor Literature*
1. What do Deleuze and Guattari mean by *minor literature*?
2. What do they mean by *state literature*?
3. Explain their concept of deterritorialization.

KEY TERMS AND CONCEPTS

KEY TERMS AND CONCEPTS

colonial discourse analysis	nationalism
colonialism	neocolonialism
cultural imperialism	oral culture
decolonization	Orientalism
the Harlem Renaissance	postcolonial culture
hybridity	slave narratives
minor literature	stereotyping
multiculturalism	universalism

ESSAY TOPICS

1. Give some of the reasons why African American (or Hispanic American, Asian American, Native American, etc.) literature should be regarded as a distinct cultural phenomenon and not merely approached as a subset of American literature as a whole.
2. In what ways might the traditional exclusion of nonwhite writers from the canon have produced a distorted view not only of American literary history but of American history as a whole?
3. In what ways might the traditional exclusion of third world writers from the Western canon have produced a distorted view not only of Western literary history but of Western history as a whole?
4. Give some of the reasons why postcolonial literature should be regarded as a distinct cultural phenomenon and not approached as merely a subset of Western literature as a whole.
5. In what ways do the insights and approaches of ethnicity and race studies resemble the insights of postcolonial studies?

VII. Interpretation/Reading Theory (1–3 weeks)

Ultimately, all literary theory and criticism is concerned, in one way or another, with the reading of literary texts. Some theoretical and critical approaches, however, have focused explicitly on the reading process and on what it means to read and interpret a literary text. Because such studies address basic concerns that are relevant to all approaches to literature, a module focusing on them can be especially useful in a course such as this one. In addition, this module offers good opportunities for cross-historical comparisons. For example, studies of the fundamental process of interpretation were especially prominent in medieval literary criticism, and those studies can be compared with modern works of hermeneutics and reader response to make clear to students that even the most basic questions about the reading and interpretation of literary texts are historically determined and not merely matters of common sense.

TEACHING TIP: Note that this module considerably overlaps with the module above on literature and the human mind. Some instructors may

wish to teach these two modules together, though each is designed to
stand alone.

Suggested Readings		
1-week module	2-week module	3-week module
Macrobius	Macrobius	Macrobius
Schleiermacher	Moses Maimonides	Moses Maimonides
Freud	Aquinas	Aquinas
Interpretation of	Schleiermacher	Dante
Dreams	Freud	Schleiermacher
Hirsch	*Interpretation of*	Freud
Fish	*Dreams*	*Interpretation of*
	Jameson	*Dreams*
	Political	Jameson
	Unconscious	*Political*
	Hirsch	*Unconscious*
	Poulet	Hirsch
	Iser	Barthes
	Fish	"Death of the Author"
		"From Work to Text"
		Allen
		Poulet
		Jauss
		Iser
		Fish

SUGGESTED READINGS AND DISCUSSION QUESTIONS

■ Macrobius, from *Commentary on the Dream of Scipio*
  Discussion questions—see chapter 2.

■ Moses Maimonides, from *The Guide of the Perplexed*
  Discussion questions—see chapter 2.

■ Thomas Aquinas, from *Summa Theologica*
  Discussion questions—see chapter 2.

■ Dante Alighieri, from *Il Convivio* and the Letter to Can Grande
  Discussion questions—see chapter 2.

■ Friedrich Schleiermacher, from *Hermeneutics*
  Discussion questions—see chapter 3.

■ Sigmund Freud, from *The Interpretation of Dreams*
  Discussion questions—see chapter 3.

■ Fredric Jameson, from *The Political Unconscious*
  Discussion questions—see chapter 3.

TEACHING TIP: For purposes of comparison, it is helpful to emphasize that Jameson uses Freud's notion of looking beneath the surface to interpret phenomenon that occur at the level of the conscious mind. In particular, Jameson's notion of the political unconscious suggests that the true significance of cultural phenomena can be understood only by digging beneath the surface to their underlying historical, political, and ideological foundations. Note that Jameson also draws on other methods of multilevel interpretation, such as the medieval notion of fourfold exegesis.

■ E. D. Hirsch Jr., "Objective Interpretation"
  Discussion questions—see chapter 3.

■ Roland Barthes, "The Death of the Author" and "From Work to Text"
  Discussion questions—see chapter 3.

TEACHING TIP: Instructors should emphasize the way in which Barthes's poststructuralist notion of authorship grants an especially active role to readers in constituting meaning in literary texts, especially in those texts he describes as "writerly." See especially S/Z (4–6). For an extended discussion of the poststructuralist emphasis on the reader, see the first chapter of Culler's *On Deconstruction*.

■ Paula Gunn Allen, "Kochirnnenako in Academe"
  Discussion questions—see chapter 3.

■ Georges Poulet, "Phenomenology of Reading"
  Discussion questions—see chapter 3.

■ Hans Robert Jauss, from "Literary History as a Challenge to Literary Theory"
  Discussion questions—see chapter 3.

TEACHING TIP: For an accessible introduction to the German reception theory represented by the work of Jauss and Iser, see Holub.

■ Wolfgang Iser, "Interaction between Text and Reader"
  Discussion questions—see chapter 3.

■ Stanley Fish, "Interpreting the *Variorum*"
  Discussion questions—see chapter 3.

KEY TERMS AND CONCEPTS

commentary

fourfold exegesis

gloss

the hermeneutic circle

hermeneutics

intention

interpretive community

meaning

phenomenology

readerly texts

reader-response theory

reception theory

writerly texts

ESSAY TOPICS

1. Write an essay that summarizes and compares the discussion of interpretation/hermeneutics in the various selections from medieval theory and criticism included in this module.
2. Describe some of the ways in which these medieval commentaries differ fundamentally from the modern discussions of reading and interpretation included in this module.
3. In what ways do the selections included in this module make you think differently about your own process of reading and interpretation?
4. Compare and contrast the approaches to reader-response criticism taken, respectively, by Iser and Fish.
5. In what ways does Allen's elaboration of a "tribal-feminist" form of interpretation suggest that many of the fundamental studies of reading and interpretation in the Western tradition are culturally determined?

VIII. *National Literatures and Vernaculars (1–3 weeks)*

The writing of literature in vernacular languages (as opposed to "official" languages, such as Latin) has been an important concern of literary theorists since the late Middle Ages. Historically, this issue took on a new relevance during the Renaissance and into the modern period: with the rise of modern nations, national literatures written in national vernacular languages often came to be seen as crucial elements in the development of national identities. And as Graff points out in *Professing Literature,* literary studies as we know them today are deeply rooted in the dramatic rise of nationalist fervor in Europe and America spurred by World War I. At that time, the formal study of modern national literatures came to be emphasized as never before as part of an effort to encourage nationalist pride and identification. In the second half of the twentieth century, nationalism was crucial to the various anticolonial movements that appeared around the world in opposition to European colonial rule over most of the earth's surface. In the postcolonial period, that nationalist orientation carried over into an emphasis on developing national literatures to help new postcolonial nations develop independent cultural identities that move beyond the colonial domination of the past. This long history makes this module well-suited for the study of historical developments in literary theory and criticism. It also serves as a good focal point for discussing the relationship between literature and society.

Suggested Readings		
1-week module	2-week module	3-week module
du Bellay	Dante	Dante
Fanon	du Bellay	Giambattista Giraldi
"On National Culture"	Ronsard	du Bellay
Ngugi et al.	Emerson	Ronsard
	Fanon	Emerson
	"On National Culture"	Fanon
	Ngugi et al.	"On National Culture"
	Anzaldúa	Ngugi et al.
		Deleuze and Guattari
		Kafka
		Allen
		Anzaldúa
		Baker

SUGGESTED READINGS AND DISCUSSION QUESTIONS

■ Dante Alighieri, from *Il Convivio* and the Letter to Can Grande
  Discussion questions—see chapter 2.

TEACHING TIP: Dante's decision to write his *Commedia* in Italian, rather than Latin, can be considered one of the important landmarks in literary history. Among other things, it marks the beginning of the end of the monological worldview of the Catholic Middle Ages and serves as a harbinger of the Renaissance. Instructors might also want to point out the similar roles played by writers such as Chaucer and Rabelais in the development of Anglophone and Francophone literature, respectively. For a brief discussion of Dante's views on language, and especially of the vernacular versus Latin, see Hollander ("Babytalk"). On this issue, see also Vance. For more general discussions of the late medieval confrontation between Latin and vernacular languages, see the volume edited by Minnis.

■ Giambattista Giraldi, from *Discourse on the Composition of Romances*
  Discussion questions—see chapter 2.

■ Joachim du Bellay, from *The Defence and Illustration of the French Language*
  Discussion questions—see chapter 2.

■ Pierre de Ronsard, "A Brief on the Art of French Poetry"
   Discussion questions—see chapter 2.

■ Ralph Waldo Emerson, from "The American Scholar" and "The Poet"
   Discussion questions—see chapter 2.

TEACHING TIP: Emerson's emphasis on developing a new national literature that is distinctively American calls attention to the way in which
American culture in the nineteenth century was, at least in a literal sense,
a postcolonial culture. Indeed, Ashcroft, Griffiths, and Tiffin argue that
"in many ways the American experience and its attempts to produce a
new kind of literature can be seen to be the model for all later postcolonial writing" (16). This may be an overstatement, given that postcolonial American culture was dominated by former settlers, while the
original native inhabitants were marginalized (and largely eradicated); but
it does suggest interesting points of comparison between American culture and third world postcolonial cultures.

■ Frantz Fanon, from "On National Culture" (*The Wretched of the Earth*)
   Discussion questions—see chapter 3.

TEACHING TIP: Fanon's complex view of the role of nationalist ideas in
the anticolonial struggle and beyond forms the baseline for all subsequent
discussions of nationalism in a colonial and postcolonial context. For
Fanon's most important statements on nationalism in this context, see
also the *NATC* selection from "The Pitfalls of National Consciousness"
(also from *The Wretched of the Earth*).

■ Ngugi wa Thiong'o, Taban lo Liyong, and Henry Owuor-Anyumba, "On
the Abolition of the English Department"
   Discussion questions—see chapter 3.

TEACHING TIP: The emphasis here on teaching African literature in
African universities represents an important statement about postcolonial
culture. Within the context of this module, it is also useful to point out
that Ngugi has been a central figure in the argument over whether
African writers should write in English, French, or other former colonial
languages or in African vernacular languages. Ngugi has, for example,
written such novels as *Devil on the Cross* (1980) and *Matigari* (1986) in
Gikuyu, even though he had previously established a major international
reputation as an Angiophone novelist. For a brief summary of this debate,
see Booker (*African Novel in English*, 14–17). For a cogent argument in
support of the use of African vernacular languages, see Ngugi's *Decolonising the Mind*. For an argument that African writers can use English effectively, see Achebe's essay "The African Writer and the English
Language."

■ Gilles Deleuze and Félix Guattari, from *Kafka: Toward a Minor Literature*
  1. What do Deleuze and Guattari mean by *minor literature*?
  2. What do they mean by *state literature*?
  3. Explain their concept of deterritorialization.

■ Paula Gunn Allen, "Kochinnenako in Academe"
  Discussion questions—see chapter 3.

TEACHING TIP: The selection from Allen, like those from Anzaldúa and Baker below, calls attention to the plurality of American culture, thus usefully problematizing the discussion of national languages and cultures in this module.

■ Gloria Anzaldúa, from *Borderlands/La Frontera*
  Discussion questions—see chapter 3.

■ Houston A. Baker Jr., from *Blues, Ideology, and Afro-American Literature*
  Discussion questions—see chapter 3.

KEY TERMS AND CONCEPTS

Anglophone literature	national literature
colonialism	neocolonialism
cultural imperialism	postcolonial culture
hybridity	vernacular language
identity politics	world literature
nationalism	

ESSAY TOPICS

1. Discuss the ways in which the emergence of national vernacular languages in the late Middle Ages marked the beginning of the end of the medieval worldview.
2. How did national languages and literatures contribute to the growth of nationalism in Europe in the eighteenth and nineteenth centuries?
3. Discuss the role played by literature and culture in the European domination of the colonial world in the nineteenth and twentieth centuries.
4. How might national literatures and cultures contribute to the attempt to develop new national identities in the postcolonial world?

IX. Literary Tradition and the Canon (1–3 weeks)

Judgments concerning literary value have long been a central concern of literary theory and criticism, though debates over these judgments have become particularly charged since the 1960s, when the civil rights, women's, and other political movements called attention to the Western canon's near-total exclusion of works written by nonwhite, female, and working-class writers. Moreover, the new kinds of criticism inspired by these political movements demonstrated that the white, male, middle- and upper-class writers who were included in the canon tended to represent nonwhite, female, and working-class people in distorted, stereotypical, and often highly offensive ways. These critics argued that works of literature often become canonical not by possessing some timeless aesthetic quality but by effectively representing certain ideological positions, especially the positions of those whose race, gender, and class place them in positions of power.

This argument about the ideological basis of canonicity has been accompanied by a growing understanding of the historicity of literary judgment. Though canons are often represented as comprising great works that have been admired through the ages, the fact is that canons change over time, sometimes dramatically. The Western canon has undergone a number of substantial revisions even in the course of the twentieth century. For example, modernist literature was generally marginalized in literary studies until the 1950s, when it suddenly moved to the very center of the Western canon and when modernist art came to be regarded as the epitome of aesthetic achievement. That the canonization of modernism was closely associated with the institutionalization of New Criticism in America further demonstrates the tenuous nature of canonicity.

Yet certain authors, such as Homer and Shakespeare, have maintained lofty reputations for centuries, and numerous theorists and critics still believe in absolute, ahistorical aesthetic qualities and assert that literary studies should focus on "great" works that embody these qualities. Not surprisingly, debates between those who believe in absolute canonicity

Suggested Readings		
1-week module	2-week module	3-week module
Arnold	Hugh of St. Victor	Hugh of St. Victor
Eliot	Arnold	Young
Ohmann	Eliot	Shelley
Graff	Bloom	Arnold
Bourdieu	Ohmann	Eliot
	Graff	Bloom
	Bourdieu	Ohmann
	Achebe	Graff
		Bourdieu
		B. Herrnstein Smith
		Ngugi et al.
		Achebe

and those who insist on the historical and ideological nature of all aesthetic judgments have sometimes become quite heated, fueling the so-called culture wars that raged through the 1990s. The selections in this module are relevant to this debate in a number of ways, and instructors may find that students' interest ignites when they realize that the material they are studying has been intensely controversial in recent years.

SUGGESTED READINGS AND DISCUSSION QUESTIONS

■ Hugh of St. Victor, from *The Didascalicon*
   Discussion questions—see chapter 2.

■ Edward Young, from "Conjectures on Original Composition"
   Discussion questions—see chapter 2.

■ Percy Bysshe Shelley, from *A Defence of Poetry*
   Discussion questions—see chapter 2.

■ Matthew Arnold, "The Function of Criticism at the Present Time" and from "Sweetness and Light" (*Culture and Anarchy*)
   Discussion questions—see chapter 2.

■ T. S. Eliot, "Tradition and the Individual Talent" and "The Metaphysical Poets"
   Discussion questions—see chapter 2.

■ Harold Bloom, from *The Anxiety of Influence*
   Discussion questions—see chapter 3.

■ Richard Ohmann, from "The Shaping of a Canon"
   Discussion questions—see chapter 3.

■ Gerald Graff, "Taking Cover in Coverage"
   1. In what ways, according to Graff, does the compartmentalization of literary studies in the current university system limit our ability to understand literature to the fullest?
   2. In what ways can Graff's essay be interpreted as a defense of "theory"?
   3. In what ways can Graff's recommendation to "teach the conflicts" be seen as a form of pluralism? What might be some of the difficulties with this seemingly commonsense approach?

■ Pierre Bourdieu, from *Distinction*
   Discussion questions—see chapter 3.

■ Barbara Herrnstein Smith, from *Contingencies of Value*
   1. Discuss the challenges to traditional literary scholarship and teaching presented by Smith's conclusions.

2. Discuss the implications of Smith's notion of the contingency of value with regard to New Criticism and other kinds of formalist criticism.

3. In what ways does Smith's essay reinforce the recent critical interest in cultural products beyond conventionally canonical works of literature, including works of popular culture, works by women, works by gay and lesbian writers, works by nonwhite writers, works by third world writers, and so on?

■ Ngugi wa Thiong'o, Taban lo Liyong, and Henry Owuor-Anyumba, "On the Abolition of the English Department"
  Discussion questions—see chapter 3.

TEACHING TIP: The selection from Ngugi et al. offers instructors the opportunity to discuss the traditional focus of the Western canon on works by white, Western, male writers and to ask whether the standards of judgment used to construct this canon are themselves culturally and historically determined.

■ Chinua Achebe, "An Image of Africa"
  Discussion questions—see chapter 3.

KEY TERMS AND CONCEPTS

aesthetics	New Historicism
canon	taste
culture wars	tradition
influence	value
multiculturalism	

ESSAY TOPICS

1. What is a literary canon and what is its function in literary studies?
2. What, in your opinion, are some of the characteristics that a work of literature should have in order to be canonical?
3. Discuss the advantages and disadvantages for literary studies of the recent expansion of the canon to include more works by women and people of color.
4. How do the recent changes in the literary canon affect our understanding of the nature and function of literary tradition?

X. The Institution and History of Academic Literary Studies (1–3 weeks)

From the 1960s forward, the rise of literary theory in the Western academy not only challenged the hegemony of older approaches but also led to debates about the fundamental nature and goals of literary scholarship and teaching. These debates, like arguments over the purpose and constitution of literary canons, have often become quite heated; but they have also often been quite productive, leading to important new insights about institutionalization, specialization, and professionalization. The selections in this module enable instructors to introduce these debates to students while making clear that similar, if sometimes less politically charged, debates over literary studies have occurred through much of the history of Western literary study.

	Suggested Readings	
1-week module	2-week module	3-week module
Ransom	Hugh of St. Victor	Hugh of St. Victor
Eagleton	Ransom	Arnold
Said	Eagleton	Ransom
Graff	Said	Eagleton
Ngugi et al.	Kolodny	Said
	Graff	Kolodny
	Fish	Christian
	Gates	Graff
	Ngugi et al.	Fish
		Gates
		Ngugi et al.

Suggested Readings and Discussion Questions

■ Hugh of St. Victor, from *The Didascalicon*
  Discussion questions—see chapter 2.

■ Matthew Arnold, "The Function of Criticism at the Present Time" and from "Sweetness and Light" (*Culture and Anarchy*)
  Discussion questions—see chapter 2.

■ John Crowe Ransom, "Criticism, Inc."
  Discussion questions—see chapter 3.

TEACHING TIP: Ransom's essay points toward the crucial role played by the institutionalization of New Criticism in the American academy in the late 1940s and 1950s in the growing professionalization of American literary studies. For more on this phenomenon, see Robbins.

■ Terry Eagleton, from *Literary Theory*
  Discussion questions—see chapter 3.

■ Edward W. Said, from *Orientalism*
  Discussion questions—see chapter 3.

TEACHING TIP: Said's delineation, in *Orientalism*, of the role played by academic studies in the growth and promulgation of colonialist and racist stereotypes represents one of the most important contributions to the debate over the ideological nature of academic (and seemingly apolitical) disciplines. Instructors might want to review that text in some detail and to remind students of its importance in the rise of postcolonial studies.

- Annette Kolodny, "Dancing through the Minefield"
  Discussion questions—see chapter 3.

TEACHING TIP: The selection from Kolodny not only provides a survey of the state of feminist criticism at its time of composition but also calls attention to the extent to which feminist approaches have gained acceptance in the Western academy.

- Barbara Christian, "The Race for Theory"
  Discussion questions—see chapter 3.

- Gerald Graff, "Taking Cover in Coverage"
  1. In what ways, according to Graff, does the compartmentalization of literary studies in the current university system limit our ability to understand literature to the fullest?
  2. In what ways can Graff's essay be interpreted as a defense of "theory"?
  3. In what ways can Graff's recommendation to "teach the conflicts" be seen as a form of pluralism? What might be some of the difficulties with this seemingly commonsense approach?

TEACHING TIP: Instructors might wish to consult Graff's *Professing Literature* or *Beyond the Culture Wars* (essentially a briefer and more accessible version of *Professing Literature*) for a fuller exposition of Graff's influential ideas on the institution and history of academic literary studies.

- Stanley Fish, "Interpreting the *Variorum*"
  Discussion questions—see chapter 3.

TEACHING TIP: Note that Fish's "interpretive communities" are largely defined by trends in academic literary studies and therefore indicate the power of the academy in determining the reception of literary texts.

- Henry Louis Gates Jr., "Talking Black"
  Discussion questions—see chapter 3.

TEACHING TIP: The selection from Gates helps indicate the way in which academic literary studies have expanded in recent decades to include a broader range of literary texts, paying much more attention in particular to works by African American and other ethnic American writers.

■ Ngugi wa Thiong'o, Taban Lo Liyong, and Henry Owuor-Anyumba, "On the Abolition of the English Department"
  Discussion questions—see chapter 3.

Key Terms and Concepts

canon	institutionalization
coverage	multiculturalism
culture wars	professionalization

Essay Topics

1. Briefly describe your understanding of the basic issues that have been at the center of recent debates over the nature and function of academic literary studies.
2. In what ways might courses such as the one you are now taking (and books such as *NATC*) contribute to the compartmentalization of literary studies that Graff and others have seen as limiting debate in the field?
3. In what ways might courses such as the one you are now taking (and books such as *NATC*) contribute to the growth of productive debates in literary studies?
4. How has studying debates about the nature and function of academic literary studies affected your own understanding of and approach to literature?

XI. Postmodernity (1–2 weeks)

The exact nature of postmodernism is still intensely debated, but it seems clear that the term describes a wide array of late-twentieth-century cultural productions, a range of contemporary modes of criticism and thought, and a distinctive historical period of postindustrial, media-saturated societies. As a contemporary phenomenon, postmodernity should seem especially relevant to many students. This module therefore serves as an effective introduction to certain contemporary trends in culture as well as in theory and criticism. This module is essentially identical to the one on postmodern theory and criticism in chapter 3, so instructors should see that module for more details.

Suggested Readings

1-week module	2-week module
Lyotard	Lyotard
Habermas	Baudrillard
"Modernity"	Habermas
Jameson	"Modernity"
"Postmodernism"	Jameson
hooks	"Postmodernism"
Deleuze & Guattari	Greenblatt
"Rhizome"	Anzaldúa
	Vizenor
	Haraway
	hooks
	Moulthrop
	Deleuze & Guattari
	"Rhizome"

CHAPTER 6

Additional Course Suggestions

The selections in *NATC* are obviously numerous and diverse enough to allow instructors to use them in any number of courses. The previous four chapters have contained detailed descriptions of some of the courses that might be taught using *NATC* as a principal text. This chapter presents several additional suggestions for courses that might be taught using *NATC*, presented as actual course outlines. Most instructors, of course, will want to use these outlines as starting points for constructing their own courses. In addition, instructors will want to add examinations, assignments, and other details as they see fit. See also the alternative table of contents in *NATC* for additional suggestions of how to group texts in teaching units.

Suggested Course Outlines
  I.   Introduction to Literary and Cultural Studies
  II. Key Issues in Modern Theory and Criticism
  III. Survey of World Literature, Theory and Criticism
       A. One-semester version
       B. Two-semester version
  IV. Survey of Modern Literature, Theory, and Criticism

Suggested Course Outlines

I. Introduction to Literary and Cultural Studies

This course is in many ways similar to the introduction to major schools of theory and criticism described above in chapter 3, which should be consulted for more detailed suggestions on teaching specific selections or on additional selections in specific categories. As with the course described there, instructors may want to supplement the readings from *NATC* with an introductory text (such as those by Booker [*Practical Introduction*], Bressler, Selden, or Tyson) that presents cogent overviews of the individual critical schools. However, the course described below is designed to be taught specifically at an introductory level, perhaps to lower-level undergraduate students who plan to major in English or another program in literature. It therefore includes significantly fewer reading assignments in theory and criticism than do the courses in chapter 3, supplemented by a few assigned readings in literature and culture. In addition, the course outlined below includes a significant historical introduction that briefly surveys the classics of theory and criticism from Aristotle through the nineteenth century. Instructors who wish to concentrate on more contemporary theoretical and critical approaches may choose to omit this segment of the course and substitute more detailed treatment of twentieth-century approaches.

Week 1—*Introduction to the Course.* Assigned reading from *NATC*: Introduction to *NATC*. *Note*: The first class session should probably be devoted to some very introductory discussions of criticism and theory, making clear to students that works of criticism and theory participate in their own discourses and therefore must be approached on their own terms. At the same time, students should be assured of the close relationship between criticism/theory and literature. The introduction to *NATC* will serve to introduce students to the notion that theoretical approaches to literature vary widely and that critics practicing different approaches may read literature in very different ways.

Week 2—*Classical Theory and Criticism.* Assigned readings from *NATC*: Aristotle, *Poetics*; Plato, from *Republic*, Book VII. *Note*: Aristotle's *Poetics* is in many ways the founding text of Western literary criticism and a text on which subsequent theorists and critics have frequently drawn. The selection from Plato can be used to introduce both philosophical idealism (which provides a philosophical background to formalism) and the notion that the nature and function of literature and culture have long been the object of considerable debate.

Week 3—*Medieval and Renaissance Theory and Criticism.* Assigned readings from *NATC*: Augustine; Aquinas; du Bellay; Sidney. *Note*: This brief treatment of medieval and Renaissance theory and criticism will at least help establish that theory and criticism *have* a history, as well as making clear to students that approaches to language and literature can vary substantially from one historical period to another. Some instructors might want to supplement the readings in theory and criticism with some sample literary works—perhaps a Renaissance sonnet by Sidney (or Shakespeare, etc.).

Week 4—*Theory and Criticism from the Enlightenment and Nineteenth Century.* Assigned readings from *NATC*: Corneille; Vico; Coleridge; Arnold. *Note*: These selections will continue to demonstrate the historical development of theory and criticism. The selection from Coleridge, which can be used to introduce Romanticism, can be usefully supplemented by in-class readings and discussions of some individual poems by Coleridge (or Wordsworth, etc.). The selection from Arnold is useful background to recent debates over the nature and function of literary studies. It also introduces the Victorian worldview and can be usefully supplemented by in-class readings and discussions of one or more Victorian poems, perhaps Arnold's "Dover Beach" (1867).

Week 5—*Formalism.* Assigned readings from *NATC*: Eichenbaum; Ransom; Wimsatt and Beardsley; Eagleton. *Note*: These selections will enable instructors to introduce both Russian formalism and New Criticism, while the selection from Eagleton should promote useful discussions of the sometimes hidden implications of formalist criticism.

Week 6—*Structuralism.* Assigned readings from *NATC*: Saussure; Jakobson, "Linguistics and Poetics"; Todorov; Bakhtin. *Note*: Saussure, Jakobson, and Todorov can be used to introduce some of the basic assumptions and methods of structuralist criticism and theory. The selection from Bakhtin shows how certain basic structuralist ideas can be extended in innovative directions.

Week 7—*Poststructuralism.* Assigned readings from *NATC*: Nietzsche, "On Truth and Lying in a Non-Moral Sense"; Barthes, "Death of the Author" and "From Work to Text"; de Man, "Semiology and Rhetoric"; Derrida, from *Of Grammatology. Note*: These selections can be used to provide a basic introduction to poststructuralism, especially in its deconstructive version.

Week 8—*Poststructuralism, cont.* Assigned readings from *NATC*: Barbara Johnson; de Man, "Return to Philology"; Foucault, from *Discipline and Punish* and from *The History of Sexuality. Note*: The selection from Johnson gives students a look at poststructuralist criticism in practice. This de Man selection can be used to introduce the ongoing debates about poststructuralist theory and its consequences. The Foucault selections suggest an application of poststructuralist ideas to social institutions and the history of ideas. (The NATC selections from Cixous and Bhabha show how poststructuralist theory and criticism can be extended to feminist and poststructuralist studies.)

Week 9—*Anglo-American Feminism.* Assigned readings from *NATC*: Woolf; Gilbert and Gubar; Kolodny. *French Feminism.* Assigned readings from *NATC*: Beauvoir; Cixous; Kristeva; Wittig. *Note*: The Beauvoir selection, which is a forerunner of the criticism of stereotypes by Anglo-American feminists, can be used to link the two types of feminist theory and criticism. The Wittig selection can be used as a transition into gender studies (week 10).

Week 10—*Gender Studies and Queer Theory*. Assigned readings from *NATC*: Zimmerman; Rich; Sedgwick; Butler.

Week 11—*Race and Ethnicity Studies*. Assigned readings from *NATC*: Du Bois; Hughes; Baker; Anzaldúa; Allen.

Week 12—*Postcolonial Studies*. Assigned readings from *NATC*: Fanon: Achebe; Said; Ngugi et al.

Week 13—*Marxism: Literature and Society*. Assigned readings from *NATC*: Marx and Engels, from *The Communist Manifesto* and from *The German Ideology*; Gramsci; Lukács. *Note*: These selections together can introduce some of the basic premises of Marxist theory as well as some of the central tendencies in Marxist criticism.

Week 14—*Marxism: Literature and Ideology*. Assigned readings from *NATC*: Benjamin; Althusser, from "Ideology and Ideological State Apparatuses"; Habermas, "Modernity—An Incomplete Project"; Jameson, from *The Political Unconscious*. *Note*: These selections extend those of week 12 to provide a broader introduction to some of the basic insights of Marxist theory and criticism. Because of the importance of Marxist ideas to cultural studies, the material from weeks 13 and 14 leads naturally to that in week 14.

Week 15—*Cultural Studies*. Assigned readings from *NATC*: Horkheimer and Adorno; Bourdieu; Ohmann; Mulvey.

Week 16—*Postmodernism*. Assigned readings from *NATC*: Lyotard; Baudrillard; Deleuze and Guattari; Jameson, "Postmodernism and Consumer Society."

II. Key Issues in Modern Theory and Criticism

Some of the greatest excitement (and most vexing problems) in recent literary studies has attended the sometimes heated debates over its fundamental nature and purpose. This course is designed to focus on some of those debates, energizing the discussion of theory and criticism in the mode recommended by Gerald Graff in call to "teach the conflicts." To further this design, most of the selections below are presented in pairs of opposing ideas on a given topic.

Week 1—*Introduction to the Course*. Assigned readings from *NATC*: Introduction to *NATC*; Graff.

Week 2—*The Value and Danger of Literature*. Assigned readings from *NATC*: Plato vs. Sidney; Peacock vs. Shelley. *Note*: The fundamental disagreement between Plato and Sidney over the value of fictional discourse and the more specific debate between Peacock and Shelley on the value of Romantic poetry should help introduce the idea of conflict in literary studies, while also making clear to students that the recent "culture wars" have significant historical precedents.

Week 3—*The World and the Text*. Assigned readings from *NATC*:

Eichenbaum vs. Bakhtin. *Note*: The selection from Eichenbaum can be used to introduce the idea of formalist criticism, while the "stylistics" of Bakhtin, though rooted in Russian formalism, describes the relationship between literature and its sociohistorical context, thus challenging the fundamental premises of formalism. For more on the Bakhtinian critique of formalism, see the essay "The Formalist Theory of the Historical Development of Literature," in Bakhtin/Medvedev's *Formal Method in Literary Scholarship*. For more on the relationship between Bakhtin and formalism, see Bennett.

Week 4—*Criticism and Ideology*. Assigned readings from *NATC*: Ransom vs. Eagleton. *Note*: Ransom's call for a sophisticated, professional literary criticism suggests that this criticism might be able to determine the "correct" readings of literary texts. Eagleton's critique of the ideological biases of New Criticism and other "nonideological" forms of Western criticism suggests that those readings, far from being scientifically correct, actually represent the interests of certain specific social groups. Note also that the formalist-Marxist opposition between Ransom and Eagleton continues the debate between Eichenbaum and Bakhtin in week 3.

    Literature and Ideology. Assigned readings from NATC: Gautier vs. Trotsky. Gautier's argument that art should remain separate from the social world opposes Trotsky's argument in favor of committed literature, thus posing another version of the formalism vs. Marxism debate while calling attention to some of the fundamental cultural debates of the past century.

Week 5—*Authorship*. Assigned readings from *NATC*: Wimsatt and Beardsley, "The Intentional Fallacy" vs. Hirsch vs. Barthes, "The Death of the Author"/Foucault, "What Is an Author?" *Note*: These four varying views of authorship should amply promote discussion of the role played by contending conceptions of authorship in the interpretation of literary texts.

Week 6—*Reading and Interpretation*. Assigned readings from *NATC*: Wimsatt and Beardsley, "The Affective Fallacy" vs. Fish vs. Knapp and Michaels. *Note*: These varying views of interpretation support discussion of the role of the reader in determining the meaning of a literary text.

Week 7—*Defining High Culture*. Assigned readings from *NATC*: Arnold vs. Althusser. *Note*: Arnold's vision of high culture as a key element in defining the values of a given culture can be usefully opposed to Althusser's treatment of ideology, which calls attention to the way in which the values conveyed by high culture may, in fact, be those not of an entire culture but merely of the ruling class. The selections from Bourdieu and Barbara Herrnstein Smith might also contribute usefully to this debate.

Week 8—*Modernism vs. Realism*. Assigned readings from *NATC*: Lukács vs. Eliot.

Week 9—*High Culture vs. Low Culture*. Assigned readings from *NATC*:

Benjamin vs. Horkheimer and Adorno. *Note*: Benjamin's view of the emancipatory potential of film opposes Horkheimer and Adorno's critique of the culture industry; this juxtaposition introduces some of the important issues that have informed studies of popular culture in recent decades.

Week 10—*Culture, Race, and Colonialism*. Assigned readings from *NATC*: Arnold vs. Said. *Note*: These selections suggest the extent to which the high culture of the West, while often presenting itself as universal, reflects values and positions that not only ignore the viewpoints of the non-Western world but are inimical to non-Western cultures, serving to justify colonialism and Western global hegemony.

Week 11—*Postcolonialism, Poststructuralism, and Politics*. Assigned readings from *NATC*: Bhabha vs. Ngugi vs. Spivak. *Note*: These three selections together introduce some of the central debates that have informed postcolonial studies in recent decades, particularly the question of whether Western poststructuralist ideas have obscured the material and political realities within which third world culture functions.

Week 12—*Anglo-American Feminism*. Assigned readings from *NATC*: Woolf; Gilbert and Gubar; Kolodny. *Note*: The last four weeks of this course focus on gender-related theory and criticism, demonstrating the variety of approaches falling under this rubric.

Week 13—*French Feminism*. Assigned readings from *NATC*: Beauvior; Cixous; Kristeva; Wittig. *Note*: The Beauvoir selection, which is a forerunner of the criticism of stereotypes by Anglo-American feminists, can be used to link the two types of feminist theory and criticism. The Wittig selection can be used as a transition into gender studies (week 14).

Week 14—*Gender Studies and Queer Theory*. Assigned readings from *NATC*: Zimmerman; Rich; Sedgwick; Butler.

Week 15—*Gender, Race, and Ethnicity*. Assigned readings from *NATC*: Barbara Smith; Allen; Anzaldúa. *Note*: The first three of these selections indicate the important contributions of gender-oriented theorists whose cultural positions differ from those of mainstream feminism, which has been dominated by middle-class, white, Western critics.

III. Survey of World Literature, Theory, and Criticism

In addition to its use in courses devoted specifically to literary theory and criticism, *NATC* can also be used very effectively in courses designed to introduce students to major works of literature, enabling instructors better to contextualize those works and to discuss various critical approaches to them. This section suggests a possible outline for either a one- or a two-semester course that surveys world literature within the context of theory and criticism. Instructors teaching on a quarter system would need to adjust the outline accordingly. Any number of literary works might be chosen for this course, and instructors will no doubt want to modify the syllabus to include their own favorites. These syllabi have given preference to literary works that are available in the 7th edition of *The Norton*

Anthology of World Masterpieces, edited by Lawall et al., which can thus provide a convenient companion text. Instructors could also construct alternative versions of this course focusing on either English or American literature, pairing *NATC* with *The Norton Anthology of English Literature* or *The Norton Anthology of American Literature.*

A. One-semester course

Week 1—*Introduction to the course.* Assigned reading from *NATC*: Introduction to *NATC*.

Week 2—*Theory and Criticism of the Classical Period.* Assigned readings from *NATC*: Aristotle, *Poetics*; Nietzsche, from *The Birth of Tragedy*. *Note*: The selection from Nietzsche, looking back on classical Greek drama from the late nineteenth century, should present excellent opportunities for comparisons and for discussion of the continuing importance of the Greek and Roman classics in Western culture. Some instructors might wish to use additional theory and criticism from the classical period, perhaps some of the selections from Plato's *Republic*.

Week 3—*Literature of the Classical Period.* Assigned reading: Sophocles, *Oedipus the King*. *Note*: As perhaps the best-known work of classical Greek drama, Sophocles' play presents an excellent example to which classical theory and criticism (especially Aristotle's *Poetics*) can be applied.

Week 4—*Theory and Criticism of the Medieval Period.* Assigned readings from *NATC*: Augustine; Aquinas; Dante.

Week 5—*Literature of the Medieval Period.* Assigned reading: Dante, *Inferno*. *Note*: Dante's poem is a late medieval work in which the breakup of the medieval worldview and movement toward the Renaissance are beginning to be visible. However, it still embodies many medieval principles; in addition, undergraduate students tend to receive it better than more purely medieval texts, such as *The Romance of the Rose*.

Week 6—*Theory and Criticism of the Renaissance and Enlightenment.* Assigned readings from *NATC*: Mazzoni; Sidney; Corneille; Dryden; Samuel Johnson, from *Shakespeare*. *Note*: The selection from Mazzoni, which addresses Dante's *Commedia*, provides a transition from the medieval segment of the course. The selections from Corneille, Dryden, and Johnson give students a context within which to look back on *Othello* (week 7) from the point of view of the Enlightenment. Moreover, the combination of the Renaissance and Enlightenment periods in this segment enables instructors to emphasize the direct historical connection between the two periods.

Week 7—*Literature of the Renaissance and Enlightenment.* Assigned reading: Shakespeare, *Othello*. *Note*: Aside from Shakespeare's crucial importance in the Western canon (and *Othello*'s crucial importance in the Shakespearean canon), this play introduces important issues such as race, class, and gender in ways that begin to be modern. Instructors who feel they have time to supplement this text with an Enlightenment work might want to choose a play, perhaps by Corneille or Molière (*Tartuffe* might be a good choice).

Week 8—*Theory and Criticism of the Nineteenth Century: Romanticism.* Assigned readings from *NATC*: Schiller; Wollstonecraft; de Staël; Coleridge; Woolf. *Note:* The selection from Woolf does not address Romanticism per se but presents the historical conditions under which women writers have traditionally worked, thereby providing an introduction to feminist approaches to Mary Shelley's *Frankenstein*, if that work is chosen for week 9.

Week 9—*Literature of the Nineteenth Century: Romanticism.* Assigned reading: Goethe, *Faust.* *Note:* Other texts, including Mary Shelley's *Frankenstein* or selections from such poets as Wordsworth, Coleridge, Keats, and Shelley, would also be good examples of Romantic literature. *Frankenstein* raises particularly useful questions about gender and about the modern hegemony of science.

Week 10—*Theory and Criticism of the Nineteenth Century: Realism.* Assigned readings from *NATC*: James; Marx and Engels, from *The Communist Manifesto*; Lukács; Althusser from "Ideology and Ideological State Apparatuses"; Foucault, from *Discipline and Punish*; Beauvoir. *Note:* These assignments are chosen to prepare students to read Flaubert's *Madame Bovary* in week 11. James's essay comments on certain technical issues, calling attention to Flaubert's own virtuosity. The selections from Marx, Lukács, and Althusser provide Marxist frameworks within which to read not only Flaubert's realistic technique but also this critique of bourgeois ideology. Foucault's work on carceral societies mounts criticisms of nineteenth-century middle-class hegemony that are in many ways reminiscent of Flaubert's. The selection from Beauvoir provides opportunities to discuss the treatment of gender in Flaubert's novel.

Week 11—*Literature of the Nineteenth Century: Realism.* Assigned reading: Flaubert, *Madame Bovary.* *Note:* A work such as Balzac's *Père Goriot* is perhaps a more paradigmatic work of literary realism, but *Madame Bovary* offers particularly rich material for discussing class, gender, and their role in the ideological construction of the subject.

Week 12—*Theory and Criticism of the Modern Period.* Assigned readings from *NATC*: Freud, from *The Interpretation of Dreams*; Eliot, "Tradition and the Individual Talent"; Said; Achebe. *Note:* The selection from Eliot enables instructors to introduce the phenomenon of modernism and its criticism—the charge that modernist art attempts to escape from history. The selection from Said introduces the topic of colonialism and the ways in which Western writers have conventionally represented the non-European world in stereotypical ways that say more about the characteristic preoccupations of Europeans than about non-Europeans. Achebe's essay does the same, while specifically addressing itself to Conrad's *Heart of Darkness*, which some instructors might wish to teach directly.

Week 13—*Western Literature of the Modern Period.* Assigned readings:

James Joyce, "The Dead"; T. S. Eliot, *The Waste Land*. *Note*: Many texts might be chosen for this segment of the course, but these two give students a good basic introduction to modernism. Students might also be referred back to the selection from Woolf in *NATC*, with a reminder of Woolf's own importance as a modernist writer.

Week 14—*Multicultural Theory and Criticism of the Contemporary Period*. Assigned readings from *NATC*: Fanon; Ngugi et al.; Barbara Smith. *Notes*: The selections from Fanon and Ngugi et al. call attention to the importance of postcolonial literature in the development of viable postcolonial cultural identities. The selection from Smith calls attention to the treatment of gender in Achebe's novel (assigned in week 15), which bears fruitful comparison to that in Conrad's novel: both books arguably take strongly masculinist positions despite their other cultural differences. On this problematic issue in Achebe, see Stratton. For more on *Things Fall Apart*, see also the chapter on that novel in Booker, *The African Novel in English*.

Week 15—*Multicultural Literature of the Contemporary Period*. Assigned reading: Chinua Achebe, *Things Fall Apart*. *Note*: Achebe's novel obviously functions as a kind of response to *Heart of Darkness*, thus supplementing his essay on Conrad. It also brilliantly exemplifies the importance in recent decades of the postcolonial novel to world culture.

B. Two-semester course

Semester 1: The Classical Period through the Renaissance

Note: This semester corresponds to the literary selections available in volume 1 of the *Norton Anthology of World Masterpieces*.

Week 1—*Introduction to the course*. Assigned reading from *NATC*: Introduction to *NATC*.

Week 2—*Theory and Criticism of the Classical Period*. Assigned readings from *NATC*: Aristotle, *Poetics*; Nietzsche, from *The Birth of Tragedy*.

Week 3—*Literature of the Classical Period*. Assigned reading: Sophocles, *Oedipus the King*.

Week 4—*Theory and Criticism of the Classical Period*. Assigned readings from *NATC*: Gorgias; Plato, from *Republic*, Books VII and X; Horace.

Week 5—*Literature of the Classical Period*. Assigned reading. Virgil, from the *Aeneid*. *Note*: The use of the *Aeneid* in this course enables instructors to introduce the topic of the epic. The poem can also be usefully taught alongside Horace's nearly contemporary *Ars Poetica*.

Week 6—*Theory and Criticism of the Medieval Period*. Assigned readings from *NATC*: Augustine; Aquinas; Dante.

Week 7—*Literature of the Medieval Period*. Assigned reading: Dante, *Inferno*.

Week 8—*Theory and Criticism of the Medieval Period*. Assigned readings from *NATC*: Macrobius; Moses Maimonides; Geoffrey of Vinsauf.

Week 9—*Literature of the Medieval Period.* Assigned reading: Chaucer, from *The Canterbury Tales.*

Week 10—*Theory and Criticism of the Renaissance.* Assigned readings from *NATC*: Boccaccio; Christine de Pizan; mazzoni. *Note*: The selections from Boccaccio, Christine, and Mazzoni all provide excellent transitions from the medieval segment of this course, while the work of Boccaccio serves as a good lead-in to that of Rabelais (week 11).

Week 11—*Literature of the Renaissance.* Assigned readings: from Rabelais, from *Gargantua and Pantagruel.*

Week 12—*Theory and Criticism of the Renaissance.* Assigned readings from *NATC*: Sidney; du Bellay.

Week 13—*Literature of the Renaissance.* Assigned reading: Shakespeare, *Othello.* From *NATC*: Samuel Johnson, from *Shakespeare.*

Week 14—*Modern Theory and Criticism of the Renaissance.* Assigned readings from *NATC*: Samuel Johnson, from *Shakespeare*; Pater, from *The Renaissance*; Eliot, "The Metaphysical Poets"; Greenblatt.

Week 15—*Literature of the Renaissance.* Assigned readings: Milton, from *Paradise Lost. Note*: Selections from the metaphysical poetry of Herbert, Donne, and Marvell also work particularly well with Eliot's essay on the metaphysical poets.

Semester 2: The Enlightenment to the Present

Note: This semester corresponds to the literary selections available in volume 2 of the *Norton Anthology of World Masterpieces.*

Week 1—*Introduction to the course.* Assigned reading from *NATC*: Introduction to *NATC*.

Week 2—*Theory and Criticism of the Enlightenment.* Assigned readings from *NATC*: Corneille; Pope.

Week 3—*Literature of the Enlightenment.* Assigned reading: Voltaire, *Candide.*

Week 4—*Theory and Criticism of the Nineteenth Century: Romanticism.* Assigned readings from *NATC*: Schiller; Wollstonecraft; de Staël; Coleridge; Woolf. *Note*: The selection from Woolf does not address Romanticism per se but presents the historical conditions under which women writers have traditionally worked, thereby providing an introduction to feminist approaches to literature assigned later, such as *Faust* and *Madame Bovary.*

Week 5—*Literature of the Nineteenth Century: Romanticism.* Assigned reading: Goethe, *Faust. Note*: Other texts, including Mary Shelley's *Frankenstein* or selections from such poets as Wordsworth, Coleridge, Keats, and Shelley, would also be good examples of Romantic literature. *Frankenstein* raises particularly useful questions about gender and about the modern hegemony of science.

Week 6—*Theory and Criticism of the Nineteenth Century: Realism.* Assigned readings from *NATC*: James; Marx and Engels, from *The Communist Manifesto*; Lukács; Althusser, from "Ideology and Ideological State Apparatuses"; Foucault, from *Discipline and Punish*; Beauvoir. *Note*: These assignments are chosen to prepare students to read Flaubert's *Madame Bovary* in week 7. James's essay comments on certain technical issues, calling attention to Flaubert's own virtuosity. The selections from Marx, Lukács, and Althusser provide Marxist frameworks within which to read not only Flaubert's realistic technique but his critique of bourgeois ideology. Foucault's work on carceral societies mounts criticisms of nineteenth-century middle-class hegemony that are in many ways reminiscent of Flaubert's. The selection from Beauvoir provides opportunities to discuss the treatment of gender in Flaubert's novel.

Week 7—*Literature of the Nineteenth Century: Realism.* Assigned reading: Flaubert, *Madame Bovary. Note*: A work such as Balzac's *Père Goriot* is perhaps a more paradigmatic work of literary realism, but Flaubert's work offers particularly rich material for discussing class, gender, and their role in the ideological construction of the subject.

Week 8—*Literature and Modernity.* Assigned readings from *NATC*: Mallarmé; Eliot; Benjamin; Habermas, "Modernity—An Incomplete Project."

Week 9—*Literature of the Twentieth Century: The Modern World.* Assigned readings: James Joyce, "The Dead"; T. S. Eliot, *The Waste Land. Note*: Many texts might be chosen for this segment of the course, but these two give students a good basic introduction to modernism. Students might also be referred back to the selection from Woolf in *NATC*, with a reminder of Woolf's own importance as a modernist writer.

Week 10—*Postcolonial Criticism.* Assigned readings from *NATC*: Said; Achebe; Ngugi et al.

Week 11—*Literature of the Twentieth Century: Non-Western cultures.* Assigned reading: Chinua Achebe, *Things Fall Apart.*

Week 12—*Literature and Society.* Assigned readings from *NATC*: Vico; Shelley; Bourdieu; Jameson, from *The Political Unconscious.*

Week 13—*Literature of the Twentieth Century: Drama.* Assigned readings: Bertolt Brecht, *The Good Woman of Setzuan*; Samuel Beckett, *Endgame. Note*: the pairing of these two dramatists encourages discussion of various theories of drama, opposing the epic theater to the theater of the absurd. Brecht's plays resonate well, of course, with Marxist criticism, though instructors might want to point out that the important Marxist critic Adorno preferred Beckett's work. Beckett's play also anticipates later developments in poststructuralist and postmodern theory.

Week 14—*Race, Gender, and the Canon.* Assigned readings from *NATC*: Gates; Baker; Vizenor; Allen; Gilbert and Gubar.

Week 15—*Literature of the Twentieth Century: Expanding the Canon.* Assigned readings: Richard Wright, "The Man Who Was Almost a Man"; Leslie Marmon Silko, "Yellow Woman."

IV. Survey of Modern Literature, Theory, and Criticism

Note that after the introduction, the weeks are paired: each week of critical/theoretical readings is followed by works of literature to which the theory and criticism is directly applicable.

Week 1—*Introduction to the course.* Reading assignment: Introduction to NATC.

Week 2—*Formalism.* Assigned readings from NATC: Eichenbaum; Ransom; Wimsatt and Beardsley.

Week 3—*Assigned reading:* T. S. Eliot, *The Waste Land.*

Week 4—*Modernism.* Assigned readings from NATC: Eliot; Woolf; Habermas, "Modernity—An Incomplete Project"; Deleuze and Guattari, from *Kafka.*

Week 5—*Assigned readings:* James Joyce, "The Dead"; Franz Kafka, "The Metamorphosis."

Week 6—*Marxism.* Assigned readings from NATC: Marx and Engels, from *The Communist Manifesto*; Gramsci; Lukács.

Week 7—*Assigned reading:* Bertolt Brecht, *The Good Woman of Setzuan.*

Week 8—*Postmodernism.* Assigned readings from NATC: Lyotard; Jameson, "Postmodernism and Consumer Society"; Foucault, from *Discipline and Punish*; Deleuze and Guattari, from "Rhizome."

Week 9—*Assigned readings:* Jorge Luis Borges, "The Garden of Forking Paths"; Samuel Beckett, *Endgame.*

Week 10—*Race and Gender.* Assigned readings from NATC: Gates; Baker; Vizenor; Allen; Gilbert and Gubar.

Week 11—*Assigned readings:* Richard Wright, "The Man Who Was Almost a Man"; Leslie Marmon Silko, "Yellow Woman."

Week 12—*Postcolonial Theory and Criticism.* Assigned readings from NATC: Said; Achebe; Ngugi et al.

Week 13—*Assigned reading:* Chinua Achebe, *Things Fall Apart.*

Week 14—*Cultural Studies.* Assigned reading from NATC: Horkheimer and Adorno; Bourdieu; Ohmann; Mulvey.

Week 15—Discussion of *Citizen Kane* and *Pulp Fiction. Note*: Instructors should arrange for a screening of these two films outside of class hours.

Works Cited

Abrams, M. H. *The Mirror and the Lamp: Romantic Theory and the Critical Tradition.* New York: Norton, 1953.

———. *Natural Supernaturalism: Tradition and Revolution in Romantic Literature.* New York: Norton, 1971.

Achebe, Chinua. "The African Writer and the English Language." *Morning Yet on Creation Day.* London: Heinemann, 1975. 91–103.

Ahmad, Aijaz. *In Theory: Classes, Nations, Literatures.* London: Verso, 1992.

Allison, David B., ed. *The New Nietzsche: Contemporary Styles of Interpretation.* New York: Delta, 1977.

Anderson, Perry. *Considerations on Western Marxism.* London: Routledge, Chapman, and Hall, 1976.

Andrew, J. Dudley. *The Major Film Theories: An Introduction.* New York: Oxford UP, 1976.

Ashcroft, Bill, Gareth Griffiths, and Helen Tiffin. *The Empire Writes Back: Theory and Practice in Post-Colonial Literatures.* London: Routledge, 1989.

———, eds. *The Post-Colonial Studies Reader.* London: Routledge, 1995.

Ashfield, Andrew, and Peter De Bolla, eds. *The Sublime: A Reader in British Eighteenth-Century Aesthetic Theory.* Cambridge: Cambridge UP, 1996.

Azim, Firdous. *The Colonial Rise of the Novel.* London: Routledge, 1993.

Bahktin, M. M. *The Dialogic Imagination: Four Essays.* Ed. Michael Holquist. Trans. Caryl Emerson and Michael Holquist. Austin: U of Texas P, 1981.

Bakhtin, M. M./Medvedev, P. N. *The Formal Method in Literary Scholarship: A Critical Introduction to Sociological Poetics.* Trans. Albert J. Wehrle. Cambridge, MA: Harvard UP, 1985.

Barolini, Teodolinda. *Dante's Poets: Textuality and Truth in the Comedy.* Princeton: Princeton UP, 1984.

Barthes, Roland. *S/Z.* Trans. Richard Miller. New York: Hill and Wang, 1974.

Beebe, Maurice. "*Ulysses* and the Age of Modernism." *"Ulysses": Fifty Years.* Ed. Thomas Staley. Bloomington: Indiana UP, 1974. 172–88.

———. "What Modernism Was." *Journal of Modern Literature* 3 (1974): 1065–80.

Beiser, Frederick C., ed. *The Cambridge Companion to Hegel.* Cambridge: Cambridge UP, 1993.

Bennett, Tony. *Formalism and Marxism.* London: Methuen, 1979.

Benvenuto, Bice, and Roger Kennedy. *The Works of Jacques Lacan: An Introduction.* New York: St. Martin's, 1986.

Berman, Marshall. *All That Is Solid Melts into Air: The Experience of Modernity.* New York: Simon and Schuster, 1982.

Berman, Russell. *Modern Culture and Critical Theory: Art, Politics, and the Legacy of the Frankfurt School.* Madison: U of Wisconsin P, 1989.

Bishop, Morris. *The Horizon Book of the Middle Ages.* New York: American Heritage, 1968.

Bloom, Allan. *The Closing of the American Mind: How Higher Education Has Failed Democracy and Impoverished the Souls of Today's Students.* New York: Simon and Schuster, 1987.

Bloom, Harold. *The Anxiety of Influence: A Theory of Poetry.* New York: Oxford UP, 1973.

———. *The Western Canon: The Books and School of the Ages.* New York: Harcourt Brace, 1994.

Bodkin, Maude. *Archetypal Patterns in Poetry: Psychological Studies of Imagination.* 1934. London: Oxford UP, 1963.

Boehmer, Elleke. *Colonial and Postcolonial Literature: Migrant Metaphors.* New York: Oxford UP, 1995.

Booker, M. Keith. *The African Novel in English: An Introduction.* Portsmouth, NH: Heinemann, 1998.

———. *Dystopian Literature: A Theory and Research Guide.* Westport, CT: Greenwood, 1994.

———. *The Modern American Novel of the Left: A Research Guide.* Westport, CT: Greenwood, 1999.

———. *The Modern British Novel of the Left: A Research Guide.* Westport, CT: Greenwood, 1998.

———. *A Practical Introduction to Literary Theory and Criticism.* White Plains, NY: Longman, 1996.

———. *Techniques of Subversion in Modern Literature: Transgression, Abjection, and the Carnivalesque.* Gainesville: U of Florida P, 1991.

———. *"Ulysses," Capitalism, and Colonialism: Reading Joyce after the Cold War.* Westport, CT: Greenwood, 2000.

————. *Vargas Llosa among the Postmodernists.* Gainesville: U of Florida P, 1994.

————, and Dubravka Juraga. *The Caribbean Novel in English: An Introduction.* Portsmouth, NH: Heinemann, 2000.

Bradbury, Malcolm, and James McFarlane, eds. *Modernism, 1890–1930.* London: Penguin, 1976.

Brannigan, John. *New Historicism and Cultural Materialism.* New York: St. Martin's, 1998.

Brennan, Timothy. *At Home in the World: Cosmopolitanism Now.* Cambridge, MA: Harvard UP, 1997.

Bressler, Charles E. *Literary Criticism: An Introduction to Theory and Practice.* 2d ed. Upper Saddle River, NJ: Prentice Hall, 1999.

Brooker, Peter, ed. *Modernism/Postmodernism.* New York: Longman, 1992.

Brooks, Cleanth. *The Well Wrought Urn: Studies in the Structure of Poetry.* 1943. Rev. ed. London: Dobson, 1968.

Burckhardt, Jacob. *The Civilization of the Renaissance in Italy.* New York: New American Library, 1995.

Cain, William E. *The Crisis in Criticism: Theory, Literature, and Reform in English Studies.* Baltimore: Johns Hopkins UP, 1984.

Calinescu, Matei. *Five Faces of Modernity: Modernism, Avant-Garde, Decadence, Kitsch, Postmodernism.* Durham, NC: Duke UP, 1987.

Callinicos, Alex. *Against Postmodernism: A Marxist Critique.* New York: St. Martin's, 1989.

Carroll, David. *Paraesthetics: Foucault, Lyotard, Derrida.* London: Methuen, 1987.

Chefdor, Monique, Ricardo Quinones, and Albert Wachtel, eds. *Modernism: Challenges and Perspectives.* Urbana: U of Illinois P, 1986.

Clark, Barrett, ed. *European Theories of the Drama: An Anthology of Dramatic Theory and Criticism from Aristotle to the Present Day.* Rev. Henry Popkin. New York: Crown, 1965.

Clark, Katerina, and Michael Holquist. *Mikhail Bakhtin.* Cambridge, MA: Belknap–Harvard UP, 1984.

Clifford, John, and John Schilb, eds. *Writing Theory and Critical Theory.* New York: Modern Language Association, 1994.

Cohen, Ted, and Paul Guyer, eds. *Essays in Kant's Aesthetics.* Chicago: U of Chicago P, 1982.

Cohen, Walter. "Marxist Criticism." *Redrawing the Boundaries: The Transformation of English and American Literary Studies.* Ed. Stephen Greenblatt and Giles Gunn. New York: Modern Language Association, 1992. 320–48.

Colish, Marcia L. *The Mirror of Language: A Study in the Medieval Theory of Knowledge.* Rev. ed. Lincoln: U of Nebraska P, 1983.

Corrigan, Timothy. *Film and Literature: An Introduction and Reader.* Upper Saddle River, NJ: Prentice Hall, 1999.

Cox, Jeffrey N., and Larry J. Reynolds, eds. *New Historical Literary Study: Essays on Reproducing Texts, Representing History.* Princeton: Princeton UP, 1993.

Culler, Jonathan. *On Deconstruction: Theory and Criticism after Structuralism.* Ithaca, NY: Cornell UP, 1982.

———. *Structuralist Poetics: Structuralism, Linguistics, and the Study of Literature.* Ithaca, NY: Cornell UP, 1975.

Davis, Lennard. *Factual Fictions: The Origins of the English Novel.* New York: Columbia UP, 1983.

DeJean, Joan E. *Ancients against Moderns: Culture Wars and the Making of a fin de siècle.* Chicago: U of Chicago P, 1997.

Demetz, Peter. *Marx, Engels, and the Poets: Origins of Marxist Literary Criticism.* Chicago: U of Chicago P, 1967.

Denning, Michael. *The Cultural Front: The Laboring of American Culture in the Twentieth Century.* London: Verso, 1996.

Derrida, Jacques. *Of Grammatology.* Trans. Gauatri Chakrovorty Spivak. Baltimore: Johns Hopkins UP, 1976.

———. *Specters of Marx: The State of the Debt, the Work of Mourning, and the New International.* New York: Routledge, 1994.

———. "Structure, Sign, and Play in the Discourse of the Human Sciences." *The Structuralist Controversy: The Languages of Criticism and the Sciences of Man.* Ed. Richard Macksey and Eugenio Donato. Baltimore: Johns Hopkins UP, 1970. 247–65.

———. *The Truth in Painting.* Trans. Ian McLeod and Geoff Bennington. Chicago: U of Chicago P, 1987.

Diamond, Irene, and Lee Quinby, eds. *Feminism and Foucault: Reflections on Resistance.* Boston: Northeastern UP, 1988.

Dirlik, Arif. *The Postcolonial Aura: Third World Criticism in the Age of Global Capitalism.* Boulder, CO: Westview, 1997.

Dodds, E. R. *The Greeks and the Irrational.* Berkeley: U of California P, 1951.

Doody, Margaret Anne. *The True Story of the Novel.* New Brunswick, NJ: Rutgers UP, 1996.

Dosse, François. *History of Structuralism.* Vol. 1, *The Rising Sign, 1945–1966.* Trans. Deborah Glassman. Minneapolis: U of Minnesota P, 1997.

———. *History of Structuralism.* Vol. 2, *The Sign Sets, 1967–Present.* Trans. Deborah Glassman. Minneapolis: U of Minnesota P, 1997.

Dworkin, Dennis. *Cultural Marxism in Postwar Britain: History, the New Left, and the Origins of Cultural Studies.* Durham, NC: Duke UP, 1997.

Eagleton, Terry. *The Ideology of the Aesthetic.* Oxford: Blackwell, 1990.

———. *Literary Theory: An Introduction.* 2d ed. Minneapolis: U of Minnesota P, 1996.

———. *Marxism and Literary Criticism.* Berkeley: U of California P, 1976.

———, ed. *Raymond Williams: Critical Perspectives.* Boston: Northeastern UP, 1989.

Eco, Umberto. *Art and Beauty in the Middle Ages.* Trans. Hugh Bredin. New Haven: Yale UP, 1986.

Ellison, Julie. *Emerson's Romantic Style.* Princeton: Princeton UP, 1984.

Ellmann, Mary. *Thinking about Women.* New York: Harcourt Brace Jovanovich, 1968.

Fiedler, Leslie A., and Houston A. Baker Jr. *English Literature: Opening up the Canon.* Baltimore: Johns Hopkins UP, 1981.

Finke, Laurie A. *Women's Writing in English: Medieval England.* New York: Longman, 1999.

Fish, Stanley. "Why No One's Afraid of Wolfgang Iser." *Diacritics* 11 (1981): 2–13.

Fokkema, Douwe. *Literary History, Modernism, and Postmodernism.* Amsterdam: John Benjamins, 1984.

Foley, Barbara. *Radical Representations: Politics and Form in U.S. Proletarian Fiction, 1929–1941.* Durham, NC: Duke UP, 1993.

Foucault, Michel. *The History of Sexuality.* Vol. 1, *An Introduction.* Trans. Robert Hurley. New York: Vintage–Random House, 1980.

Fowler, Alasdair. *Kinds of Literature: An Introduction to the Theory of Genres and Modes.* Cambridge, MA: Harvard UP, 1982.

Freund, Elizabeth. *The Return of the Reader: Reader-Response Criticism.* London: Methuen, 1987.

Gandhi, Leela. *Postcolonial Theory: A Critical Introduction.* New York: Columbia UP, 1998.

Gates, Henry Louis, Jr. *Loose Canons: Notes on the Culture Wars.* New York: Oxford UP, 1992.

———. *The Signifying Monkey: A Theory of Afro-American Literary Criticism.* New York: Oxford UP, 1988.

Gilbert, Sandra M., and Susan Gubar. *The Madwoman in the Attic: The Woman Writer and the Nineteenth-Century Literary Imagination.* New Haven: Yale UP, 1979.

———. *No Man's Land: The Place of the Woman Writer in the Twentieth Century.* Vol. 1, *The War of the Words.* New Haven: Yale UP, 1988.

Goldberg, Jonathan, ed. *Queering the Renaissance.* Durham, NC: Duke UP, 1994.

Goldgar, Anne. *Impolite Learning: Conduct and Community in the Republic of Letters, 1680–1750.* New Haven: Yale UP, 1995.

Goldstein, Jan, ed. *Foucault and the Writing of History.* Cambridge, MA: Blackwell, 1994.

Gottlieb, Roger S., ed. *An Anthology of Western Marxism: From Lukács and Gramsci to Socialist-Feminism.* New York: Oxford UP, 1989.

Graff, Gerald. *Beyond the Culture Wars: How Teaching the Conflicts Can Revitalize American Education.* New York: Norton, 1992.

———. *Professing Literature: An Institutional History.* Chicago: U of Chicago P, 1987.

Gray, John. *Enlightenment's Wake: Politics and Culture at the Close of the Modern Age.* London: Routledge, 1995.

Greenberg, Mitchell. *Corneille, Classicism, and the Ruses of Symmetry.* Cambridge: Cambridge UP, 1986.

Greenblatt, Stephen. *Renaissance Self-Fashioning: From More to Shakespeare.* Chicago: U of Chicago P, 1980.

————. *Shakespearean Negotiations: The Circulation of Social Energy in Renaissance England.* Berkeley: U of California P, 1988.

Grossberg, Lawrence, Cary Nelson, and Paula Treichler, eds. *Cultural Studies.* New York: Routledge, 1992.

Guillory, John. *Cultural Capital: The Problem of Literary Canon Formation.* Chicago: U of Chicago P, 1993.

Gutting, Gary, ed. *The Cambridge Companion to Foucault.* Cambridge: Cambridge UP, 1994.

Guyer, Paul, ed. *The Cambridge Companion to Kant.* Cambridge: Cambridge UP, 1992.

Habermas, Jürgen. "The Entwinement of Myth and Enlightenment: Re-Reading *Dialectic of Enlightenment.*" *New German Critique,* no. 26 (1982): 13–30.

Harland, Richard. *Literary Theory from Plato to Barthes: An Introductory History.* London: Macmillan, 1999.

Harvey, David. *The Condition of Postmodernity: An Enquiry into the Origins of Cultural Change.* Oxford: Blackwell, 1990.

Hassan, Ihab. "POSTmodernISM." *New Literary History* 3 (1971): 5–30.

Hawkes, Terence. *Structuralism and Semiotics.* Berkeley: U of California P, 1989.

Hawkins, Hunt. "The Issue of Racism in *Heart of Darkness.*" *Conradiana* 14.3 (1982): 163–71.

Hebdige, Dick. *Subculture: The Meaning of Style.* London: Methuen, 1979.

Held, David. *Introduction to Critical Theory: Horkheimer to Habermas.* Berkeley: U of California P, 1980.

Hobsbawn, Eric. *The Age of Capital, 1848–1875.* New York: Scribner's, 1975.

————. *The Age of Empire, 1875–1914.* New York: Pantheon, 1987.

————. *The Age of Revolution, 1789–1848.* London: Weldenfeld and Nicolson, 1962.

Hoggart, Richard. *The Uses of Literacy.* London: Chatto, 1957.

Holland, Norman N. *5 Readers Reading.* New Haven: Yale UP, 1975.

————. *Poems in Persons: An Introduction to the Psychoanalysis of Literature.* New York: Norton, 1973.

————. "Unity Identity Text Self." *Reader-Response Criticism: From Formalism to Post-Structuralism.* Ed. Jane P. Tompkins. Baltimore: Johns Hopkins UP, 1980. 118–33.

Hollander, Robert. *Allegory in Dante's "Commedia."* Princeton: Princeton UP, 1969.

————. "Babytalk in Dante's *Commedia.*" *Studies in Dante.* Ravenna: Longo Editore, n.d. 115–29.

Holub, Robert C. *Reception Theory: A Critical Introduction.* London: Methuen, 1984.

Horkheimer, Max, and Theodor W. Adorno. *Dialectic of Enlightenment.* Trans. John Cumming. New York: Seabury, 1972.

Houlgate, Stephen. *Freedom, Truth, and History: An Introduction to Hegel's Philosophy*. London: Routledge, 1991.

Howe, Irving. *The American Newness: Culture and Politics in the Age of Emerson*. Cambridge, MA: Harvard UP, 1986.

Huizinga, Johan. *The Autumn of the Middle Ages*. Trans. Rodney J. Payton and Ulrich Mammitzsch. Chicago: U of Chicago P, 1996.

————. *The Waning of the Middle Ages: A Study of the Forms of Life, Thought, and Art in France and the Netherlands in the Fourteenth and Fifteenth Centuries*. 1924. New York: St. Martin's 1985.

Hulme, T. E. "Romanticism and Classicism." *Speculations: Essays on Humanism and the Philosophy of Art*. Ed. Herbert Read. 1924. New York: Harcourt Brace, 1961. 111–40.

Hunter, J. Paul. *Before Novels: The Cultural Contexts of Eighteenth-Century English Fiction*. New York: Norton, 1990.

Hutcheon, Linda. *A Poetics of Postmodernism: History, Theory, Fiction*. London: Routledge, 1988.

Hutchinson, George. *The Harlem Renaissance in Black and White*. Cambridge, MA: Belknap–Harvard UP, 1995.

Huyssen, Andreas. *After the Great Divide: Modernism, Mass Culture, Postmodernism*. Bloomington: Indiana UP, 1986.

Irwin, David G. *Neoclassicism*. London: Phaidon, 1997.

Iser, Wolfgang. "Talk Like Whales." *Diacritics* 11 (1981): 82–87.

Jameson, Fredric. *The Political Unconscious: Narrative as a Socially Symbolic Act*. Ithaca, NY: Cornell UP, 1981.

————. *Postmodernism, or, The Cultural Logic of Late Capitalism*. Durham, NC: Duke UP, 1991.

Jancovich, Mark. *The Cultural Politics of the New Criticism*. Cambridge: Cambridge UP, 1993.

JanMohamed, Abdul R. "The Economy of Manichean Allegory: The Function of Racial Difference in Colonialist Literature." *"Race," Writing, and Difference*. Ed. Henry Louis Gates Jr. Chicago: U of Chicago P, 1986. 78–106.

Jay, Martin. *The Dialectical Imagination: A History of the Frankfurt School and the Institute of Social Research, 1923–1950*. Boston: Little, Brown, 1973.

Jones, Richard F. *Ancients and Moderns: A Study of the Rise of the Scientific Movement in Seventeenth-Century England*. 2d ed. Gloucester, MA: Peter Smith, 1961.

Kaminsky, Jack. *Hegel on Art: An Interpretation of Hegel's Aesthetics*. Albany: State U of New York P, 1962.

Kellner, Douglas. *Critical Theory, Marxism, and Modernity*. Baltimore: Johns Hopkins UP, 1989.

Kemp, John. *The Philosophy of Kant*. New York: Oxford UP, 1968.

Kennedy, George Alexander, ed. *The Cambridge History of Literary Criticism*. Vol. 1, *Classical Criticism*. Cambridge: Cambridge UP, 1989.

Kennedy, William J. *Rhetorical Norms in Renaissance Literature*. New Haven: Yale UP, 1978.

Kermode, Frank. *Romantic Image.* New York: Macmillan, 1957.

Kurzwell, Edith. *The Age of Structuralism: Lévi-Strauss to Foucault.* New York: Columbia UP, 1980.

Laclau, Ernesto, and Chantal Mouffe. *Hegemony and Socialist Strategy: Towards a Radical Democratic Politics.* London: Verso, 1985.

Lanham, Richard. *The Motives of Eloquence.* New Haven: Yale UP, 1976.

Lauter, Paul. *Canons and Contexts.* New York: Oxford UP, 1991.

Lawall, Sarah, et al., eds. *The Norton Anthology of World Masterpieces.* 2 vols. New York: Norton, 1999.

Leitch, Vincent. *American Literary Criticism from the 1930s to the 1980s.* New York: Columbia UP, 1988.

———. *Cultural Criticism, Literary Theory, Poststructuralism.* New York: Columbia UP, 1992.

———. *Deconstructive Criticism: An Advanced Introduction.* New York: Columbia UP, 1983.

Lentricchia, Frank. *After the New Criticism.* Chicago: U of Chicago P, 1980.

Levine, Lawrence W. *The Opening of the American Mind: Canons, Culture, and History.* Boston: Beacon, 1996.

Lukács, Georg. *The Historical Novel.* Trans. Hannah Mitchell and Stanley Mitchell. Lincoln: U of Nebraska P, 1983.

———. "Narration vs. Description: A Contribution toward the Discussion of Naturalism and Formalism." Trans. S. Altschuler. *International Literature* 6 (1937): 96–112; 7 (1937): 85–98.

———. *Studies in European Realism.* New York: Grosset and Dunlap, 1964.

Lunn, Eugene. *Marxism and Modernism: An Historical Study of Lukács, Brecht, Benjamin, and Adorno.* Berkeley: U of California P, 1982.

Lyotard, Jean-François. *The Postmodern Condition: A Report of Knowledge.* Trans. Geoff Bennington and Brian Massumi. Minneapolis: U of Minnesota P, 1984.

McClintock, Anne. *Imperial Leather: Race, Gender, and Sexuality in the Colonial Conquest.* New York: Routledge, 1995.

———, ed. *Dangerous Liaisons: Gender, Nation, and Postcolonial Perspectives.* Minneapolis: U of Minnesota P, 1997.

Mack, Maynard. *Alexander Pope: A Life.* New Haven: Yale UP, 1985.

MacKenzie, John M. *Orientalism: History, Theory, and the Arts.* Manchester: Manchester UP, 1995.

McKeon, Michael. *The Origins of the English Novel, 1600–1740.* Baltimore: Johns Hopkins UP, 1987.

McLellan, David. *Ideology.* Milton Keynes, UK: Open UP, 1986.

———. *Karl Marx: His Life and Thought.* New York: Oxford UP, 1973.

———. *The Thought of Karl Marx.* New York: Oxford UP, 1971.

McLuhan, Marshall. *The Gutenberg Galaxy.* Toronto: U of Toronto P, 1962.

Mandel, Ernest. *Late Capitalism.* Trans. Joris De Bres. London: NLB, 1975.

Maxwell, William. *New Negro, Old Left: African-American Writing and Communism between the Wars*. Urbana: U of Illinois P, 1999.

Megill, Allan. *Prophets of Extremity: Nietzsche, Heidegger, Foucault, Derrida*. Berkeley: U of California P, 1985.

Miller, J. Hillis. *Poets of Reality: Six Twentieth-Century Writers*. Cambridge, MA: Belknap–Harvard UP, 1965.

Miller, Toby. *The Well-Tempered Self: Citizenship, Culture, and the Postmodern Subject*. Baltimore: Johns Hopkins UP, 1993.

Millett, Kate. *Sexual Politics*. Garden City, NY: Doubleday, 1970.

Minnis, A. J., ed. *Latin and Vernacular: Studies in Late Medieval Texts and Manuscripts*. Woodbridge, UK: Boydell and Brewer, 1989.

Moi, Toril. *Sexual/Textual Politics: Feminist Literary Theory*. London: Methuen, 1985.

Mongia, Padmini, ed. *Contemporary Postcolonial Theory: A Reader*. London: Arnold, 1996.

Montrose, Louis. "New Historicisms." *Redrawing the Boundaries: The Transformation of English and American Literary Studies*. Ed. Stephen Greenblatt and Giles Gunn. New York: Modern Language Association, 1992. 392–418.

Moore-Gilbert, Bart. *Postcolonial Theory: Contexts, Practices, Politics*. London: Verso, 1997.

Moretti, Franco. *The Way of the World: The Bildungsroman in European Culture*. London: Verso, 1987.

Morson, Gary Saul, and Caryl Emerson. *Mikhall Bakhtin: The Creation of a Prosaics*. Stanford: Stanford UP, 1990.

Mumford, Lewis. *The Story of Utopias*. New York: Viking, 1962.

Murphy, James F. *The Proletarian Moment: The Controversy over Leftism in Literature*. Urbana: U of Illinois P, 1991.

Nelson, Cary, ed. *Theory in the Classroom*. Urbana: U of Illinois P, 1986.

Ngugi wa Thiong'o. *Decolonising the Mind: The Politics of Language in African Literature*. Portsmouth, NH: Heinemann, 1986.

Nicholls, Peter. *Modernism: A Literary Guide*. Berkeley: U of California P, 1995.

Nicholson, Linda J., ed. *Feminism/Postmodernism*. New York: Routledge, 1990.

Norris, Christopher. *Derrida*. Cambridge, MA: Harvard UP, 1987.

Outram, Dorinda. *The Enlightenment*. Cambridge: Cambridge UP, 1995.

Parrinder, Patrick. "*Heart of Darkness*: Geography as Apocalypse." *Fin de Siècle/Fin du Globe*. Ed. John Stokes. New York: St. Martin's, 1992. 85–101.

Pater, Walter. *The Renaissance: Studies in Art and Poetry*. 1877. New York: Oxford UP, 1998.

Pinkus, Philip. "Swift and the Ancients-Moderns Controversy." *University of Toronto Quarterly* 29 (1959): 46–58.

Poster, Mark. *Foucault, Marxism, and History: Mode of Production versus Mode of Information*. Cambridge: Polity, 1984.

Postgate, Raymond. *The Story of a Year: 1848*. London: Cassell, 1955.

Ragland-Sullivan, Ellie. *Jacques Lacan and the Philosophy of Psychoanaly-sis*. Urbana: U of Illinois P, 1986.

Robbins, Bruce. *Secular Vocations: Intellectuals, Professionalism, Culture*. London: Verso, 1993.

———, ed. *Intellectuals: Aesthetics, Politics, Academics*. Minneapolis: U of Minnesota P, 1990.

Robertson, Priscilla. *Revolutions of 1848: A Social History*. Princeton: Princeton UP, 1952.

Ross, Andrew, and Constance Penley. "Cyborgs at Large: Interview with Donna Haraway." *Technoculture*. Ed. Constance Penley and Andrew Ross. Minneapolis: U of Minnesota P. 1–20.

Rudé, George. *The French Revolution*. London: Phoenix, 1988.

Russell, D.A. *A Criticism in Antiquity*. Berkeley: U of California P, 1981.

Ryan, Michael. *Marxism and Deconstruction: A Critical Articulation*. Baltimore: Johns Hopkins UP, 1982.

Sadoff, Dianne F., and William E. Cain, eds. *Teaching Contemporary Theory to Undergraduates*. New York: Modern Language Association, 1994.

Said, Edward. *Culture and Imperialism*. New York: Knopf, 1994.

——— *Orientalism*. New York: Vintage–Random House, 1979.

San Juan, E., Jr. *Beyond Postcolonial Theory*. New York: St. Martin's, 1998.

Sawicki, Jana. *Disciplining Foucault: Feminism, Power, and the Body*. New York: Routledge, 1991.

Scholes, Robert. *Textual Power: Literary Theory and the Teaching of English*. New Haven: Yale UP, 1985.

Scholes, Robert, Nancy R. Comley, and Gregory L. Ulmer. *Text Book: An Introduction to Literary Language*. 2d ed. New York: St. Martin's, 1995.

Selden, Raman. *A Reader's Guide to Contemporary Literary Theory*. 2d ed. Lexington: U of Kentucky P, 1989.

Sheppard, Richard. "German Expressionism." *Modernism, 1890–1930*. Ed. Malcolm Bradbury and James McFarlane. London: Penguin, 1976. 274–91.

Showalter, Elaine. *A Literature of Their Own: British Women Novelists from Brontë to Lessing*. Princeton: Princeton UP, 1977.

Sidnell, Michael J., et al., eds. *Sources of Dramatic Theory*. 2 vols. Cambridge: Cambridge UP, 1991–94.

Singh, Frances. "The Colonialistic Bias of *Heart of Darkness*." *Conradiana* 10 (1978): 41–54.

Spearing, A. C. *Criticism and Medieval Poetry*. New York: Barnes and Noble, 1972.

Spears, Monroe K. *Dionysus and the City: Modernism in Twentieth-Century Poetry*. New York: Oxford UP, 1970.

Spencer, Jane. *The Rise of the Woman Novelist: From Aphra Behn to Jane Austen*. Oxford: Blackwell, 1986.

Spivak, Gayatri Chakravorty. *In Other Worlds: Essays in Cultural Politics.* New York: Methuen, 1987.

Stock, Brian. *The Implications of Literacy: Written Language and Models of Interpretation in the Eleventh and Twelfth Centuries.* Princeton: Princeton UP, 1983.

Stoler, Ann Laura. *Race and the Education of Desire: Foucault's "History of Sexuality" and the Colonial Order of Things.* Durham, NC: Duke UP, 1995.

Stratton, Florence. *Contemporary African Literature and the Politics of Gender.* London: Routledge, 1994.

Taylor, Ronald, ed. *Aesthetics and Politics.* London: Verso, 1977.

Therborn, Göran. "Dialectics of Modernity: On Critical Theory and the Legacy of Twentieth-Century Marxism." *New Left Review,* no. 215 (1996): 59–81.

Thompson, E. P. *The Making of the English Working Class.* New York: Vintage–Random House, 1966.

———. *The Poverty of Theory: And Other Essays.* London: Merlin, 1978.

Todorov, Tzvetan. *Mikhail Bakhtin: The Dialogical Principle.* Trans. Wlad Godzich. Minneapolis: U of Minnesota P, 1984.

Tompkins, Jane, ed. *Reader-Response Criticism: From Formalism to Post-Structuralism.* Baltimore: Johns Hopkins UP, 1980.

Trinh, T. Minh-ha. *Woman, Native, Other: Writing Postcoloniality and Feminism.* Bloomington: Indiana UP, 1989.

Tucker, Robert C., ed. *The Marx-Engels Reader.* 2d ed. New York: Norton, 1978.

Tyson, Lois. *Critical Theory Today: A User-Friendly Guide.* New York: Garland, 1999.

Vance, Eugene. *Mervelous Signals: Poetics and Sign Theory in the Middle Ages.* Lincoln: U of Nebraska P, 1986.

Veeser, H. Aram, ed. *The New Historicism.* New York: Routledge, 1989.

Viswanathan, Gauri. *Masks of Conquest: Literary Study and British Rule in India.* New York: Columbia UP, 1989.

Wald, Alan M. *The New York Intellectuals: The Rise and Decline of the Anti-Stalinist Left from the 1930s to the 1980s.* Chapel Hill: U of North Carolina P, 1987.

Walder, Dennis. *Post-Colonial Literatures in English: History, Language, Theory.* Oxford: Blackwell, 1998.

Walsh, Chad. *From Utopia to Nightmare.* Westport, CT: Greenwood, 1972.

Watt, Ian. *The Rise of the Novel: Studies in Defoe, Richardson, and Fielding.* Berkeley: U of California P, 1957.

Weisbuch, Robert. *Atlantic Double-Cross: American Literature and British Influence in the Age of Emerson.* Chicago: U of Chicago P, 1986.

Wetherbee, Winthrop. *Chaucer and the Poets: An Essay on Troilus and Criseyde.* Ithaca, NY: Cornell UP, 1984.

Wheen, Francis. *Karl Marx: A Life.* New York: Norton, 2000.

Wilde, Alan. *Horizons of Assent: Modernism, Postmodernism, and the Ironic Imagination*. Baltimore: Johns Hopkins UP, 1981.

Williams, Patrick, and Laura Chrisman, eds. *Colonial Discourse and Post-Colonial Theory: A Reader*. New York: Columbia UP, 1994.

Wright, Elizabeth. *Psychoanalytic Criticism: Theory in Practice*. London: Methuen, 1984.

Žižek, Slavoj. *The Fright of Real Tears: The Uses and Misuses of Lacan in Film*. London: British Film Institute, 1999.